TRAFALGAR CHRONICLE

Dedicated to Naval History in the Nelson Era

New Series 7

Journal
of
THE 1805 CLUB

Edited by
JUDITH E PEARSON AND JOHN A RODGAARD

In association with The 1805 Club

Seaforth
PUBLISHING

Text copyright © individual authors 2022

First published in Great Britain in 2022 by
Seaforth Publishing,
A division of Pen & Sword Books Ltd,
47 Church Street,
Barnsley S70 2AS

www.seaforthpublishing.com

British Library Cataloguing in Publication Data
A catalogue record for this book is available from the British Library

ISBN 978 1 3990 9046 9 (paperback)
ISBN 978 1 3990 9047 6 (epub)
ISBN 978 1 3990 9048 3 (kindle)

Pen & Sword Books Limited incorporates the imprints of Atlas, Archaeology, Aviation, Discovery, Family History, Fiction, History, Maritime, Military, Military Classics, Politics, Select, Transport, True Crime, Air World, Frontline Publishing, Leo Cooper, Remember When, Seaforth Publishing, The Praetorian Press, Wharncliffe Local History, Wharncliffe Transport, Wharncliffe True Crime and White Owl.

Designed and typeset in Times New Roman by Mousemat Design
Printed and bound in the UK by CPI Group (UK) Ltd, Croydon, CR0 4YY

Contents

Biographical Portraits

Articles of General Interest

President's Foreword

In last year's edition of the *Trafalgar Chronicle*, I recognised that it was a truly unique volume. The individual authors, together with the editorial team, overcame the hurdles placed in front of them by the COVID-19 pandemic. Despite being denied access to archives, libraries and museums, they produced submissions of high quality, and the editorial team maintained the high standards one expects in The 1805 Club's flagship periodical. The 2022 issue of the *Trafalgar Chronicle* is no exception.

As with the 2021 issue, this year's *Trafalgar Chronicle* has a central theme: scientific and technological advances in the navies of the Georgian era. The editors conveyed to me their delight that they received so many proposals and the subsequent superb quality of submissions in this year's edition.

I was personally elated to see that the lead article on the life of Samuel Bentham and his inventions was co-authored by my old shipmate, Captain John Wills RN, Rtd. Back in the day, John was my engineering officer when I took command of the Royal Navy's first Type 23 frigate, HMS *Norfolk*. He and his co-author, Mr Ken Flemming, a noted naval engineer in his own right, and one of the founders of The 1805 Club, have shown us how consequential Bentham's inventions and manufacturing efficiencies were to the successes that the Royal Navy enjoyed during the great Anglo-French wars of the Georgian era.

The Bentham article is joined by articles with subjects covering the development of gunnery, hydrography, medical advances and signalling. One would be remiss not to include fellow club member Tom Fremantle's work on the great naturalist Sir Joseph Banks, and the influence he had within the Admiralty: influence that gave the Royal Navy's leadership a greater understanding of the natural world.

I believe you will come away with an appreciation that the scientific and technological advances presented within these pages helped to lay the foundation for the development of the greatest military industrial complex the world had seen, until it was surpassed by America's own military industrial complex of the twentieth century.

I wish to convey my warm congratulations to the editors and the writers who have contributed to another engaging *Trafalgar Chronicle* — BZ!

In closing, I want to recognise the passing of one of the *Trafalgar Chronicle*'s prolific contributors, Charles Fremantle. As with his cousin Tom, also a frequent contributor to the *Chronicle*, Charles was a direct descendant of a long line of Fremantles who served with distinction in the Royal Navy. This included another Thomas Fremantle who was 'Nelson's Right Hand Man'. With his retirement in 1991, Charles could boast that the Fremantles had 214 years of unbroken service in the Royal Navy. You are relieved, Sir. We have the watch.

ADMIRAL SIR JONATHON BAND GCB DL
Former First Sea Lord
President of the 1805 Club

Editors' Foreword

When we chose the theme for this issue, 'Scientific and Technological advances in the Navies of the Georgian Era', we had no inkling we would get so many impressive proposals – all on pertinent topics relevant to naval history at the dawning of the Industrial Revolution. This year's contributors gave us quality content on inventions and innovations that facilitated the evolution of naval sea power, particularly in the Royal Navy during the Napoleonic wars. We felt gratified that our talented authors gave us more than meticulous research; they fashioned dramatic stories of exploration and adventure, achievement and folly, death and survival, and the accomplishments of geniuses.

Our lead article by fellow 1805 Club members, Captain John Wills RN, Rtd, and Kenneth Flemming, documents the life of Samuel Bentham, Royal Navy engineer, a brigadier-general for Russia under Catherine the Great, and the Royal Navy's Inspector General of Naval Works, 1796 to 1805. In the latter position he invented a fresh water system for ships at sea, developed steam power machinery for slitting timber, improved dockyard firefighting methods and dredging operations, and mechanised the manufacture of ships' blocks, while expanding dockyard facilities, personnel and efficiencies.

Lieutenant-Colonel Aaron Bright, US Army, and professor at the US Naval War College, Newport, Rhode Island, tells a searing tale about cannons that exploded in battle, maiming and killing the sailors who manned them. A young officer in the Royal Artillery, Thomas Blomefield took on the problem, making cannons safer and more efficient, and Royal Navy firepower more formidable. Frequent contributor Anthony Bruce details the life of Benjamin Robins, mathematician, engineer, and England's expert in the science of naval gunnery, who invented the carronade and gave the Royal Navy more accurate artillery.

Retired US Navy Commander and naval historian Christopher Pieczynski tells the story of a weapon that the British hated: Robert Fulton's torpedo. In the War of 1812, while the British cursed these 'infernal machines', Yankees copied Fulton's blueprints to devise ways to sink HM ships. And most of us remember Fulton only for his steamboat!

Fellow 1805 Club member, Captain Michael Barrett RN, studies the history of hydrography and cartography. Readers will enjoy his piece on improvements to naval charts during the Georgian era. Canadian Paul Martinovich, a retired museum planner, provides a biography of Peter Heywood, a 'scientific sailor' who became an oceanic surveyor and hydrographer, first with the Royal Navy and then with the East India Company. He charted about 350 locations around the Indian Ocean, surveyed South Atlantic islands and the River Plate, and perfected the use of chronometers for determining longitude, while commanding HM ships during the Anglo-French wars 1793–1815.

Naval historian Andrew Venn examines the increased reliance on signalling in naval battles from the Seven Years War through to the Battle of Trafalgar and analyses how that reliance influenced the decisions of various naval commanders as they shifted between centralised and decentralised command styles. He concludes that Nelson's 'tactical revolution' struck the perfect balance between those two styles.

In the Age of Sail, more sailors died from diseases and infection than from battle wounds. It's amazing that the shipboard mortality rate from illness dropped from one in eight, in 1780, to one in thirty in 1812. Linda Collison, a retired registered nurse, describes some of the advances in shipboard care hospital medicine that brought about this change.

The 1805 Club stalwart, Tom Fremantle, has two distinguished ancestors who were naval officers in the time of Nelson. Mr Fremantle acquaints readers with Sir Joseph Banks, a navy naturalist who was influential with the Admiralty, the Navy Board and officers assigned to distant posts and unexplored lands.

Club members Barry Jolly and Lily Style contribute to our section on 'Biographical Portraits' of Nelson's contemporaries. Mr Jolly writes a follow-on to his piece in the 2021 issue on Sir Harry Neale, Baronet GCB, Member of Parliament, burgess, mayor, and a Lord Commissioner of the Admiralty. In this year's issue of the *Trafalgar Chronicle*, Mr Jolly tells of the controversy surrounding the name by which Sir Harry would be remembered after his death. The controversy stemmed from a stipulation in his wife's grandfather's will! Mr Barry goes on to solve three mysteries that emerged after Sir Harry's death, involving a Canadian inlet, a telescope and a sword. Lily Style, a descendant of Lord Nelson and Emma Hamilton, writes about her ancestor, George Matcham, Nelson's brother-in-law, who made his fortune with the East India Company. Matcham and his family provided a home for Emma's daughter, Horatia, when she became orphaned.

Under 'General Interest', we are delighted to host Canadian naval history scholar, author and teacher, Nicholas Kaiser. His article gives readers a new appreciation of single ship actions in the War of 1812. Jakob Seerup, a museum curator in Denmark, describes a futile Danish expedition to Morocco. Let it suffice to say that the Moroccans did not play nicely with the visiting Danish navy! His article was presented at the 2021 Biannual McMullen Naval History

Symposium at the US Naval Academy, Annapolis, Maryland and sponsored by The 1805 Club.

Thirteen well-written, engaging articles by superb authors from four countries! Enough to warm an editor's heart! We thank these authors for their acumen as historians, and their expertise in making history memorable and rich in detail. We admire the depth of their research, their selection of illustrations, and the quality of their writing. They were all marvellously obliging and co-operative with our questions and suggestions for revisions or clarification. They made our work as editors easy and enjoyable.

The 1805 Club is a non-profit organisation with members across the globe. To honour our international membership, we have chosen the theme for the 2023 issue: 'International Perspectives on the Navies of the Georgian Maritime Era.' We want to know about events and personalities that shaped the navies of the world, 1714–1837. If you like to write and conduct historic research about all manner of things pertaining to the navies and maritime world of the Georgian era, send us a proposal and/or get on our email list of potential contributors. Contact us at tc.editor@1805Club.org.

To our readers: we welcome your comments, questions, ideas, and suggestions about this issue and future issues. Please tell your friends and colleagues about the *Trafalgar Chronicle*. Our publisher, Seaforth Publishing, welcomes purchases from individuals, organisations, universities, institutes, and libraries. 1805 Club members receive this journal as well as the *Dispatches* digital newsletter and the bi-annual *The Kedge Anchor* magazine as benefits of membership. If you aren't a member of The 1805 Club, please join by completing an application at our website, www.1805Club.org.

JUDITH E PEARSON, PHD
BURKE, VIRGINIA

JOHN A RODGAARD, CAPTAIN USN, RET
MELBOURNE, FLORIDA

Sir Samuel Bentham – Civil Architect and the First Engineer of the Royal Navy

John Wills and Kenneth Flemming

Machinery set in motion by inanimate force was the significant contribution of Sir Samuel Bentham (1757–1831), a brigadier-general who in 1813 wrote officially to the Admiralty to propose his innovation to mechanise the making of blocks for ships' rigging. England led the world in the Industrial Revolution of the late 1700s. In naval shipbuilding and support, Bentham is an icon of that revolution, with much the same effect as George Stephenson (1781–1848) with the introduction of steam railways for land-based transportation.

Bentham's early life

Born in London, the youngest of the seven children of Jeremiah Bentham (1712–1792), an attorney, and his wife, Alicia Woodward Whitehorne Grove (*d*1759), Samuel and his more famous brother Jeremy Bentham (1748–1832), philosopher, jurist and reformer, were the only two children in the family to survive infancy. The two brothers were exceptionally close, and their lives were frequently intertwined. Jeremy's education is worth noting as he tutored Samuel at an early stage.

For the first sixteen years of his life, Jeremy was described as exceedingly small, puny and feeble. He acquired a knowledge of musical notes at five. He learned to write and play the violin and was subsequently initiated into Latin grammar. He gained distinction at Westminster School, London, for writing Latin and Greek verses. At twelve, he was entered as a commoner at Queen's College, Oxford. Samuel also attended Westminster from age six, leaving there in 1771 at fourteen to become a naval apprentice to William Grey, the best master shipwright in the Royal Dockyard at Woolwich. His parents paid Grey the substantial sum of £50 per year for Samuel's boarding, besides paying a large apprentice fee. It was doubtless primarily due to Jeremy's persuasions that their father agreed to let Samuel pursue his enthusiasm for naval architecture rather than go to Oxford.[1]

Jeremiah Bentham was an intelligent businessman who had added considerably to his legacy by land speculations and leases, allowing both surviving sons to continue their education and placements. Samuel continued his apprenticeship with Grey when Grey transferred to Chatham Dockyard. It was there that Samuel soon found he was inclined towards the administrative and constructional work of the navy. During his apprenticeship, Samuel was allotted time to study mathematics, chemistry, electricity, painting, grammar, and especially the French language at the Royal Naval Academy, Portsmouth; all skills connected with a naval education.

During this period, he went to sea as a volunteer in the Third Rate HMS *Bienfaisant* (64), under Captain MacBride, aiming to learn more about constructional issues arising from the movement of ships. Captain Bazely had previously carried him from Chatham to Portsmouth in the Second Rate *Formidable* (90), in which Bentham proposed an improvement to the steering gear later adopted by John Jervis (Earl St Vincent) in the Second Rate *Foudroyant* (80). Jervis had inspected *Formidable* with Bentham while both were taking passage in the ship at the same time.

Housed in the Portsmouth Dockyard, the Royal Naval Academy opened in July 1733 for the education and training of future naval officers due in part to the Admiralty's dissatisfaction with the previous shipboard instruction, which was dependent on the calibre of the captain with whom the boy entrants sailed. Accordingly, students were selected on an exclusive basis: boys between the ages of twelve and fifteen who were the sons of noblemen or gentlemen. Moreover, no boy was to be admitted unless he produced a certificate to the effect that he had made considerable progress in Latin. The students enjoyed separate rooms, and each paid the master £25 a year for their board. The length of stay was to be not less than two years and no more than three.[2]

The Academy did not flourish during the first forty years, and it seems something of an impressive failure for the whole of its duration. From the outset, it was plagued by poor food and discipline problems from the young gentlemen: breaking the rules and drunkenness. The relative dullness of life of studying at the shore-based institution could not bear comparison with the excitements of a life at sea aboard a man-of-war.

Nevertheless, Samuel's father sent him to the Academy to be schooled under the principal, George Witchel, an astronomer and mathematician who designed tables for determining longitude by the moon and was responsible for compiling the *Nautical Almanac*. Witchel tutored the entire school. The Admiralty paid his tuition fees. Jeremiah Bentham also paid Witchel a retainer. Witchel became a Fellow of the Royal Society in 1767. By 1766 the number of scholars had fallen to the smallest since its establishment, remaining so until its closing in February 1806 on the recommendation of the great seaman and naval reformer, John Jervis, Earl St Vincent.

Finally, on 11 January 1778 Samuel came of age, and his apprenticeship finished at the month's end. He was soon as fertile in ideas for improvement in shipbuilding as brother Jeremy was in ideas for improvement in the law. Samuel's education, although unusual, was well-rounded, with the accomplishments expected of a gentleman added to the more practical expertise of a shipbuilder. Despite this education, however, he failed to find a suitable position in the Royal Dockyards.

Bentham begins his naval service
In 1779, due to Samuel's rising abilities and connections, Lord Howe, First Lord of the Admiralty, suggested he should visit various ports and dockyards in northern Europe to study their facilities and practices in shipbuilding. So, armed with seventy letters of recommendation, those indispensable social passports of the time, he set off in August 1779 for Holland, visiting naval establishments and various ports on the Baltic Sea. For the next two years he journeyed to Russia on a fact-finding mission, where he toured the Black Sea area, eastwards into Siberia and ultimately as far as the frontiers of China.

Returning to St Petersburg, he enjoyed the patronage of the British ambassador, Sir James Harris, and became known at the imperial court of Catherine the Great. In February 1783 he made her a formal offer of his services, asking for the rank of brigadier and a salary of 1,000 roubles. Finally, in September of that year he entered the service of the empress, with the equivalent rank to lieutenant-colonel. Brother Jeremy visited him in 1785, staying for almost two years.

In 1787, during the Russo-Turkish War, Samuel Bentham commanded a flotilla based at Kherson on the Dnieper River. He devised a new system for fitting guns without recoil, allowing him to arm his boats with far heavier armament than the enemy could expect them to be carrying. His system called for mounting 36pdrs and 48pdrs in pairs so that the recoil of one gun drew out the other, thus diminishing the recoil. Gun crews could then reload effectively with no time lost in replacing the gun to its firing position. The resulting rapid and heavy fire was so devastating for the Turks that Bentham was awarded the Military Cross of St George, advanced to the rank of full colonel, and received a gold-hilted sword of honour.[3] In a letter of 10 August 1788, Robert Hynam, watchmaker to the empress, sent Jeremy the news after Samuel's return to St Petersburg:

Petersburgh, 30 Jly OS

I am extremely happy to inform you, Sir, that your brother is promoted to the rank of Colonel for his valour and prudence in two successful attacks against the Turks upon the Nieper. He is in good health. The publick papers here have announced his praise.[4]

However, an earlier, less complimentary letter from George Wilson and James Trail, dated 26 February 1787, to Jeremy Bentham highlights the character of both brothers. Wilson wrote:

With one-tenth part of your genius, and a common degree of steadiness, both Sam and you would long since have risen to great eminence. But your history, since I have known you, has been to be always running from a good scheme to a better. In the meantime, life passes away and nothing is completed.[5]

Matthew Anderson, one of the first authors to write about Samuel Bentham in the mid twentieth century said of this same letter:

This criticism was abundantly justified. Brilliant, volatile, headstrong, unbusinesslike, Samuel Bentham was not marked out for great material success in any society. His correspondence nevertheless shows us, with remarkable fidelity and completeness, the reactions of an intelligent nonofficial observer confronted by the vast and half understood phenomenon of the empire of Catherine II. It illustrates a phase in the career of a very remarkable man. It also illumines a small corner of the eighteenth-century Europeanization of Russia.[6]

Bentham took charge of Prince Potemkin's factories, which at that time were badly mis-managed. As there were few skilled workers, Bentham started working on the problem of improving workers' skills and using machines. He thought it should be possible to replace skilled workers with machines that could be

Sir Samuel Bentham (1757–1831). A half-length portrait to the left shows Bentham in a Russian lieutenant-colonel's uniform, consisting of a green coat with red lapels and gold buttons and epaulettes. He also wears a gold-laced waistcoat and a grey tie wig. Artist unknown. (© National Maritime Museum, Greenwich, London, Greenwich Hospital Collection) operated by unskilled labour, producing the same products in the same amount of time and at the same cost.

His time in Russia gave him many other opportunities to apply his talents as an engineer and inventor, constructing machinery for industrial use and experimenting with processes such as steelmaking. He designed and built many novel vehicles, including an amphibious vessel and an articulated barge for Catherine the Great. He later campaigned for the introduction of watertight compartments, an idea that, he acknowledged, came from seeing large Chinese vessels on the Amur River on the Siberian border with China. He was further raised in rank to brigadier-general and received a knighthood from the Tsarina for his services to Russia.

He returned home in 1791 at age thirty-four, after what may be considered an exceptionally long and continuing education, in time to see something of his father before his father's death in 1792. He remained in England, touring the dockyards under the authority of the Admiralty, with the objective of suggesting improvements in construction and organisation, receiving permission from King George III to use his Russian titles.

Inspector General of Naval Works, 1796–1805
In 1796 the Admiralty appointed Samuel Bentham Inspector General of Naval Works, creating this office especially for him. In this position, he continued his work in naval modernisation with the introduction of steam power and mechanising production processes in the dockyard. His office employed specialists as assistant mechanists (engineers), draughtsmen, architects, chemists and clerks.

Bentham was a man of drive, whose innovations continued to adapt the products of Britain's Industrial Revolution to the Royal Naval Dockyards, reflecting his ingenuity, leadership and engineering prowess. His inventions, adaptations and improvements often took years to complete, and his many projects overlapped with each other over a span of nine years during his time as inspector general. For that reason, the following subsections are organised, not chronologically from 1796 to 1805 when his position was abolished, but project by project, so that the reader might more fully appreciate each of Bentham's major innovations in full.

Maintaining fresh water
In early 1796 Bentham had devised a practical way of maintaining fresh water for long periods at sea. To demonstrate this capability, he conducted an experiment for the forerunner of the Royal Society for the Arts. For the experiment, the Navy Board authorised him to have constructed at Redbridge,

on the River Test, seven small vessels, uncontrolled by any Navy Board or dockyard officer, built to his own specifications. The vessels were to be two sloops of war, *Arrow* and *Dart*, both of 28 guns, and four war schooners, *Nelly*, *Eling*, *Redbridge* and *Milbrook*, all of 16 guns, together with an unnamed water vessel.[7] He sent the results to the society in a letter on 27 January 1801, in which he wrote:

The method I conceived Fresh Water might be preserved sweet, was merely by keeping it in vessels of which the interior lining at least should not be acted upon by the water, so as to become a cause of contamination. Accordingly on board the two ships here alluded to [*Arrow* and *Dart*], the greater part of the water was kept, not in casks, but in cases or tanks, which, though they were made of wood, on account of strength, were lined with metallic plates, of the kind manufactured by Mr. Charles Wyatt of Bridge Street under the denomination of tinned copper-sheets; and the junctures of the plates or sheets were soldered together.

The shape of these cases was adapted to that of the hold of the ship, some of them being made to fit close under the platform, by which means the quality of the water stowed was considerably greater than could have been stored, in the same space, by means of casks; and thereby the stowage room on board ship was very much increased.

After the water kept in this manner had remained on board a length of time which was deemed sufficient for the experiment, it was used out, and the tanks were replenished as occasion required: but in some of the tanks, on board one ship at least, the original water had remained three years and a half, as appears on the certificates herewith in-closed.[8]

A certificate from Captain William Bolton, commander of HM Sloop *Dart*, dated 28 June 1800 at Sheerness, accompanied this letter, stating that the water delivered to the society was taken from a tank holding about 700 gallons, and which his predecessor Captain Portlock had informed him had been poured into this tank in December 1796, except about thirty gallons added in 1798, and had remained good during the whole time.[9]

In a further letter, Bentham also stated that:

... the water which had been preserved sweet on board his Majesty's sloops *Arrow* and *Dart*, was taken from the well at the King's Brew House at Weevil, from whence ships of war lying at or near Portsmouth are usually supplied with water for their sea store, as well as present use.[10]

Public recognition for this innovation resulted in the Premium Award of a gold medal in 1801 to Samuel Bentham from the forerunner of the Royal Society of Arts.[11]

Steam power

Bentham developed an interest in steam technology when he toured the country, observing various industries. He wanted to see for himself how this inanimate force was replacing manual labour. He saw workers using machines to lift water out of the mines, spin cotton, and roll metal into sheets.

After his tour, Bentham designed and built steam-powered machinery that would replace manual labour in HM dockyards. However, Bentham needed to persuade the dockyard officials and labourers to accept the innovation of steam machinery. One persuasive application that revolutionised naval engineering was applying steam-powered machinery to slitting timber.

While touring the country, Bentham had seen that England had no sawmills for slitting timber. He devised and introduced a steam-powered machine for slitting and shaping timber planks. By the year 1812, sawyers could cut 4in and 5in timber planks in Portsmouth Dockyard at the rate of 9,000 to 10,000ft per week.[12] With this success, Bentham further applied his ingenuity and leadership in pursuit of greater efficiency in other dockyard processes.

Improvements to firefighting

A naval industrial site such as a dockyard, with timber-built ships at various stages of completion or repair, does not exist without risk of catching fire. Processing large volumes of timber entailed a constant fire hazard from accumulated sawdust. Bentham deduced the need for a more efficient firefighting capability in the Portsmouth Dockyard. In 1797 he introduced a system of distributing water to the at-risk parts of the dockyard's industrial site.

He achieved this by constructing an elevated static water reservoir into which water from a well was raised during meal hours and in the evening, by either of the two steam engines in daily use in the wood-mills. From this reservoir, the water was distributed throughout the dockyard by a system of pipes passing by all the principal buildings, and by the sides of the docks and to the jetties; upon these pipes, outlets were provided at intervals of from 50 to 200ft for speedily affixing fire hose, jet and branch pipes.

This system of pipes was arranged so that water flowed through them by two different courses. Thus, should any temporary interruption occur, the supply of water at any point would be effected by the other course. In addition to this supply, always ready to be instantaneously applied to extinguishing a fire in any part of the dockyard, and with a force sufficient to throw the water into the first floors of buildings, the steam engines also raised either fresh water from the well, or an immense supply of seawater, forcing this water, fresh or salt, into the fire.[13]

Dredging operations

Crucial to maintaining the operations of a naval port is for the harbour seawater level to be kept at a depth that enables ships to remain afloat at low tide. Seabed levels are continually scoured by the ebb and flow of the tide, which in turn deposits silt. The gunnery school HMS *Excellent* on Whale Island, Portsmouth, was built predominantly on reclaimed land, using the deposits dredged from Portsmouth harbour during the nineteenth century, increasing the land harbour area by about 125 per cent. The island was constructed with the labour of many prisoners taken during the Napoleonic Wars.

As ships became larger, they required deeper water to remain alongside dockyard wharfs. In 1800 Bentham applied his engineering mind to this challenge with his invention of a steam-powered dredging machine. He calculated that his apparatus, when constructed, would raise 1,000 tons of soil a day. He sent an estimate to the Navy Board for the cost of the apparatus and for barges for carrying away soil.[14] The Navy Board approved construction.

The dredging machine fulfilled its promise, allowing wharf walls to serve as viable alongside-berths for ships, instead of ships having to anchor off in the deeper midstream. In addition, sailors had the benefit of being able to walk aboard their ships when loading and offloading stores and ammunition. Bentham's 'floating engine for digging underwater' found application at Portsmouth, as well as the other naval ports on the Thames and Medway.

Manufacture of ships' blocks

Ships' blocks were indispensable components of a ship's rigging. With ropes, blocks served as pulleys and tackles for hoisting or trimming sails. Even before becoming inspector general, Bentham set about to mechanise the sawyers' processes of constructing these wooden blocks. In 1793 Bentham took out a patent, which has been called one of the most remarkable patents ever issued by the British Patent Office. It set forth the whole scheme of introducing steam-powered woodworking machinery for making ships' blocks.[15] Working with Sir Marc Brunel in the design, Samuel Bentham introduced a factory in Portsmouth that automated the manufacture of pulley blocks.

It is worth noting that Bentham and Brunel's innovation threatened the sawyers, who feared that such an attempt to mechanise their trade would jeopardise their livelihoods. Under the direction of a Mr Burr, of the inspector general's office, some dockyard labourers were trained to work the machinery

Original ships' blocks made at the mill and retained in Portsmouth Dockyard.
(Picture courtesy of English Heritage)

and were encouraged by some small extra allowances to exert themselves in this employment.[16]

By 1794, government representatives had started taking an interest, and Lord Melville (Henry Dundas, 1st Viscount Melville, 1742–1811), then Secretary at War (1794–1801), recognised the greater efficiencies and speed of manufacture that Bentham's design provided for these essential components of the nation's warships. In the House of Commons, Melville championed the work of Bentham, whom the Admiralty subsequently appointed to visit all His Majesty's dockyards to expand the deployment of his mechanisation.

In considering the functioning of a sailing warship, pre-Industrial Revolution, the humble wooden block stands out as one of the most essential components a ship would have needed for its propulsion and manoeuvrability, as these simple devices kept its rigging 'running'. A First Rate ship of the line such as *Victory* required 768 blocks of various types.

In battle, not unlike modern yacht racing, captains and sailing masters would contest for wind advantage by a superior choice of course and the effective setting of their sails. Consider, for example, Nelson's closing approach to the enemy at Trafalgar, where, with the wind advantage, his fleet 'crossed the T' of the combined

Block mills in Portsmouth Dockyard. (Picture courtesy of English Heritage)

French and Spanish fleets and so enabled both his port and starboard guns to come to bear on the enemy. Hundreds of humble blocks would have enabled the fleet's sheets to be veered and hauled with superior speed and efficiency.

It was Bentham, a true engineer, who not only thought through the problems, but devised engineering-based solutions on a mass scale that revolutionised the manoeuvrability of the fleet. Indeed, it could be argued that the mass production of the wooden block was as important an innovation to the Georgians as the microchip has been for today's Elizabethans!

Students of naval and industrial history can easily recognise the block mills in Portsmouth Naval Base, even today. Within this group of buildings, a remarkable set of machine tools designed by Bentham's colleague, Sir Marc Brunel, laid the foundations for the subsequent worldwide development of industrial production lines that used ever more sophisticated machinery to replace the work of

Original block building mechanism retained in Portsmouth Dockyard.
(Picture courtesy of English Heritage)

Interior of block mill in Portsmouth Dockyard showing the overhead drive belt system used to power the manufacturing machinery. (Creavtive Commons)

individual craftsmen. They have rightly become regarded as one of the seminal buildings of the British Industrial Revolution. Importantly, they are also the site of the first stationary steam engines used by the Admiralty.

Expansion of dockyard facilities, personnel and efficiency

In 1798 Bentham drew up a report to the Lords of His Majesty's Council recommending a host of improvements to the management of naval dockyards. The report stated, among other items, that each dockyard needed an additional officer who was conversant with the principles of mechanics as well as with the business of the millwright, capable of implementing the recommendations of the surveyors on all mechanical subjects.

The man for the job was Simon Goodrich. He had been with Bentham's office since 1796, first as a draughtsman, and then promoted to the post of machinist. He became Bentham's deputy, responsible for managing the installation of machinery at the Portsmouth block mills, and for the metal mills and millwright's shop at Portsmouth. Later he was also responsible for the mechanical engineering work at all the other naval dockyards and travelled incessantly on naval business as engineer to the Navy Board.[17] Due to Bentham's absence in Russia in 1805, it was Simon Goodrich who actually brought all the block mills into full production.

Bentham's report stated that, as the inspector general, he had to submit, in writing, all proposals for reorganisation and improvements, along with a complete account of the supporting reasons, to the First Sea Lord and the Navy Board. This process required lengthy and time-consuming explanations for even the most minor proposals. Samuel's letters, explaining the reasoning behind his proposed changes, often ran into tens of pages. His reports were by no means unusual in their length or the wealth of detail. Such documents must have taken up a considerable amount of Samuel's time while inspector general. One cannot fail to conclude that Samuel's professional life at this stage was marked by almost constant frustration and frequently thwarted by petty bureaucracy.[18]

Bentham also designed and built a mortar mill that facilitated the construction of numerous brick and stone buildings required to house a range of stores, offices and factories within the Portsmouth Naval Base and Dockyard. Bentham took further measures to create what transpired to be the introduction of a branch of millwrights to work metals, as well as timber, who, it could be argued, were the forerunners of today's marine engineers. By February 1805, wood mills and metal mills were established, each with specialist millwrights.[19]

Bentham's retirement and death

In 1805 the Admiralty sent Bentham back to Russia in the audacious hope that the Tsar would allow British warships to be built at Archangel to overcome the shortage of oak timber in England. The Admiralty had agreed to an allowance sufficient to cover all his expenses, taking his family with him and various 'shipwright men', together with a surgeon and his principal assistant, Mr Helby, who worked as a quartermaster in Portsmouth Dockyard.

The Russian government and Admiral Techitchagoff did not take the Admiralty and the British government's appeal as a civil diplomatic request. After repeated and lengthy discussions, Russia consented to the building of the ships, under the condition that for every vessel laid down for the English government, a similar one should be laid down for Russia; that Bentham should equally supervise the one as the other during construction; and that all improvements in naval construction should be introduced and exemplified in the ships for Russia.

Bentham's wife, Mary Sophia, found the experience of living in Russia rather trying. She occupied herself with the children, their education and other pursuits, while continuing to be a supportive assistant to Samuel. After many delays and transiting between the British and Russian governments, Bentham returned home two years later at the end of 1807, fatigued by many constant obstacles from both governments and without having achieved any of the apparent official objectives.

During his absence, the Naval Commissioners recommended that the inspector general become a member of the Navy Board, 'with the title of civil architect and engineer'. Accordingly, the office of inspector general was abolished in October 1807, a decision Bentham discovered on his return. The family came to believe that he had been sent to Russia to get him out of the way while the post was abolished.

Bentham's many attacks on abuses and mismanagement in the dockyards naturally did not serve to make him popular. Inevitable in a time of modernisation, some inflexible and narrow-minded working practices persisted in the yards during this early phase of industrialisation. Standpipes were provided for supplying fresh water to ships lying in the basin or at the jetties, but for some years these new standpipes were not used, as ships were required to shift berth because watering ship was the victualling yards' responsibility. Other practices included each dockyard department being separated by a fence in case of pillage or loss: no equipment, not even basic timber planking, could be moved to other sections of the yard.[20]

Bentham was appointed to the Navy Board with his new title where, unfortunately, his relations with his colleagues were strained further by various divergences of opinion and personality. In 1812, at the age of fifty-five, he was retired with a pension of £1,500 a year, equal to his full pay. There is no doubt that the frustrations and difficulties of petty officialdom and workplace tensions influenced this outcome.

In 1814 Bentham moved with his family to France, settling eventually in the neighbourhood of Montpellier. Shortly after their departure, the family suffered a tremendous blow when the elder son, Samuel junior, died, aged seventeen. On this occasion, Bentham himself and his wife wrote to Jeremy, informing him of the sad event.[21]

Both letters were moving expressions of the grief of bereaved parents. Samuel wrote: 'at ½ past 5 in the afternoon I lost my boy, my friend and companion from whom for the last twelvemonth I had no secret and in whom I found the most correct judgement.' Bentham recorded that his son's last words were 'my breather pipe is stopt', a not inappropriate comment for the son of an engineer. In 1827 George, Bentham's younger son, was to write to his elder sister Mary Louisa: 'It is a sad thing to think how those whom I have most loved and confided in have been separated from me, my poor brother whom I had never quitted a single day till his last fatal illness.'[22]

Samuel returned with his family to London, spending most of his time writing on various naval matters, his last being on the influence of the shape of a ship's hull on its speed and direction. He died in 1831, a year before his brother Jeremy, with whom his life had been intertwined.

In 1854 his widow, now aged ninety-three, wrote her husband's biography, in an effort to vindicate his memory of various accusations. It was published four years after her death in 1858. In the preface of this work, she correctly wrote:

> To him are to be traced some of the most important changes in Naval Administration; and to him we are indebted for many inventions which have effected an incalculable saving in public expenditure, as well as for Dockyard and other reforms which closed the sources of many long-continued and most pernicious abuses. Official opposition, which sought to uphold all vested interests, prevented him from carrying out many things which he had at heart; while, even in that he was enabled to accomplish, he had to struggle with the obstacles furnished by a passive resistance.

One might add that Bentham's inventions did much to enable the Royal Navy to prevail at sea during the great Anglo-French wars of 1793 to 1815.

It is generally acknowledged that today's world of factory mass production had its origins in the Portsmouth block mill, a Georgian building that still stands within the heart of Portsmouth's Royal Naval Dockyard. Discerning contemporaries recognised the importance of Bentham's pioneering work, and the

Samuel Bentham, Naval Architect (c1795–1800), by Henry Edridge. Inscription: 'The sitter's son, George Bentham, (1800–84), botanist, president of the Linnaean Society 1861–74; in 1854 presented his family collections and books to Kew, where he worked with both Sir Walter and Sir Joseph Hooker who sold much Bentham material to the British Museum, including NPG 3069 in 1897; transferred to the NPG in 1939.' (National Portrait Gallery, London) building swiftly became an object of pilgrimage for many, its fame assured by its inclusion in major nineteenth-century encyclopedias. Block-making ceased there in 1965, but several machines still survive, in Portsmouth and in the London Science Museum, while the building remains much as it was completed in the first decade of the nineteenth century with the interiors little altered. The block mills have not been in use for many years, although many of the original pulley systems remain in situ.

In her 1999 PhD thesis on Bentham, Felicity Wilkin wrote:

These advances were primarily due to a small group of men led by Samuel Bentham who became the First Engineer of the Navy. For their innovative use of new technologies and their management skills, these men can justifiably claim their place in the history of the Navy and of technology. More importantly, the applications of technology in Portsmouth Dockyard made a significant contribution to the industrial revolution in Britain and Imperial history during the period.[23]

Portsmouth's Royal Naval Dockyard No. 2 Dock dates from 1799–1801. It forms one of six docks designed by Sir Samuel Bentham. No. 2 Dock represents another visible legacy to his improvements to the Royal Dockyard. The first steam-powered engine in the dockyard was used there to empty and fill the docks. The docks are protected by law as a Grade I Listed Structure and as part of the Portsmouth Royal Naval Dockyard Scheduled Monument. HMS *Victory* entered the dock in 1922 where she remains to this day. We are sure Bentham would be pleased.

The Blomefield Cannon

Aaron Bright

On 23 September 1793 the Second Rate HMS *Princess Royal* (98) arrived to relieve the Second Rate *St George* (98) of her task to bombard the town of La Seyne and the batteries along the route to Toulon. Captain John Purvis began a bombardment that would keep the *Princess Royal* busy for the next two months.[1] In the lower gun decks of his three-deck ship, the work of his, or any gun crew, was as difficult as it was dangerous, requiring skill, practice and teamwork. On 23 October one of the crews of the lower deck finished another reload of their Armstrong 32pdr cannon and hauled it back into firing position. The gun captain looked along the length of the gun towards his target. Satisfied with his aim, he pulled its lanyard one last time. The spring-loaded piece of flint on the gunlock released towards the touch hole atop the cannon's breech. At the moment of ignition, the firing train began.[2] Sparks lit the small amount of fine-grain powder, which carried its heat, fire and pressure down to the main charge resting inside the bore behind a wad and a cannonball brimming with potential energy. When the individual, coarser granules of the main charge ignited, each one struggled to encompass three times as much space in gas form as it had when it was a solid. The rapid need for space started pushing the cannonball toward the muzzle to alleviate the pressure inside.[3] Before it could, however, the pressure found another way out.

In a split second, three tons of cannon ripped itself apart. Close in to the explosion, four members of the crew died instantly, possibly never knowing what happened. Those in the immediate area not burned or lacerated by flying iron would have at least suffered internal issues from the concussive effects of the shockwave. A large hunk of cannon iron took flight upwards, carrying enough inertial force to tear itself through not only the deck above it but also the deck above that, overturning an 18pdr on its way through the second deck. The master and the master's mate were also killed as a result of the blast. Two lieutenants and twenty-nine other members of the ship's crew were badly wounded.[4] Nearly everyone on board would have existed in a state of shock at the unexpected loss of a limb, a friend, their hearing, or faith in their own gun. It was a catastrophe, with the only saving grace being that *Princess Royal* was not in action with another ship. Others ships of the line across the empire were not so lucky, as British cannons were becoming increasingly more dangerous at both ends.

Any person unacquainted with the intricacies of British iron cannons in the Age of Sail would be hard-pressed to identify how they changed over time. All of them are essentially hollowed-out tubes of metal, closed off at one end (the breech) and open at the other (the muzzle). A closer study, though, reveals important but subtle innovations that after the turn of the nineteenth century made British cannons the most reliable in the world. Explosions like the one that tore through the *Princess Royal* became increasingly rare on British ships, contributing to their superior combat performance in the Napoleonic Wars. While this particular story is one that cannot help but contain some technical aspects of metallurgy, internal ballistics, and Age of Sail fighting tactics, it also involves penny-pinching politicians, profiteering and patronage. More than anything, this is the story of what one man, Sir Thomas Blomefield, did to right a wrong committed against common sailors and marines like those of the *Princess Royal*. It is as much his story as it is of the cannon design which bears his name.

Blomefield's predecessor, Jon Armstrong

In 1722 Jon Armstrong, originally a cavalry officer, officially took over the task of the Crown's gun designer as the head of the Surveyor of Ordnance. In the opinion of the late Adrian Caruana, the foremost expert on guns in the Age of Sail, Armstrong was a fantastic administrator. He added a much-needed structure to the Ordnance Board. As a gun designer, though, he was a disaster. More an engineer than a gunner, he replaced Albert Borgard who had held the position since 1716, and not necessarily because he was the best qualified. When Borgard's patron, the Duke of Marlborough died, it was not Armstrong's gunnery knowledge, but rather his influential friends who seated him in the job that same year.[5] Even more so than it is today, who you knew could be your ticket to the top. Armstrong died of a stroke after holding the position for twenty years, but his basic design carried on through the Seven Years War and American War of Independence with only minor alterations. At first glance this would seem a testament to a superior gun design. While the Armstrong guns were an evolution from their predecessors, they were created for the moment with little regard for progressive improvements in gunpowder and fighting techniques that were continually evolving. Follow-on designers tended to compensate for the perceived deficiencies of Armstrong's design by adding more iron.[6] This made the various sized models heavier and less manageable. It was the gun that the Royal Navy took *completely* into the American War of Independence and *primarily* into the French Revolutionary Wars. It was during the former that these cannons revealed themselves for the dangerous pieces they were, and that a change was necessary.

Thomas Blomefield and the Royal Artillery

A young Thomas Blomefield started his military service as a midshipman in 1755 at the age of eleven, when his father placed him into naval service on board the Third Rate HMS *Cambridge* (80). Evidently not thrilled with life at sea, he secured a cadetship at the Royal Military Academy at Woolwich. Showing incredible aptitude in mathematics and chemistry, he secured a commission into the Royal Artillery (RA) at the beginning of 1759. His scientific aptitude plus his previous naval experience made him a prime candidate for directing army artillery with the navy. The RA assigned him to a bomb ketch, where the fifteen-year-old became a waterborne artillery expert. He progressed through the ranks, and as a staff officer became a key member of establishing what would later become the Royal Arsenal in Woolwich. He committed himself to the study and experimentation of artillery, but soon tired of staff work. Upon his request, he returned to the field.[7] During the American War of Independence, at the Battle of Bemis Heights on 7 October 1777, he was grievously wounded. Ten days later General Burgoyne capitulated after losing the Battle of Saratoga. In her memoir of the war, Baroness von Riedesel, who was travelling with her officer husband, children and the army, recounted tending to his wounds.

At one time I was nursing a Major Bloomfield [*sic*], aide to General Phillips, who had a bullet shot through both cheeks, smashing his teeth and grazing his tongue. He could not keep anything in his mouth; the pus almost choked him, and he could not take any nourishment at all except a little bouillon or other liquid. We had some Rhine wine. I gave him a bottle, hoping that the acid would cleanse his wounds. He took a little of it in his mouth, and this alone had such a fortunate effect that his wounds healed entirely, and I gained a further friend.[8]

This American's bullet, the baroness saving his life with a bottle of wine, and Blomefield's subsequent two-year convalescence in England keeping him out of the line of fire, proved to be one of the most fortuitous combinations for the future of the Royal Navy and Great Britain. By 1779, cannons bursting had hit a climax and the King himself wanted to know why his naval guns were wreaking havoc on his own ships. The next year Blomefield took on the task when the RA assigned him to the post of Inspector of Artillery. Here he began his pivotal role in fixing the Armstrong design and in devising a new system for testing the structural integrity of cannons.

When he accepted his appointment in 1780, it was part of a bigger reform of the Office of Ordnance. The duties assigned to him were previously those of a civilian department within the Office of the Surveyor General. His new office's primary tasks were the proof of new guns and the supply of ordnance to the army and navy.[9] The shift from a civilian authority to a military one turned out to be the right move. It had been wishful thinking to believe that a group of entrenched bureaucrats could maintain all their scruples in such a situation. Pinched between the contractors providing the 'carrot' and the government wielding the 'stick', temptation and threat loomed in equal measure. Large sums of money came to contractors if their creations could pass the test these men put the guns through and the government applied pressure to get as many guns to pass and out to ships as fast as possible. The results of this simultaneous carrot and stick were that thousands of guns passed proof that never should have. Sailors and marines paid with their lives and ships bore the scars. It seemed that it was more than just the industry which had a vested interest in the status quo.

'Proof' tests for cannons

A 'proof' was the test of a cannon after it left the foundry and arrived in London. If it passed, it went to one of the five ports where it would fill a gap in a ship's establishment.[10] The gunfounder who forged it did not get paid in full if his cannons failed to 'pass proof'. When Blomefield took over, what he found was that nearly any gun could pass the standard in place. It required a cannon to fire two rounds, one cannonball each, with a proof charge.[11] What he wanted, and implemented, was a test that bore a closer resemblance to combat conditions.[12] Blomefield's new proof called for a gun to fire thirty rounds, double-shotted[13] with service charges. It was much closer to what a gun would endure on a ship in action. In Blomefield's first year, 496 brand new cannons exploded during proof.[14] The new standard was set, and initially for the profiteers of the iron industry, it was nearly unattainable.

Gunfounders were understandably less than enthusiastic about the new system. It was a meticulous and lengthy process to create a gun to exact specifications. A gunfounder had first to heat his furnace to a certain temperature, which included the time and cost of sourcing the fuel to do it. Depending on the process they used, getting the foundry hot enough could take anywhere from three months to a year. They had to build a one-time-use gun mould to precise specifications for each cannon – a painstakingly detail-oriented process itself – only then to break it off the completed gun. Once the iron cooled after several days, they drilled out the bore; another long, tedious, 'boring' procedure.

On average, it took about seven to eight months to produce a gun.[15] The finished product was then moved to Woolwich for proof, usually first by land to a waterway where it was loaded on a vessel; land and water transportation being two additional costs in production. One can imagine, then, the frustration at having built several cannons according to the government's instructions, only to have the new Inspector of Ordnance destroy or condemn them shortly after arrival. Complaints were made, but initially they fell on deaf ears.[16] Thomas Blomefield had the attention of everyone who mattered, and more changes were coming.

There were a few reasons so many guns failed the new proof. Much of it had to do with a metallurgical problem that was impossible to understand fully at the time. *Full* understanding, though, was unnecessary. During the middle of the century, manufacturing started moving much of its operations from the continually deforested Weald in southeastern England to places further north such as the Midlands, Wales and Scotland.[17] Theoretically, the location of production should not have mattered, but northern guns turned out to be quite different. On a molecular level, northern iron was strongest when it was cool, the opposite of Wealden iron. The second difference was in production. Northern iron needed a higher temperature to get it to pour and flow properly within the mould. Gunfounders developed a way to get a hotter hearth by changing the fire's fuel to coke. Little did they realise the problem they introduced.

Coke was the mineral coal and it gave them the hotter furnace they needed. The hotter the fire, the quicker one can start making a gun. Quicker also meant cheaper, and cheaper to the penny-pinching government was always attractive. As the military saying goes, never forget that your weapon came from the lowest bidder. This had a secondary consequence of being the final straw that decimated the southern competition and by 1787 only three Wealden foundries remained.[18] Unfortunately, the coke contaminated the iron with sulphur. It became a kind of adhesive impurity within the guns. Before Blomefield's arrival, the proof tested the new northern Armstrong guns at their cold and strongest state. Combat tested them at their weakest.

Newton's second law of thermodynamics tells us that some of the energy generated from firing a cannon transfers in the form of heat to the gun.[19] When the firing train meets and ignites the main charge, the internal explosion spikes somewhere between 2,000 and 2,500°C. This flash of heat transfers a percentage of itself to the gun, which absorbs it, as does the heat from the friction of multiple cannonballs racing for the muzzle.[20] This heat compounds with every shot when the gun is not given sufficient time to cool. In action, one of the most important aspects of gunnery was the rate of fire, so to allow for cooling was not an ideal option. As the northern Armstrong guns warmed from continuous volleys, the sulphur, which was essentially acting as a glue holding the iron together, began to break down. It was just a matter of time and temperature until the bonds between iron and sulphur became too weak to withstand the pressure, and the cannon ruptured violently.

In 1787 Samuel Walker – Blomefield's trusted gunfounder who started prototyping his new designs – after much trial and error solved the contamination problem on a hunch. By melting down an old Wealden Armstrong gun, and mixing it 50:50 with northern iron, it dissipated the sulphur content adequately to create a gun strong enough to withstand the new proof. It was a new metal in gunfounding and a recipe that only the British knew how to make.[21] Walker and Blomefield were on their way to a safe and functional gun.

During Blomefield's first three years, his proofing system drastically raised gunfounding standards. The situation got worse – or better, depending on the point of view – in 1783 when he was given even further latitude. He had a trusted team by this point: Lieutenant William Robe was his proofmaster, Captain Fage his assistant inspector, and Sergeant Bell was his master searcher. Together with their clerks and labourers, these four men did the yeoman's work of proofing guns. In 1783 Blomefield expanded the proofing operation, splitting them into two teams. He and Lieutenant Robe continued testing new guns as they came in to Woolwich, while Captain Fage and Sergeant Bell went on the road to proof the navy's guns already in operation. The effort took three years, and the results were unnerving. From April to November of 1787, at the Portsmouth gun wharf alone, Fage and Bell condemned to scrap 436 guns. They further removed from use another 449 for needing repairs to make them serviceable.[22] This put Portsmouth in a 632-gun deficit to fill the required ship establishments for which it was responsible. If we assume a comparable situation at all four of the five ports[23] that Fage and Bell checked, the total number of fratricidal guns climbs to around 3,500.[24] This figure could certainly be high, seeing as Portsmouth was the largest, but when considering it excludes the hundreds of guns Blomefield and Robe reduced to chucks of iron during this same period, 3,500 may actually be a low number. In his zealous pursuit to fix one issue, unfortunately Thomas Blomefield created another in supply. Though Britain's ships and dockyards would be in a far better state following the after-effects of the reform work by Sandwich, First Lord of the Admiralty up to 1782, the Royal Navy was quietly vulnerable in firepower.[25] Luckily for Britain, 1783–92 was a time of relative peace.

Weaknesses in Armstrong's cannons – and Blomefield's solutions

In all the shattered pieces of Armstrong guns scattered throughout the various proving grounds – and in a few instances, in Blomefield's own garden – patterns emerged. Guns mostly failed along two areas of the barrel: the 'cascabel' and the 'ring of the first reinforce'. The cascabel is the back end of the cannon that resembles the top of a baby's bottle. The first reinforce is the area from the cascabel to the ring where the gun took its first step down in diameter (see illustration below). Though Blomefield could not have completely understood the science of *why* it was happening at those two regions – because nobody did for another half-century – he could draw conclusions from cause and effect, experience, and intuition.

Back to 1723 when Armstrong started, he and his team attempted to make guns lighter and more manageable, a worthy cause. In doing so, his initial design introduced weak points – later called 'planes of weakness'. At first, even his designs made from the stronger Wealden iron failed miserably. He added back weight, but they too failed because the design was still so bad. He finally fixed it essentially by cheating, increasing the bore's diameter. This increased the windage, lowering the internal pressure, which reduced the stress on the first reinforce, but created a gun that wasted precious powder and further decreased its accuracy.[26] While reducing the diameter of the gun at the first reinforce ring was a well-established, weight-saving practice, it produced a

Vocabulary of a 9' Single-shot-loaded Armstrong 24 pdr.

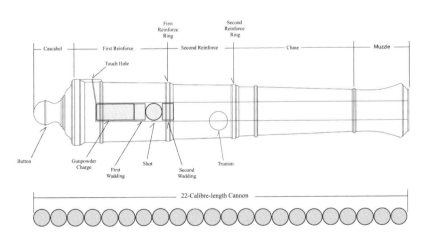

Armstrong-pattern 24pdr gun. Cross-section drawing by the author.

31

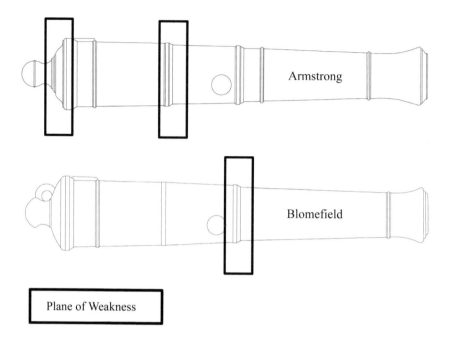

Armstrong and Blomefield 24pdr comparison showing the relative planes of weakness. Digital drawing by author from primary source drawings.

plane of weakness. What a gun designer cannot do is have any plane of weakness occur inside what is called the 'area of greatest pressure'.

Neither the terms 'plane of weakness' nor 'area of greatest pressure' were fully understood until Robert Mallet published his discoveries in 1856, making what Blomefield did all the more impressive.[27] The area of greatest pressure, as the name implies, is where the greatest amount of strain occurs along the length of the gun. It measures from the cascabel, through the breech, the charge, the first wadding, the shot, the second wadding, plus one calibre length.[28] Had Blomefield possessed the next century's vocabulary, he would have concluded that the Armstrong design had *two* planes of weakness within the area of greatest pressure and that is why they burst. Since his first reinforce ring ran around the second wadding, Armstrong unknowingly broke what would become a fundamental rule of gun design. The weakness of the design and the situation only got worse with changes in iron, gunpowder and fighting tactics. Northern iron made them weaker, gunpowder started getting stronger, and captains started seeing the benefits of double-shotting their payloads, which lengthened the area of greatest pressure.[29]

The cascabel's problem was a similar issue. Armstrong designed it with an eye towards decoration vice efficiency. It had a complicated series of ring flourishes that made it look like ripples from a water drop. Each of those beautiful flourishes was another plane of weakness.[30] When a gunpowder charge explodes, it does as all other explosions do, pushing pressure out equally in all directions. The purpose of a gun is to direct and reflect as much of the pressure and energy as possible in a singular direction. Like water, pressure finds the path of least resistance – in this case, through the cascabel towards the man pulling the lanyard.

Of all the changes the Armstrong guns required, these two problems bore the largest percentage of weakness Blomefield addressed. Where the first reinforce of the Armstrong had been conical, Blomefield made it near-completely cylindrical, making it strong throughout. He moved the first reinforce ring forward to a point where it was beyond the area of greatest pressure. Where the first reinforce met the second, there was no longer a steep drop in the diameter. He widened it to the same thickness and this is where the cannon would start its more noticeable conical tapering. The first abrupt step down in diameter now came at the second reinforce ring instead of the first, three calibre lengths beyond the area of greatest pressure[31] (see illustration on page 32). There was no significant change in weight, and the over-engineering ensured that it would last through future progressions in gunpowder and fighting techniques.

For the cascabel, it was a simpler fix. He removed the ornamentation from it, rounding the breech of the gun more evenly, removing the planes of weakness they caused.[32] He also increased the thickness of the breech at the touch hole. The strain was now evenly distributed and pressure could remain concentrated in one direction. In June 1786 Sam Walker and Blomefield proofed their first prototype in Woolwich, an 18pdr. Though it performed well, by July Blomefield thought they could do better.[33] With the cascabel and first reinforce fixed, he made one more addition that had nothing to do with making it stronger. The addition of the ring on the cascabel became the signature of a Blomefield-patterned gun and makes it easily distinguishable from its predecessors.

In adding a loop, or vertical ring, between the cascabel and the button he solved a problem associated with moving a gun to the left and right during action. Today this is called deflection. To revisit Newton, here the concern is his third law of motion: for every action, there is an opposite and equal reaction – in this case, recoil. Cannons of this time were built with a typical shot-to-gun weight ratio of 1:100.[34] The lower you make the second number, the more violent the recoil, yet another trade-off when determining gun weight. Allowing

Blomefield replica onboard HMS *Victory* showing the breeching rope run from the rings on the hull and through the loop on the cascabel to limit the gun's recoil travel. (Author's photo)

Blomefield replicas onboard HMS *Victory.* Each has a breeching rope run from the rings on the hull and through the loop on the cascabel to limit their recoil travel. (Author's photo)

a 32pdr to recoil unrestrained, it will travel backwards just over 50ft, or about the length of a typical lorry.[35] For this reason, a cannon had to have a 'breeching rope' to stop it. This rope was three times the length of the gun and hooked to rings bolted to the hull, on both sides of the cannon. That same 32pdr now came to a sudden stop at 11ft, giving the gun crew room to reload and haul it back into position. The strain placed on these two points was immense: 8 imperial tons per ringbolt. From this, the idea of a rippling fire broadside came into fashion to save the fibres of the hull from the concentrated shock of all guns firing simultaneously.[36] This modification prolonged the life of the ship and kept it sturdy where it counted most.

With Blomefield's addition of the cascabel ring, the breeching rope and the gun were now integrated. Before, the gun crew had to splice or loop the rope around the button where it was fixed. Having it pass through a metal loop allowed the rope to run free, making left and right deflection easier. Now, when a cannon fired in anything other than 90 degrees to the keel, it maintained a near-50:50 distribution of its 16 tons of recoil force since the rope's slack was no longer tighter on one side. This came in handy when an entire gundeck prepared for a broadside that converged all its shots on a single point. Each gun position had markers specific to it, above the gun, to line up such a concentrated and devastating broadside.

The breeching rope loop was a challenge to forge. Letters between Blomefield and Walker tell the story of the difficulties Walker encountered, but Blomefield pushed hard and eventually Walker figured it out.[37] Walker's trial and error over the course of several years was an emotional period for him. In addition to the stress of dealing with Blomefield's uncompromising standards and working out all the many nuances of making a gun by the new recipe, he suffered other delays. He had several guns burst in proof, his gunsmith was badly burned when he fell in a casting pit, and his daughter died of illness.[38] By 1796, though, he seemed to have ironed out most of the imperfections. The Blomefield pattern of guns went into full production and started trickling into service at a quicker pace from 1798 when the number of contractors climbed to nine.[39] Where the Armstrong had failed, the Blomefield would not. The Armstrong had been fragile to begin with, but its fatal flaw had been that it left no room for improvements in technology or doctrine. Blomefield and his team fixed that. Iron, brass, long versions, short versions, mortars, cannons of all sizes from 3pdrs to 42pdrs, it was a family of ordnance that would make Britain more than formidable once these armaments were in the hands of the Royal Navy in sufficient numbers.

Their biggest test came at Trafalgar. While not every gun in Nelson's fleet by October of 1805 was a Blomefield, the overwhelming majority were. British

Jan Verbruggen's casting pits at his foundry, possibly drawn by Pieter Verbruggen. This shows six guns being cast at once vertically. (Flickr, commercial use authorised)

gun crews had an expectation of one round every sixty to ninety seconds, and at Trafalgar most pulls of the lanyard were double-shotted, and at times treble-shotted.[40] Doing so slowed the shots' velocity for Nelson's up-close tactics, cutting a more ragged hole that was harder to repair. Slow and heavy cannonball penetrations turned portions of enemy hull into foot-long splinters of whirling projectiles, killing and maiming along their paths. Many a shot cut through only one side, ricocheted off the opposite hull, and remained inside the ship. Barefooted gun crews avoiding dozens of hot and heavy enemy cannonballs rolling around their ankles was a significant hazard in itself. Sustaining such a volume of multiple-round shots would not have been possible with Armstrongs. British gun crews delivered two or three broadsides for each one from a French or Spanish ship throughout that day, chewing up ships and crews at an alarming pace for four hours.[41] The *Victory* herself took 105 guns with 120 tons of solid iron shot ammunition into Trafalgar. Of that, her gun crews expended 27 tons of it – 2,669 cannonballs.[42] Had Nelson's fleet been equipped with Armstrongs instead of Blomefields, victory would have been questionable. Nelson was the right man, with the right tools, at the right time. Britain knows well the significant debt it owes Nelson. It should also be aware of the one due to Baroness von Riedesel and her bottle of wine.

Jan Verbruggen's boring machine, see colour plate 1

Benjamin Robins and the Science of Naval Gunnery

Anthony Bruce

Benjamin Robins (1707–1751) was an English mathematician, military engineer and pamphleteer who was a key figure in the eighteenth-century ballistics revolution and a significant influence on the development of naval gunnery. As a result of his work, which was based on practical experiments, 'the killer application of science [gave] the West a truly lethal weapon: accurate artillery.'[1] According to an artillery officer writing in 1789, 'before Robins, who was in gunnery what the immortal Newton was in philosophy, the founder of a new system deduced from experiment and nature, the service of artillery was a mere matter of chance, founded on no principles, or at best, but erroneous ones.'[2]

Robins – mathematician, engineer and polemicist

Robins was born in Bath in 1707 to Quaker parents living in modest circumstances and during his early years he was largely or wholly self-taught.[3] Robins soon demonstrated his abilities in languages and mathematics and was advised to move to London, where he studied mathematics under Dr Henry Pemberton, who was preparing the third edition of Sir Isaac Newton's *Principia* for publication at the time. Robins's talent for mathematics, especially Euclidean geometry, enabled him to support himself by working as a tutor to prospective university students. He also helped to clarify basic concepts in calculus and his early publications in the field of pure mathematics led to his election as a fellow of the Royal Society, Britain's most prestigious scientific institution in 1727, when he was only twenty years of age.

In the 1730s Robins gave up teaching to become an engineer and specialised in the construction of bridges, mills and harbours. He also developed an interest in artillery and fortifications and toured Flanders, where he studied castles and other defensive structures. During this period Robins established a reputation as a polemicist, engaging in lengthy debates with fellow mathematicians before turning his attention to political issues, particularly the policies of Sir Robert Walpole's administration towards Spain. The arguments he deployed in a series of pamphlets added to the public pressure that led to war with Spain in 1739, the War of Jenkins's Ear.[4] Following Walpole's departure from office in 1741,

Robins, who was now in favour with the Tory opposition, served as secretary of a secret committee that was established to investigate the former prime minister's conduct.[5] In 1749 he wrote an apology for the Battle of Prestonpans (1745), in which Jacobite forces under Charles Edward Stuart defeated British troops commanded by Sir John Cope, who was alleged to have shown cowardice in the face of the enemy. It was published anonymously as the preface to the *Report of the Proceedings and Opinion of the Board of General Officers, on their Examination into the Conduct ... of Lieutenant-General Sir John Cope.*[6]

These political activities may explain why Robins's application for the post of Professor of Fortification at the new Royal Military Academy, Woolwich, was unsuccessful, but he turned the course material he had prepared into the *New Principles of Gunnery* (1742), which formed the basis of all future work on the theory of artillery.[7] The work summarised the results of his early discoveries on internal and external ballistics – the motion of a lead or iron ball before and after it leaves the cannon's muzzle – and included an account of the progress of modern fortification, the invention of gunpowder and the theory of gunnery. It described the results of his experiments on the force of gunpowder, the resisting power of air, the velocity of a projectile as it left the muzzle and the mechanics of projectiles in free flight.

Experiments in gunnery

At the time the book was published, gunnery 'was still held to be an art and a mystery', rather than a science, and with no range-tables to guide him, the naval gunner could only rely on his own practical knowledge and skills. Textbooks had been published, but they were based on theory rather than practical experiment and could not help him in making practical calculations of aerodynamic forces. Based on theories developed by Galileo, Tartaglia and Newton, it was believed, incorrectly, that a shot travelled in a parabola – a symmetrical, U-shaped curve – from the muzzle to the target and was unaffected by the resistance of the air. These misconceptions, combined with design weaknesses, meant that the cannon was 'a singularly inefficient weapon', although at sea it could deal 'its powerful blows at close quarters, double-shotted and charged lavishly, with terrible effect. It was then that it was most efficient.'[8]

In order to test these earlier theories, Robins invented the ballistic pendulum, a device which, for the first time, accurately measured the velocity of a cannon shot at high speeds. It consisted of a heavy pendulum suspended in a metal frame with a wooden block acting as a weight and a measuring tape at the bottom. When a ball was fired into the block, its energy was transferred to the block and caused the pendulum to swing. From the subsequent swing angle,

The Ballistic Pendulum: a machine for determining the velocity of projectiles, an ink and wash drawing by Benjamin Robins, c1742. (Royal Picture Society)

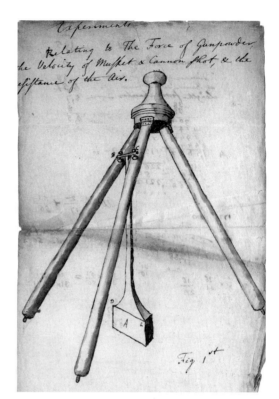

The Whirling Arm: a mechanism for determining aerodynamics and drag, an ink and wash drawing by Benjamin Robins, c1746. (Royal Picture Society)

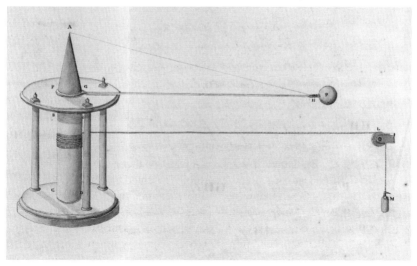

Robins was able to calculate the striking velocity of the ball. By repeating the experiment at varying ranges, he was able to determine the loss of velocity as a result of the resistance of the air and gravity. The device was soon adopted by other countries and remained in use for more than a century.

The air's resistance was far greater than Robins had expected. For example, its resistance to a 24lb ball fired with 16lbs of powder was as much as twenty-four times the weight of the projectile itself. He was the first to discover the effect of the sound barrier on aerodynamic drag, when he found 'a most extraordinary, and astonishing increase of the resistance, and which seems in a manner to take place all at once, and this when the velocity comes to be that, of between eleven and twelve hundred feet in one second of time.'[9] With these findings, Robins refuted the idea that a cannon ball's trajectory was a parabola, instead demonstrating that it veered off to the right or left of the intended line of fire. This was caused by the side forces exerted on the ball during its whirling motion in flight. Of all Robins's discoveries, 'the enormous and complex function of air-resistance force encountered by high-speed projectiles caused the greatest sensation in the 18th century [and] made the practical mathematical analysis of high-speed ballistic motion possible'.[10]

Robins's experiments brought him to the attention of George Anson (later Lord Anson) shortly after his return to England in 1744 at the end of his voyage round the world. Soon to be a leading member of the Admiralty Board, and from 1751 First Lord of the Admiralty, Admiral Anson became his friend and most important patron.[11] He commissioned Robins to complete the official account of his circumnavigation, which Richard Walter, his chaplain on the voyage, had originally been asked to undertake. Robins worked closely with Anson as he finalised a draft and received a fee of £1,000 for his labours. Published in 1748, *A Voyage Round the World* appeared under Walter's name, even though the text was largely Robins's work.[12] It became an international bestseller and was reprinted four times in the first year.

In view of the book's success, Anson asked Robins to produce a second volume of nautical observations, but it would never appear. In October 1749 Anson wrote to Robins to ask whether the manuscript would be finalised before he left for India to take up an appointment with the East India Company.[13] Although Robins's reply has not survived, it is known that he took a draft with him when he left England, but it does not appear to have been completed, and when he died suddenly a year later, it could not be found.

Lord Anson's patronage greatly facilitated Robins's experimental work on naval gunnery in the late 1740s. His support was of 'great benefit to him, not only in securing for him the means of varied experiment with all types of guns in use in the Royal Navy, but by the encouragement which his lordship gave

Lord George Anson, 1st Baron Anson (1697–1762), friend and patron of Benjamin Robins, a painting by Thomas Hudson, before 1748.
(© National Maritime Museum, Greenwich, London, BHC2517)

him to publish his opinions even when they were in conflict with the orthodox professional opinion of the day.'[14] Robins also collaborated with Anson in efforts to speed up the process of loading naval guns, which included plans to fit gunlocks (a modified version of the flintlock musket's firing mechanism) and to use flannel instead of paper for making cartridges.[15]

In 1746 Robins produced a gunnery table which demonstrated the impact of air resistance on the range of heavy artillery and demonstrated that his measurements were sufficiently accurate for the naval weapons of his time. He gave the example of a 13in sea mortar which fired a shell weighing 231lbs over a distance of 3,350yds and compared it to his own calculation of the range, which was 3,230yds, a difference of only 120yds.[16] He also investigated low-speed air resistance using the whirling arm, a device he had invented, which was to influence aeronautical testing for the next 150 years until it was replaced by the wind tunnel.[17] It consisted of a drum spun rapidly by a falling weight, which in turn revolved an arm (4ft in length) attached to the conical head of the device. Shot was attached to the arm and as it rotated, the impact of air resistance could be measured. Robins summarised the results of these experiments in a paper presented to the Royal Society in 1746.[18]

In 1747, the year in which he received the Royal Society's Copley Medal for his work on ballistics, Robins produced a pamphlet entitled *Of the Force of Fired Gunpowder*. Published with Anson's encouragement, it criticised efforts to optimise gunpowder charges and barrel lengths in order to maximise a projectile's muzzle velocity.[19] He argued that the barrel length and charge weight should be set to provide the minimum muzzle velocity necessary to destroy the target in question. Later the same year, Robins deployed these arguments in *A Proposal for increasing the strength of the British Navy, by changing all guns from 18pdrs downwards into others of equal weight but of a greater bore*, which proved to be an important influence on the future development of naval gunnery.[20]

Based on a series of experiments beginning in 1742, Robins decided to publish the results only when he discovered that the French had been conducting similar trials. Their results were described in a paper found on the French Third Rate *Mars* (64) when she was captured by the Fourth Rate HMS *Nottingham* (60) in October 1746 as she was returning to France after the failure to capture Louisbourg. The French had found that a 24pdr cannon elevated to 5 degrees had a range of 790yds with an 8lb charge, and only 277yds more with a 20lb charge. They also discovered that the more the shot weighed, the further it travelled with the same proportion of powder but, as Robins pointed out, 'this circumstance of ranging farther … is perhaps the least inconsiderable pre-eminence of heavy shot; for the uncertainty in this practice, especially at sea, is so great, that it has been generally discounted by the most skilful commanders, as tending to waste ammunition.'[21] Lord Anson passed the paper to Robins, who found that the French shared his ideas about gun dimensions and powder-charges. Previously, he had hesitated to publish them because, as he explained, 'not being regularly initiated into the profession of artillery, he would be considered a visionary speculatist.'[22]

In his paper, Robins stated that the greatest advantage of larger shot was that, 'with the same velocity, they break out holes in all solid bodies in a greater proportion than their weight.' For example, 'a twenty-four pound shot will, with the same velocity, break out a hole in any wall, rampart, or solid beam, in which it lodges, above eight times larger than will be made by a three pound shot.' The 24pdr, which was twice the diameter of the 3pdr, would make a 'superficial fracture' more than four times the size and would penetrate to more than twice the depth. This meant that 'in ships the strongest beams and masts are hereby fractured, which a very great number of small bullets would scarcely injure.'[23] Warships were, therefore, armed with the largest cannon they could safely bear and it was necessary to ensure that the weight of metal in a ship's ordnance was deployed to the best advantage. During the previous century, the weight of cannon had generally been reduced, enabling ships to carry guns of a larger bore. Robins argued that cannon should weigh no more than was necessary to avoid the danger of bursting, overheating and to ensure they 'shall not recoil too boisterously'. When these conditions were met, 'all addition of metal beyond is not only useless but prejudicial.'

Robins then stated that there is a law of comparison to which the dimensions of guns should conform and their weights should be calculated. For every pound of shot, a certain weight of metal for the gun could be determined. He took the 32pdr, which was the heaviest naval gun then in general use, as having the correct proportions, which meant 'that for each pound of bullet there should be allowed one hundred and two thirds of metal only.'[24] This enabled him to establish the weight and size of every other piece from 24pdrs to 6pdrs and meant, for example, that a 12pdr should be reduced from a maximum of 34 hundredweight (cwt) to 20cwt.

He also demonstrated that the smallest guns had the greatest relative weight, with the 6pdr weighing as much as 24cwt when, according to Robins's calculations, it should only weigh 10cwt. The excess weight of smaller pieces was due to their barrel length: 'when guns are used in batteries on shore, their length cannot be in proportion to the diameter of their bore, because the parapet being of a considerable thickness, a short piece would by its blast ruin the embrasures.'[25] He recommended that the redundant weight should be used to increase the calibre of smaller guns. Although this would mean a reduction in range, most naval engagements were fought at close quarters, while the destructive effect of a cannonball increased disproportionately to its increase in size.

He also proposed that the powder-charge should be reduced to one-third the weight of the shot for all calibres, which was far less than the proportion then used in 32pdrs (seven-sixteenths of the weight of the ball). This would produce a considerable saving in ammunition, and would keep the guns cooler and quieter without any significant reduction in performance compared to larger charges. He pointed out that the 'sides of the strongest ship, and the greater part of her timbers, are of a limited thickness, insufficient to stop the generality of cannon bullets, fired at a reasonable distance', even with the reduced charge he proposed.[26]

In a letter to Lord Anson, read at the Royal Society in October 1749, Robins reported on the results of his extensive experiments with an 18pdr cannon at Chatham Naval Dockyard during the previous July. He explained that the subject of his experiments 'relates to a matter about which I have formerly troubled your lordship; I mean, the diminishing the allotment of powder for heavy cannon, and thereby facilitating the reduction in the weight of those pieces.'[27] The results modified the conclusions he had presented in his earlier pamphlet on increasing the strength of the Royal Navy.

From these experiments, he concluded that much smaller powder-charges were far more effective than had been generally believed (or he had previously proposed). Beyond a certain charge (for example, 3.5lbs of powder in an 18pdr),

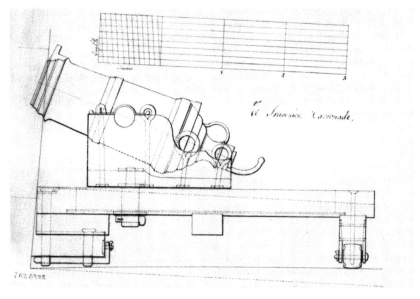

18-pounder Trunnion Carronade on its Slide Mounting, 1790s, an ink drawing. (© National Maritime Museum, Greenwich, London, ZAZ6988)

'all addition of powder will create but an inconsiderable change either in the range at an elevation, or in the force at a distance: And that the penetration of an 18pdr with 3 pound of powder is [at almost 33in] more than sufficient for traversing the sides of the stoutest ships.'[28] Increasing the velocity of the bullet 'is not only an [sic] useless, but a prejudicial practice; since, in penetrating solid bodies, that bullet which has but just force enough to go through, will produce much greater effect, than a bullet, which has a considerable velocity after it has got through.'[29]

Despite Lord Anson's support and some expressions of interest from the navy, Robins's proposals for reducing the weight and increasing the calibre of guns were not adopted quickly. The explanation may be the 'erroneous opinions at present prevailing among the practitioners of artillery', according to Robins's own assessment of his contemporaries' conservative attitudes. A practical design was eventually developed by General Robert Melville (1723–1809), who worked on improvements in ordnance and shell delivery. Influenced by Robins's arguments, he designed a new 'short seven-calibre weapon, [which] delivered a slow-moving, heavy shot which upon impact with timber caused a large irregular hole and massive splintering'.[30]

However, there was a considerable delay in adopting Melville's design as its production depended on other innovations, notably the process of boring out barrels cast as solid pieces of iron, a process not invented until 1769. Previously, cannon had been cast in a mould enclosing a core and then bored to remove imperfections, while the new technique enabled guns to be made with much less windage – the space between the shot and the surface of the bore – and meant that they were lighter, required a smaller charge of powder (which made reloading quicker) and fewer men to operate them. As Robins had found, reduced windage meant that a projectile would deviate less in flight.

In 1774 the Carron Iron Works of Falkirk installed a cylinder-boring machine and four years later it produced the first prototype based on Melville's design, naming it the carronade.[31] Reflecting Robins's ideas, carronades were much shorter, about seven calibres (seven times the diameter of their bores) and some 30 per cent lighter than the equivalent long gun. In their original form they closely resembled a mortar. The new design was adopted by the Admiralty in 1779 and remained in service until the 1840s. Although it had a mixed operational record, the carronade has been described as 'perhaps the most important innovation in naval ordnance since the introduction of bronze guns at sea in the sixteenth century',[32] its length to calibre to weight ratio representing a significant technological advance.

England had been slow to recognise the benefits of rifling in small arms and ordnance and Robins addressed the issue in a paper on the 'nature and advantage of a rifled barrel piece', presented to the Royal Society in 1747. He explained theoretically why rifling – spiralled groves in the interior of the bore – produced greater accuracy of fire compared to the smoothbore gun – and why bullets should be egg-shaped rather than spherical, as this would give them the same stability seen in arrows. Robins emphasised the importance of applying rifling to heavy ordnance as well as to small arms.

Robins was aware of the strategic implications of his analysis as well as its scientific significance and concluded with the following prophecy: 'whatever state shall thoroughly comprehend the nature and advantages of rifled barrel pieces, and ... shall introduce into their armies their general use ... will acquire a superiority, which will almost equal any thing, that has been done at any time by the particular excellence of any one kind of arms.'[33] But his words were to have little practical effect before the mid nineteenth century because of the difficulties in manufacturing rifled ordnance. Thus rifling did not come into general naval use until after the Crimean War (1853–56).

Robins also investigated the potential use of rockets for naval and military purposes. In a paper read to the Royal Society in May 1749, he reported that one of the rockets fired during an official fireworks display in Green Park, London, which had been organised to celebrate the end of the War of the Austrian Succession (1739–48), had reached a maximum height of 615yds. Such rockets typically reached about 440yds and three had risen to 526yds. He calculated that the rockets could be seen more than fifty miles away 'if their light be sufficiently strong, and the air be not hazy'.[34]

Soon afterwards, Robins conducted his own experiments to establish how far rockets could rise, as well as the distance from which they could be seen. He fired several single-pound rockets and found that they could reach a height of between 450 and 500yds after an ascent of just under seven seconds. These experiments were to lead to the development of purpose-built signal rockets for naval use. The rockets, which discharged white stars, were manufactured for the Royal Navy by the Royal Laboratory, Woolwich, and production to the same specifications continued well into the nineteenth century.

Robins's work on the science of ballistics was brought to an end when he left England in December 1749 to take up his appointment as Engineer General for the East India Company, with Lord Anson expressing regret at his departure. Arriving in India in July 1750, his responsibilities were to make 'plans of fortifications and propose expedients where he deems improvements necessary, and ensure there is proper training in the use of cannons and mortars and the proper allotment of ammunition.'[35] He made preparations for the defence of Madras (Chennai) and Fort St David before dying of a fever in July 1751, just over a year after his arrival in India.

Robins's legacy

The results of Robins's gunnery experiments were widely disseminated and proved to be highly influential. A late eighteenth-century mathematician, Charles Hutton, who continued Robins's experimental work, referred to the *New Principles of Gunnery* as 'the first work that can be considered as attempting to establish a practical system of gunnery, and projectiles, on good experiments, on the force of gunpowder, on the resistance of the air, and on the effects of different pieces of artillery.'[36] Three years after its publication in London, Frederick the Great commissioned Leonard Euler, the eminent Swiss mathematician, to produce a German translation and it soon also appeared in French. In the German edition, published in 1745, Euler significantly improved the original text by adding a series of tables, which gave the velocity, range, maximum altitude and flight time for a projectile fired at certain velocities and elevation angles.[37]

The work of Robins and later mathematicians led to significant improvements in the accuracy and impact of naval artillery. Practical guides to gunnery, based on mathematics and geometry, which were inspired by his work – and sometimes offered critical comment – soon appeared.[38] The development of the carronade, which had been inspired by Robins's proposals for guns of larger calibre and lower weight, produced a significant increase in the Royal Navy's firepower. His ideas may have also influenced the design of the standard long gun, with the Armstrong-Frederick pattern (1760) using a reduced powder-charge of one-third the weight of shot in line with Robins's original recommendations. Its successor, the Blomefield canon, which the navy adopted in 1794, had a lower weight as a result of reducing the thickness of the tube. Although the gunlock, which Robins had advocated, was not widely adopted during his lifetime, it had become a standard fitting on naval ordnance by the late eighteenth century and proved to be an 'important aid to disciplined firing'.[39]

The effect of these innovations, stimulated by Robins's work, were to give England a significant advantage during the French Revolutionary and Napoleonic Wars when combined with changes in naval tactics. As economist-historian John Nef has pointed out, 'typical older battles of the period of limited warfare – Beachy Head in 1690, Malaga in 1704, and Toulon in 1744 – were battles of slow attrition and meagre results. By concentrating ships and fire on a section of the enemy line … English admirals of the Napoleonic period … were able to modify naval tactics, to break up the enemy's fleet, and to win decisive victories at sea.'[40]

Robert Fulton's Infernal Machines

Christopher Pieczynski

In modern usage, the employment of floating or moored mines in maritime warfare offers a significant offensive and defensive advantage over a superior maritime power. Even the mere possibility of the presence of mines is enough to cause hesitancy in maritime operations (save, of course, for the famous 'Damn the Torpedoes' incident of the American Civil War). The initial introduction of such weaponry, originally called 'torpedoes', met with reluctance from some naval commanders.

One of the most prolific developers of early undersea weapons was an American named Robert Fulton. Both an artist and inventor, Fulton initially sought to improve upon the design of the first submarine by David Bushnell, called the *Turtle*. It was not until Fulton sold rights to a newly patented invention for moving boats between levels of a canal without a lock, called the inclined plane, that Fulton finally had the requisite funding necessary to begin building his improved submarine.[1] Seeking to patent the inclined plane in France, Fulton found himself caught up in the Napoleonic Wars with a unique opportunity – to aid in the French invasion of Great Britain.

Robert Fulton, drawing by Charles G Crehen, 1850.
(Library of Congress, public domain)

Fulton in France and Britain

Initially, Fulton built his submarine, or 'plunging device', with the intent of using its submerged stealth to place an explosive device of his design, called a torpedo, on the hulls of British ships. His submarine vessel, the *Nautilus*, propelled by hand, was limited by speed, unable to make more than two or three knots. While the venture proved unsuitable for attacking ships under sail, it held possibility for ships at anchor. Fulton identified needed modifications to improve the *Nautilus'* performance but was stymied by the ever-changing political dynamics in France. Supporters within the government who offered official sanction for the scheme were often replaced, quickly, by others who wanted nothing to do with the venture. He was finally able to secure 10,000 francs for repairs and modifications and was offered certain bounties for ships sunk based on the number of cannon.[2]

Fulton finally had his chance in September 1800 off the harbour of Growan, near Isigny, when he attempted to approach two British brigs at anchor. For reasons unknown, both ships weighed anchor, denying Fulton his opportunity to sink a vessel with his invention.[3] News of his endeavours reached British shores, where ships were now ordered to avoid lingering in an area too long lest more of Fulton's machines be lurking. Before Fulton could find another opportunity, the Treaty of Amiens ended the hostilities in 1802, rendering his services and invention no longer needed.

Not without merit, Fulton's concepts eventually caught the attention of Napoleon himself. Napoleon lamented, 'Citizen Fulton's proposal that you sent to me much too late, in that it can change the face of world.'[4] Napoleon was talking more about Fulton's steam navigation experiments and the idea of using steam-powered ships to tow landing barges across the English Channel to invade England. The limited speed obtained during Fulton's steam experiments and the requirement for calm seas and light winds limited the options for using this means of attack, but Napoleon recognised that perhaps a combination of steam, submarine and torpedoes was worth further investigation.

The peace would not last long. When hostilities recommenced, France found itself losing a unique capability. Ever the opportunist, Fulton had immediately offered his services, including his submarine and torpedo devices, to the British government. He was now in Great Britain conducting experiments on steam propulsion. Although the government had brought Fulton under contract, it was not without some hesitation. Prime Minister William Pitt surmised that since England's pride and strength was in her navy, Fulton's invention could make the Royal Navy sailing warships obsolete, thus damaging England's symbol of power and prestige in the process.[5]

England conducted an initial attempt against the French fleet at Boulogne in September 1804. Small boats launched several torpedo devices against the French fleet at anchor. A few of the machines exploded, but not near their intended targets, and several appear to have washed ashore intact. George Elphinstone, Admiral Lord Keith, who led the attack, lamented that 'the enemy sustained very little, if any injury, our machines not answering the purpose for which they were intended [...] I heartily wish we had never taken them.'[6]

To put any doubts about the utility of his weapon design to rest, Fulton demonstrated his torpedo against the former 200-ton Danish brig *Dorothea*. In the experiment off Deal, near the residence of William Pitt, trial runs proved that the torpedo, carried by the tide, would perform as desired. When the actual live-fire test was ready on 15 October 1805, Pitt and Lord Melville, First Lord of the Admiralty, were away on business and unable to observe the experiment. Had they been present, they would have witnessed the *Dorothea* lifted about 6ft out of the water and broken in two in the centre before disappearing below the water, all in the course of about twenty seconds.[7]

'Sinking the *Dorothea* with a Torpedo', in Robert Fulton, *Torpedo and Submarine Explosions*, 1810. (Project Gutenberg, public domain)

While this test proved the ability and effectiveness of Fulton's torpedo, the need, or even desire, for such a weapon changed a week later with Vice Admiral Horatio Nelson's glorious victory off Cape Trafalgar. With a combined French-Spanish maritime threat greatly reduced, there appeared to be little penchant for such an innovative, if not ungentlemanly, system. As a result, Fulton's contract, which included a stipend of £200 per month and a reward of £40,000 for each vessel sunk with his system, was nullified. It was not clear whether the contract provision not to divulge 'any part of his principles to any person whatever for the space of fourteen years' was still binding.[8]

Fulton nonetheless tried to re-engage with Pitt whom, he believed, could be a key influencer in securing British backing for the weapon. In an unpublished memoir to Pitt, Fulton presented his case as one of using science to obtain peace in the world. Fulton surmised that any nation using his weapons, the submarine and the torpedo:

> … them all in equal safety, affords no inducement for tyrannising, puts an end to maritime dreadful, catalogue of crimes which they entrain, the barbarous impressment of seamen, the unbridled passion for violence & plundre [*sic*], other immoralities which are now let loose with every war, & are so difficult to restrain at the return of peace. On the ruins of these may arise the liberty of commerce & the harmony of nations.[9]

Fulton returns to the US

Fulton never sent the letter but continued his 'peace through weaponry' message in later publications and writings. Following rebukes from both the French and British governments, Fulton returned to the United States to continue pursuing a potentially more lucrative endeavour – the steamship. The idea to use steam as ship propulsion was not a new idea. Early inventors such as James Rumsey, John Fitch and Samuel Morey were unable to perfect a propulsion system capable of generating enough speed for a ship. Fulton devised a way to overcome this difficulty with the side paddlewheel system and demonstrated it in the *Clermont*.[10]

No sooner had Fulton refocused his attention on steamships than the next phase of possible torpedo use came into view. On 21 June 1807 Americans were outraged and threatened war against Britain when the Fourth Rate frigate HMS *Leopard* (50) fired upon the Fifth Rate frigate USS *Chesapeake* (38) as she was departing Hampton Roads, Virginia, on a cruise to the Mediterranean. The British believed *Chesapeake* had four British deserters who had joined the crew in Norfolk. A boarding party from *Leopard* refused surrender of the *Chesapeake* and instead searched the ship and removed the four suspected deserters. The incident was one of many instances where seamen, suspected of being British citizens, were impressed into the Royal Navy, but the first such incident against an American warship.

The war looming, American responses ranged from calls for expulsion of all British vessels from American ports to an all-out declaration of war. Fulton suggested that his torpedo concept would be effective in enforcing British expulsion from ports through the use of both floating torpedoes against violators and moored torpedoes to establish exclusion areas. Even an anonymous letter to the editor of the New York-based *Balance and Columbian Repository* signed by 'Archimedes' called for torpedo use, stating: 'the wooden walls of Old England may be entirely demolished.'[11] Was 'Archimedes' really Fulton?

Although President Thomas Jefferson was lukewarm regarding the idea, the defence committee in New York City was not. Fulton conducted a demonstration in which he sank a brig in New York harbour, launching the torpedoes from gunboats and using the tide to sweep them toward the target vessel. The resulting explosion caused the target to sink and, as Fulton described it, provided 'the best and most simple mode of using it with the greatest effect in maritime wars.'[12]

Fulton returned to his steamship operation, but not before publishing his undersea warfare concept in hopes of garnering more interest in his project. *Torpedo War and Submarine Explosions*, published in 1810 and dedicated to President James Madison, detailed the various uses and implementation methods of torpedoes for offensive and defensive purposes. Presenting a detailed analysis of situations in which torpedoes could be useful, and addressing number and placement, targeted ship size, cost, and even probable effectiveness, Fulton's publication sparked discussions in Congress on utilising torpedoes for defending ports and harbours. The concept was a natural complement to Jefferson's gunboat strategy in which ports and harbours were defended by a series of coastal fortifications, operating in conjunction with gunboats. Why not augment the system with torpedoes? While not everyone was receptive to the idea, Congress ordered experiments to determine 'how far the Torpedo, or submarine explosions, may be usefully employed as engines of war', allocating $5,000 for the experiment.[13]

Fulton conducted an experiment in New York harbour in much the same manner as the sinking of *Dorothea* in 1805. Using the US Brig *Argus* (20), and blank torpedoes so as to not damage the vessel, Fulton tested a variety of delivery techniques including spar delivery, floating torpedo, moored torpedo, and harpoon assisted delivery.[14] All methods showed a semblance of possibility, but met with mostly failure. *Argus'* crew demonstrated effective countermeasures against torpedoes with passive defences such as nets over the sides to snare the torpedo or any other floating objects. The best defence against the torpedo delivery vessel proved to be *Argus'* 24pdr cannon firing grapeshot at suitable range to destroy the delivery vessel before torpedo launch could occur.[15]

American captains Isaac Chauncey and John Rodgers witnessed the proceedings. Rodgers was critical of the concept and he showed his contempt for the torpedo equally with his contempt for Fulton himself. Rodgers viewed Fulton as one who had already 'exerted himself to impose a belief on the minds of the Citizens of the UStates [*sic*] that his project was calculated to supersede the necessity of a Navy.' Rodgers concluded that torpedoes were 'comparatively of no importance at all; consequently that they ought not to be relied on as a means of national defense.'[16] Turning again to steamship development, Fulton all but abandoned his undersea ventures.

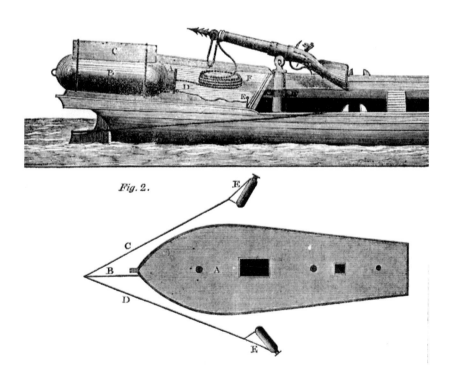

'Torpedo launching system using a harpoon', in Robert Fulton,
Torpedo and Submarine Explosions (1810). (Project Gutenberg, public domain)

Torpedoes in the War of 1812

The United States declared war on Great Britain on 18 June 1812, at a decided disadvantage with only a handful of oceangoing warships and an army steadily declining in size and readiness. While issuing letters of marque for privateers proved successful, with more than five hundred captures of British merchant vessels in just the first six months of the war, the Royal Navy was beginning to tighten the noose of the blockade at many of the major ports.[17] With the Delaware and Chesapeake bays now finding British warships in their waters, the Jeffersonian coastal defence plan was quickly proving its inadequacy. The US resurfaced older means of attack, namely fire-ships and floating powder kegs, to counter the British fleet threatening Hampton Roads and their attempt to capture the Fifth Rate frigate USS *Constellation* (38), chased into the Elizabeth River off Norfolk.[18]

Rear-Admiral George Cockburn's early raids up the Chesapeake forced the US Congress to act. Military resources were stretched thin, leaving many coastal cities and ports utterly defenceless. The government looked elsewhere and incentivised civilians to sink British vessels in the Act to Encourage the Destruction of the Armed Vessels of War of the Enemy. The Act stated:

> it shall be lawful for any person or persons to burn, sink, or destroy, any British armed vessel of war [...] and for that purpose to use torpedoes, submarine instruments, or any other destructive machine whatever: and a bounty of one half the value of the armed vessel so burnt, sunk, or destroyed.[19]

The Act, specifically citing the use of 'torpedoes, submarine instruments, or any other destructive machine', appeared to offer Fulton another opportunity for his torpedo. Fulton, however, finding success and increasing demand with the steamship, opted out of this challenge. Even though Fulton's design was not patented but published with great details on how the machines were built and operated, certain technical aspects, known only to Fulton, remained a challenge to the casual weapon builder. In particular, the clockwork mechanism that activated the powder proved to be extremely delicate. In theory, the clock would be activated by removing a pin from the device. The clock would be set for a specified time starting from when the pin was released (generally, by the boat crew pulling a line, thereby launching the torpedo). At the end of the set time, the clockwork would activate a flintlock that ignited the powder in the torpedo, causing the explosion.[20] The delay was theoretically long enough for the torpedo to float into position on or under the target ship and allow the launching boat to escape to a safe distance.

One of the first attempts under the Act occurred in Long Island Sound and was carried out by John Scudder, Jr, a businessman of curiosities. Scudder took the schooner *Eagle*, loaded the vessel with explosives hidden under a variety of other materials worthy of capture, and rigged the ship to explode. The Third Rate HMS *Ramillies* (74), Captain Thomas Hardy, was on patrol in the Sound and the *Eagle* was positioned as a vessel that looked abandoned by its crew. It was hoped that the boarding party would see the prize goods and bring *Eagle* alongside *Ramillies* for offloading. The materials were rigged to explode when moved, thus destroying or damaging *Ramillies* during the offloading.[21]

The explosive device worked as planned. However, it was not *Ramillies* that was alongside during the explosion. Another small vessel was sent alongside instead to offload the cargo and it was this vessel that was destroyed. Eleven British sailors were killed in the explosion.[22] Scudder had rigged *Eagle* with ten kegs of powder mixed with sulphur, with two gun flintlocks rigged so that any movement, such as moving the barrels, would trigger the gun-lock. To increase the expected explosion, barrels of turpentine were added for flammability. Scudder cited his reasons for creating the device as more for retribution for British instigation of the native population in the Ohio Valley (where Scudder had family), rather than financial reward offered by the government for sinking a British warship.[23]

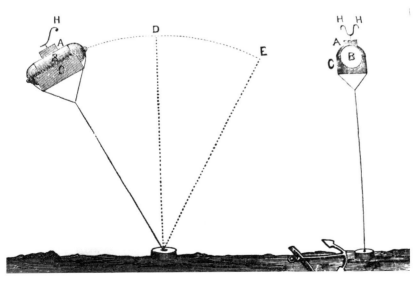

'Moored torpedo configuration' in Robert Fulton, *Torpedo and Submarine Explosions* (1810). (Project Gutenberg, public domain)

Meanwhile, local officials in New York City, remembering the 1811 torpedo tests and demonstrations, opted for the moored torpedo version. Fixed torpedoes were moored in the Narrows with their presence well-publicised to act as a deterrent. An inspection of one of the torpedoes weeks later showed the 'powder was perfectly dry', testimony to the viability of the weapon.[24]

Another entrepreneur, Elijah Mix, tried his hand at destroying a British warship as the fleet operated off Annapolis. This time the US Navy was a little more receptive to the scheme, offering a boat, six men and 500lbs of powder.[25] Mix, a merchant captain, had gained familiarity with several former Fulton devices located at the Washington Navy Yard (with Fulton's permission) and was appointed a US Navy sailing master in 1812, which might account for the navy's co-operation.[26] When the British fleet moved back to the Chesapeake Bay entrance, Mix had to relocate his preparations to Norfolk, finding the Lynnhaven Inlet anchorage area a target rich environment.

Mix had difficulty pulling off his plan. His chosen target was the Third Rate HMS *Plantagenet* (74), which he reported anchored in the same vicinity in Lynnhaven Inlet for almost a month. Operating from an open boat named *Chesapeake's Revenge*, his first attempt on the night of 18 July 1813 was discovered by a lookout. Trying again on the 19th, he was under the bow of the ship readying the device when a sentinel called out 'Boat ahoy?' As Mix made his escape, the sentinel:

… fired his musket, which was followed by a rapid discharge of small arms. Blue lights were made to find the boat, but failed, they then threw rockets in different directions, which illuminated the water for a considerable width as far as they were thrown, and succeeded in discovering the position of the nocturnal visitor; when the ship commenced a rapid fire of heavy guns, slipped her cables and made some sail, while her boats were dispatched in pursuit.[27]

Mix got away. He was persistent, however, trying again on four other nights to sink *Plantagenet*, all without success.

However, the evening of 24 June was the closest Mix and *Chesapeake's Revenge* came to sinking *Plantagenet*. As Mix manoeuvred to:

Within 100 yards distance in a direction with her larboard bow, he dropped the fatal machine into the water just as the centinel was crying all's well. It swept along with the tide, and would have completely effected its errand, but for a cause not proper to be named here, but which may be easily guarded against in future experiments, it exploded a few seconds to soon. The scene was awfully sublime! It was like the concussion of an earthquake, attended with a sound louder and more terrific than the heaviest of thunder. A pyramid of water fifty feet in circumference was thrown up to the height 30 or 40 feet, its appearance was a vivid red, tinged at the sides with a beautiful purple. On ascending to its greatest height, it burst at the top with a tremendous explosion, and fell in torrents on the decks of the ship, which rolled into the yawning chasm below, and had nearly upset; impervious darkness again prevailed. The light occasioned by the explosion, though fleeting, enabled Mr. M. and his companions to discover that the fore channel of the ship was blown, and a boat which lay alongside with several men in her, was thrown up in the dreadful convulsion of the waters. Terrible indeed must have been the panic of the ship's crew, from the noise and confusion which appeared to our adventurers to prevail on board; and they are certain that nearly the whole ship's crew betook themselves to the boats.

The damage was minimal, but it gave the British concern that their anchorage in Lynnhaven Inlet, while convenient, was anything but safe. The *Norfolk Herald* ended their coverage of Mix's attempt with: 'Since the Torpedo explosion on Saturday night, the Plantagenet has been guarded by a 74 and 2 frigates, which, with 2 or 3 tenders, comprise all the shipping at present in Lynnhaven.'[28]

One of Mix's torpedoes recovered by the Third Rate HMS *Victorious* (74) was dissected and described as:

... six barrels of gunpowder, to which a lock is affixed; and attached to the lock is a line, reaching to the person or boat that has the execution of the design. It is next suspended to a stage of planks, at each end of which are about 50 fathoms of small line, with a buoy at each end.[29]

The British were not amused by the attempts. Admiral George Cockburn reported that by using a 'Powder Machine' the 'American Government [is] intending thus to dispose of us by wholesale Six Hundred at a time.' Cockburn further characterised these as 'infernal Machines' and lamented that, 'I have now closed with His Majesty's Ships towards Hampton Roads, which will enable the Enemy to try further humane Experiments with us with much more facility to himself and much less risk to the Public at large.'[30]

Elijah Mix's action in Lynnhaven Inlet was not the only attempt to use torpedoes or mines on British warships, but it was the closest that any attempt came to success. Reports of attempted torpedo attacks against the blockading fleet at the Delaware Bay resulted in two individuals with British sympathies warning Commodore Beresford on the Third Rate HMS *Poictiers* (74). The British barred fishing boats in the area from leaving port as these were suspected of delivering the torpedo devices.[31] Prisoners taken in a raid on New London, retribution for the *Eagle* attack, were publicly announced as being on the British ships as a means of preventing additional torpedo attacks lest American citizens be killed in the attempts.[32] Hardy even ordered a raid into East Hampton to detain Joshua Penny, a 'non-combatant' suspected of plotting another *Eagle*-type attack.[33] Hardy further threatened to destroy any town where a torpedo was fitted out.[34]

The British reaction to the new weapons was varied, but mostly verging on outrage. It did not help that Americans viewed the torpedo as a fairly useful weapon – and even called for its expanded use. This was even prior to the War of 1812. Following the *Chesapeake–Leopard* Affair in 1807, poetry emerged touting the use of the torpedo. A line from one such poem cited:

See the British squadron comes!
All asleep it is supposed –
Burst torpedoes! Ocean foams!
And the squadron's 'decomposed.'[35]

Such open, public support, even up to and during the war, served to legitimise the use of such weapons.

The attempts in Long Island Sound and Lynnhaven Inlet drew a host of criticism from the British. In a letter to the editor of the *Naval Chronicle*, a writer identified only as 'Albion' surmised that with the continued trend of using 'unnatural' weapons, the war would 'become one of unprecedented cruelty'. He placed the blame for this shift on the Americans, highlighting that:

we have, conscious of our superiority, forborne to commit hostilities beyond the capture of sheep and oxen, even on that part of their coast where their newly invented torpedos were preparing for the destruction of our navy. To forbear reprisals under these circumstances, was no doubt magnanimous, as we could perhaps have only punished the innocent inhabitants, whilst those actually fitting out these infernals might have escaped the vengeance of justly incensed enemies.[36]

Another British officer called 'this species of warfare, unmanley, and I might say assassin-like.' The same officer, however, noted that the outcry generated by the American use of such 'dastardly proceedings' was potentially hypocritical since the 'example had been first set by England.'[37]

The use of the American 'infernal machine' saw the rise of a variety of British counter-torpedo weapons and ideas – some realistic, some farcical. Without a viable torpedo defence, the added caution while operating in American waters reduced the effectiveness of British operations for fear of an infernal machine attack. Both the Scudder attack in Long Island Sound and the Mix attack in Lynnhaven Inlet were against easy targets – they were anchored or largely stationary. This caused commanders in both areas to issue orders restricting the idleness of vessels in and around ports and rivers, forcing constant manoeuvring in shallow or constrained waters, thus increasing risk and wearing on ships' crews. Anticipating such attacks based on intelligence, additional small boat patrols and increased watches, particularly at night, added to the wear.[38]

One counter-torpedo weapon was a British submarine device reportedly under construction by the government. A contributor to the *Naval Chronicle* described the device as 'porpoise'-shaped, 27ft in length and 5ft in diameter, capable of making 4 knots (almost twice the speed of Fulton's submarine).[39] Able to resist a 12pdr shot at 'point-blank shot', the submarine was specifically built to 'counteract the torpedo system of America'. There is no indication that the British government ordered such a system and the inclusion of this letter may have been a simple psychological countermeasure against further torpedo employment. The simple physics of a vessel able to make that speed and withstand that amount of direct fire seem impossible based on the technology of that day.

Many officers of the day expressed a belief that further reinforced the reluctance to adopt this technology. 'Let us hope that in future wars the nation will evince a more chivalric spirit, and abandon for ever a system which, to all generous minds, must ever appear mean as well as dastardly.'[40] By dismissing Fulton's idea, this lost opportunity would see several more decades pass before the Royal Navy embraced mine warfare as something other than a peripheral weapon, ceding the technological advantage to the United States in the interim.

'The Yankey Torpedo', see colour plate 2

Charts 'sent by the ever to be lamented Lord Nelson': Some Reflections on Navigational Practice in the Georgian Royal Navy

Michael Barritt

The chart is a key aid for the planning and execution of a campaign or voyage. But how has it been used throughout the centuries, not least in the era of Nelson? In the lifetime of the author it remained a reference document in some merchant vessels, stowed away in the chart-house at the back of the bridge, to be taken out and consulted alongside pilot books and navigational tables. In the Royal Navy in which the author served, the chart had long since transitioned into a plotting surface as well as a repository of information. It was central to a rigorous navigational routine. During planning, the navigating officer laid down tracks on the charts with ancillary information such as the rate and direction of the tidal stream. By plotting frequent fixes, he could ensure adherence to those tracks in the course of a voyage.

Theoretical works from earlier ages throw little light on chart usage. A few images made onboard ships suggest that, from the time of the early medieval portolan chart through to the nineteenth century, charts were generally rolled and stowed below decks. The format of most commercially published charts, through to the renowned blue-back charts of the nineteenth and twentieth centuries, was designed to aid visual pilotage with reference to leading and clearing marks. Many were designed, like today's car satnav systems in 'heads up' mode, to show the coast as the mariner would view it during his approach, and few coastal charts had graticules of latitude and longitude.

A lack of examples hinders analysis. Charts worn by usage were discarded and destroyed. The best source of early evidence is the MEDEA-CHART Database hosted by the Faculty of Sciences, University of Lisbon, Portugal.[1] This database identifies some ninety-seven examples of charts created between 1492 and 1798 on which navigational annotations have been made. Some of these can be identified confidently as plotted positions, with some connected by a track. Rare survivals which can be analysed more closely will generally be associated with a prominent historical personality or event. Thus it is that we can examine several charts which were onboard the First Rate HMS *Victory*

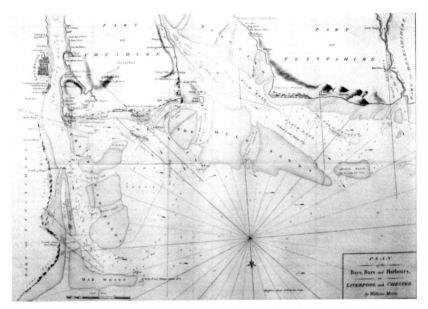

A chart from the turn of the eighteenth and nineteenth centuries in the style preferred by many mariners operating from Liverpool. South is at the top, thus showing the coast as the approaching navigator would see it. There is no graticule of latitude and longitude. Leading marks and transits are highlighted with vignettes. (Author's collection)

(100) during Lord Nelson's command in the Mediterranean leading up to the Trafalgar campaign.

Recording the track made good and the gathering of hydrographic information
In a report to the Board of Admiralty, their hydrographer, Alexander Dalrymple, noted that Nelson had sent a number of manuscript charts to the Hydrographical Office, the loss of whose interest was 'ever to be lamented'.[2] Nelson had been only too ready to respond to the request of his old friend Thomas Troubridge during the latter's tenure as a commissioner on the Board. Troubridge, too, had shown an acute awareness of the importance of hydrographic intelligence, and his correspondence with Nelson at the time confirms this:

My Lord, I have sent you a few Charts of what we have finished, and by giving them to intelligent men with directions to make remarks and correct any errors we shall in time make them good […] I sent a lot of what was done I think 20 copies of each by the *Seahorse* […] it is a great thing to know any information you may send me. I will add to our collection.[3]

Troubridge had been alert for the plans coming from Rear-Admiral Sir Richard Bickerton, senior officer in the Mediterranean during the short-lived Treaty of Amiens. He had orchestrated a campaign of data-gathering round the coasts of Sardinia. Troubridge had passed these without delay to Dalrymple. He had them swiftly engraved in the simple format of his East India Company charts. Sufficient copies for despatch to the Mediterranean fleet were then run off on the Boulton and Watt proofing press which the Admiralty had purchased for the Hydrographical Office.

Bickerton had encouraged the sharing of manuscript copies of surveys whilst awaiting the charts from London. One of these manuscripts was a survey of the Maddalena Archipelago made by Midshipman (later Captain) Alexander Becher RN in 1789. This manuscript had been given to Captain George Ryves of the Third Rate *Agincourt* (64) when Bickerton despatched him to make a further examination of a promising fleet anchorage. Nelson praised this anchorage and christened it 'Agincourt Sound'.[4] The manuscript chart that guided Nelson on his first entry to the anchorage is preserved in the archive of the United Kingdom Hydrographic Office (UKHO).[5]

Boulton and Watt proofing press. This one is on display in the office of George Washington, Mount Vernon, Virginia. (Photo by Judith E Pearson)

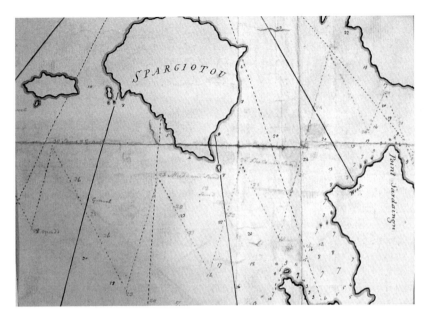

Thomas Atkinson's plot of the track of HMS *Victory*, with soundings and seabed samples, added to Captain Ryves's manuscript survey. (UK Hydrographic Office, reference m13 on Ry)

This Agincourt Sound chart is a clear example of a chart in use as a reference document, giving guidance to the navigator regarding safe water, alerting him to dangers, and enabling the selection of head marks and clearing marks as *Victory* beat upwind at the head of the squadron. But, as another invaluable survival in the British Library makes clear, the chart was also in use as a plotting surface. Nelson recorded in a little pocket book every one of the alterations of course shown on the chart, together with the hydrographic information, the sounding and sample of the seabed, which his crew obtained as the great ship went about.[6] One can imagine the master of *Victory*, Thomas Atkinson, seeing the ship safely on its new course and then diving into his adjacent day cabin to plot the track and information shown in the illustration above.

Dalrymple included the tracks of the squadron on his published charts for this area.[7] His East India Company charts reflected this established practice, which was designed as an encouragement to other captains and masters to render track plots with their deductions of ocean currents and their fixing of coastline and soundings when in uncharted waters. John Hamilton Moore and others laid down this methodology in textbooks. Article VII of Part Three of the Royal Navy's *Regulations and Instructions* gave the responsibility for this task to the master, as navigational specialist. Expanded directions were issued in Admiralty circulars. In 1805, during his administration as Lord of the Admiralty, John Jervis, the 1st Earl of St Vincent, issued a particularly comprehensive circular that detailed guidance from Dalrymple on formats and symbols for remark books and charts.[8]

Such guidance was necessary. When Dalrymple's successor, Thomas Hurd, was briefing the first 'Admiralty Surveyor' to deploy into theatre, he noted that he had an abundance of plans thanks to the initiative of the flag officers on station. These were pragmatic documents, mostly compiled by the masters in the fleet. They were the result of compass surveys, and most would indicate a value for variation. Some might record latitude for a feature on the chart. Yet others contained no positional information at all, clearly expecting that at least the name of the location was known to others serving in the theatre. Hence Hurd lamented that he could not compile all this data into a chart of the whole sea, since 'he was greatly at a loss for latitudes and longitudes to dress it by.' The surveyor, William Henry Smyth, would list in his famous books the precise positions for landfalls and other important places that he had obtained by astronomical observation.[9] They helped Hurd to extend the coverage of the small-scale charts to include the Mediterranean, coverage that was essential for campaign and voyage planning.[10]

Selecting and following safe tracks
In 1805 a set of small-scale charts for the Mediterranean was available in Britain. Captain John Knight had compiled these charts. He had assisted in the campaign of hydrographic surveys conducted in North America after the Seven Years War (1756–63), and thereafter was assiduous in gathering data throughout his active service, ensuring timely promulgation by London's commercial chart publishers. Knight had served as flag captain in the Mediterranean at the outset of the French Revolutionary War (1793) and the charts indicate clearly the coasts with which he had personal knowledge. He undoubtedly used the charts himself in 1805 when, as a newly promoted rear-admiral, he commanded the escort of a vital troop-carrying convoy, conducting it safely into the sea and despatching it onwards to Malta. A portfolio of the charts, entitled 'Knight's Atlas', is preserved in the Naval Historical Branch in Portsmouth.[11] It belonged to Lord Keith, Nelson's precursor as commander-in-chief in the Mediterranean. It contains annotations plotted on the sheets. Significantly, they record a reported danger in the approaches to the Strait of Sicily at the extremity of Knight's coverage. Having no experience of the eastern basin of the sea, he had not attempted to include it.

Hence, when preparing for redeployment to the Mediterranean as sailing

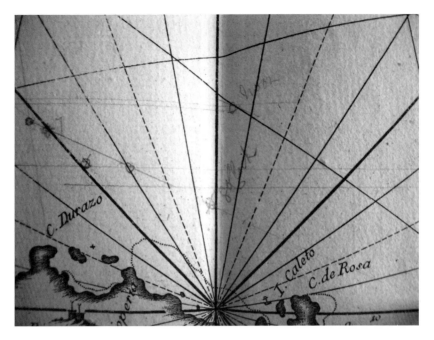

Thomas Atkinson's plotted positions on landfall on the North African coast for 0700h, 1200h, and 2000h (adjusted) on 5 February 1803. (© National Maritime Museum, Greenwich, London)

master of *Victory* at the resumption of hostilities against Napoleon's France, Thomas Atkinson resorted to an old atlas of charts by Joseph Roux, which he had taken from one of the French ships after the Battle of the Nile. This atlas is another invaluable survival, preserved in the National Maritime Museum.[12] Its sheets are annotated with his plotted positions and tracks for the first entry of *Victory* to the Mediterranean in 1803, seeking out the fleet. They also reveal how he used these small-scale charts in the hunt for Villeneuve's fleet across the Eastern Mediterranean in 1805.

When news reached Nelson in Agincourt Sound on 19 January 1805 that the French fleet had sailed from Toulon, he set off for Alexandria. In the early morning of 5 February, after an 800nm run from Messina with a steady WNW wind, Nelson's fleet made landfall on what Atkinson described as a 'very low' coast. His Roux chart showed off-lying rocks, and he could not be certain how accurate the representation was. Comparison with modern charts justifies his caution. The extended pencil lines on his plot showing latitude reflect that caution – how close is that coast? The fleet 'hauled up on the larboard tack' and set an easterly course.[13]

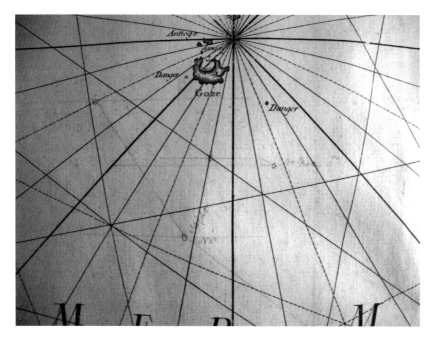

Thomas Atkinson's track plot on approaching Crete and offlying dangers, showing the
elongated lines of observed and estimated latitude at noon on 9 February.
(© National Maritime Museum, Greenwich, London)

Another rare survival provides a striking revelation that throws further light
on Atkinson's decision-making. The library of Pembroke College, Oxford,
holds a small pocket notebook in which he kept additional navigational
information for this period, amplifying the record in the ship's logs.[14] This
shows that whilst Atkinson was confident of his latitude, confirmed by a sight
at noon, the longitude indicated by the position circles was based on dead
reckoning. *Victory* was not carrying a chronometer. This would suggest an
oversight by Captain Samuel Sutton, to whom the preparation of the flagship
had been delegated as hostilities loomed. Nelson, who eventually elected to set
out ahead in the Fifth Rate frigate *Amphion* (32), declared himself 'anxious and
hurried in getting the *Victory* to sea'.[15] Hence, when a signal was made to the
ships of the fleet to report their positions on the morning of the landfall, that
rendered by Captain Henry Bayntun in the Third Rate *Leviathan* (74), who did
have a chronometer, was nearly 2 degrees (98nm) further west than Atkinson's
reckoning.[16] In other words, the noon position in the illustration on page 65
should be moved virtually to that shown for 0700h. Atkinson's plotted position

for 8 o'clock (2000h) has been adjusted accordingly. At 0700h the following morning, Atkinson observed lunar distances and his computation of longitude confirmed Bayntun's navigational record.

As the hunt for Villeneuve progressed, we see clear evidence confirming that charts were used as plotting surfaces to assist ships in keeping clear of danger. The French were not at Alexandria, and Nelson turned back to the west. With the prevailing wind, the fleet's best course was northwest by north, taking them towards Crete and the off-lying island of Gavdos (Goze on Roux's chart). As can be seen in the illustration on page 66, Roux also showed 'dangers' in the vicinity. These were vigias (a warning of a hazard) resulting from false reports in an area of abyssal depths shown on modern charts. Clearly, Atkinson could not know this. Hence at noon on 10 February he plotted two positions, again with elongated lines of latitude, one derived 'by account' and one 'by observation'. At noon on the 11th the crew sighted the great snow-covered Mount Ida on Crete. The wind now came into the northwest and the fleet made slow progress; hence the other extended latitude lines scribed on the chart to confirm that the ships remained clear of the Cretan coast. When they worked themselves clear of Gavdos on the 15th, they had come within four miles of its shore.

Having reviewed this evidence of use of the chart as a plotting surface for hazard avoidance, it is instructive to look at Atkinson's navigation in the vicinity of the most significant danger in the Mediterranean Sea, the Esquerques (Skerki Bank), which lies athwart the western approach to the Sicilian Channel. The record in his logs shows that he was aware of this danger, recording estimates of its bearing and distance whenever in the vicinity.[17] The bank is indicated on the earliest surviving portolan charts, and in remarkable detail in charts from the fifteenth century.[18] Yet its very existence, let alone its accurate position and extent, was called into question by some British navigators at the turn of the eighteenth and nineteenth centuries. At the subsequent court martial of the survivors from the Third Rate HMS *Athenienne* (64), which struck on the bank in October 1806 and became a total loss, it was confirmed that the late Captain Raynsford had a copy of a survey ordered by Lord Keith in 1802.[19] Yet it was said that, just moments before the ship struck, he had remarked, 'If the Esquerques shoals do exist we should now be upon them.'[20] Significantly, the verdict of the court martial was that 'the course was certainly too near consistently with safety.' What was needed to assist in the selection of a safe course was a graduated chart at the right scale to cover the approaches to the Sicilian Channel, such as the one Captain William Durban, who had conducted the 1802 survey, published in 1810.[21]

Dalrymple and his engravers had found it hard work to compile charts from Durban's field sheets, and it was not until September 1805 that twenty-five copies of a chartlet showing the reef were despatched to the Mediterranean Fleet.[22] In the meantime, positional information had indeed been promulgated in theatre, and the Roux atlas shows that Atkinson had plotted it (see illustration on page 69). The reported position lay to the southwest of where Roux depicted the danger. We will see that this confirmed Atkinson's practice of always planning to pass well to the north and east of the bank.

Though the annotation is now faint, the track of *Victory* on entry to the Mediterranean in 1803 can be traced on sheet five in Roux's atlas (see illustration below). Inbound for Malta, after landfall on the south coast of Sardinia, Captain Sutton manoeuvred at the southern end of the Tyrrhenian Sea to intercept shipping and gain intelligence of Nelson's whereabouts with the main body of the fleet. On completion of this sweep, Atkinson's plot in the atlas gave him the confidence that his ship had navigated a sufficient distance to the east, and that he could turn south for a landfall. His log for 7 July records his sighting, in succession, of the lofty islands of the Egadian group: at 1940h Levanzo, which rises some 912ft above sea level, and at 2100h the summit of Maritimo some 2,251ft (686m) above sea level.[23] The illustration on page 69 shows how he then charted a course to pass east and inshore of Maritimo. The return track from Malta can also be traced. *Victory* kept clear of the notorious shoals off Cape Granitola, where the brig-sloop *Raven* (18), which led the way in that first entry into Agincourt Sound, had been wrecked the previous year. Atkinson then kept *Victory* within 12–15nm of the coast of Sicily, taking soundings as he entered the Sicilian Channel. He then used bearings and estimated distances off Maritimo to give him confidence that he was passing

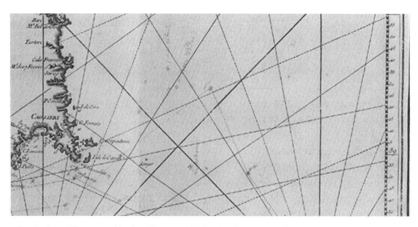

Track plot of *Victory* seeking intelligence of Nelson's whereabouts from shipping in the southern part of the Tyrrhenian Sea. (© National Maritime Museum, Greenwich, London)

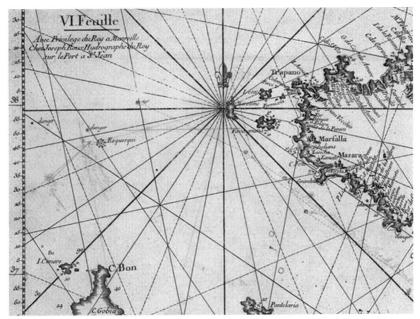

Thomas Atkinson's plot of the positions of Keith Reef and the Esquerques (Skerki Bank), as established by the Royal Navy's survey, and tracks of *Victory* in 1803 and 1805 in the vicinity. (© National Maritime Museum, Greenwich, London)

well to the northeast of the Esquerques as successive alterations of course to westwards were made on 17 and 19 July.

The importance of Maritimo as a navigational reference point is confirmed by the string of positions recorded in Captain Sutton's log.[24] Returning to the western basin in 1805 in the hunt for Villeneuve, Atkinson sounded his way into the Sicilian Channel rather further offshore, but then passed within five to six miles of Maritimo bound for Pula Bay and then Toulon.[25] It is noteworthy that the compilers of the portolan charts drew the attention of mariners to Maritimo by depicting it in brilliant colour.[26]

Subsequent improvements in charts
These survivals underscore the significance of the Admiralty charts subsequently produced under the direction of Thomas Hurd, and particularly the improved smaller-scale sheets for the Mediterranean and other seas: charts that were constructed on a network of precise positions for landfalls observed by RN hydrographic surveyors. Hurd had lost no time in putting chart supply on a proper footing. The captains and masters who had hitherto been responsible

for acquiring appropriate charts for their operations, with limited central provision, now received boxes of charts tailored for their station.

Hurd had the charts pasted onto linen for greater durability. Dalrymple had opposed this practice on the grounds that it could lead to distortion and loss of accuracy.[27] Hurd also issued charts for the Channel and Mediterranean bound in atlases. This suggests that any plotting on the charts in this period was no different from the early examples in the MEDEA-CHART Database, or from Thomas Atkinson's practice. It was a retrospective plot of fixes and tracks. The latter will have been selected by reference to and measurement on the chart, but planned tracks – or, more realistically in a square-rigged sailing ship, a mean track – were almost certainly not plotted before the voyage.

Published works of reference on navigation provide another source of evidence. Though by mid century power-driven vessels could penetrate and operate in waters that larger sailing warships would have avoided, manuals such as Henry Raper's *The Practice of Navigation and Nautical Astronomy* merely developed earlier guidance on the keeping of a reckoning on ocean passage. The *Notes Bearing on the Navigation of HM Ships*, published by the Admiralty in 1892, contained guidance on the assessment of charts and surveys, and advice on fixing and plotting, but nothing on planning and preparation of the chart.[28] The first indications of a rigorous plotting routine do not appear until the first edition of *The Admiralty Manual of Navigation* in 1914, suggesting that specific technological advances, especially the advent of the gyro compass, brought about major improvements. The story of the development of the practice of chartwork in the Royal Navy and further afield is well worthy of further research and sharing of evidence. Perhaps readers of the *Trafalgar Chronicle* can contribute more information?

Peter Heywood: Scientific Sailor

Paul Martinovich

During the French Revolutionary and Napoleonic Wars, a new breed of naval officer emerged in the Royal Navy – the 'scientific sailor'. In earlier years scientifically inclined officers, men such as Cook, Bligh and Vancouver, had navigated discovery vessels to remote parts of the globe. The new scientific sailors commanded warships and fought the enemy at sea, at the same time as they were collecting, recording and circulating information gathered during their voyages. Of course, the Admiralty required all its captains to record the events of their commissions in logbooks. But whenever the opportunity allowed, the scientific sailor went far beyond the dry information of the log, investigating his surroundings and then recording the results, often in a private journal. Naturally, these officers focused much of their energy on charting the sea (hydrography), but they also collected information on many other aspects of the environment. One such sailor was Peter Heywood (1772–1831).

Mutiny on HMS *Bounty*

Early in his service, it had seemed unlikely that Heywood would reach his twenty-first birthday, let alone survive long enough to make his reputation as a scientific sailor. He was born on the Isle of Man in 1772,[1] son of a once-prosperous merchant now down on his luck. With the support of his uncle by marriage, Captain Thomas Pasley, he joined the crew of HMS *Bounty* as a prospective midshipman. During the famous journey to Tahiti to obtain breadfruit for transplantation to the Caribbean, Heywood became friendly with Master's Mate (later Acting Lieutenant) Fletcher Christian, second in command to Captain William Bligh. When Christian led a mutiny after the ship departed Tahiti, Heywood did not accompany the deposed captain in the ship's launch, instead staying on board the *Bounty* with the bulk of the crew. Heywood's actions during this critical time have been extensively discussed, but it is hard to see him as anything other than a misguided youth, influenced by his friendship with the charismatic Christian, and perhaps carried away by the excitement of the event.

Under Fletcher Christian's command and after several changes of plan, the mutineers eventually divided into two groups. Two-thirds (including Heywood) remained in Tahiti, while Christian took the ship and the remaining men (as well as a number of Polynesians) off to find an uncharted island where they could be safe from the long arm of the Royal Navy. Heywood spent the next nineteen months on Tahiti, adopting local ways – building a house, taking a partner and fathering a child. When the ship sent to find the *Bounty*, the Sixth Rate *Pandora* (24), arrived off the island, he raced out to welcome his countrymen, but was promptly clapped in irons and imprisoned, along with the other Bountys still on Tahiti.[2]

The journey home was an ordeal of cruel mistreatment, hunger, and near drowning when the *Pandora* wrecked on Australia's Great Barrier Reef. Heywood escaped from the deckhouse (nicknamed Pandora's Box) into which the mutineers were crammed, thanks only to the kindness of two of the ship's crew, who refused to let the shackled prisoners drown. On their return to England in 1792, he and nine other surviving mutineers (four had died trying to escape from Pandora's Box) were put on trial for mutiny, the penalty for which was death. After six days of testimony, the assembled panel of admirals and senior captains found Heywood and several of his shipmates guilty. There was conflicting evidence about his role in the mutiny, but in the harsh view of the law, his failure to oppose the mutineers or to join Bligh in the launch made him culpable. Nevertheless, the panel recommended the young man to the King's mercy. A concerted campaign by the Heywood family and their well-connected friends resulted in a pardon, making Heywood a free man, but with a sensational history that would follow him for the rest of his life.[3]

Peter Heywood was well-educated, serious and intelligent – when his cousin and future friend Pulteney Malcolm visited him before the court martial he described the prisoner as 'very clever and much the gentleman'.[4]

An undated portrait of Peter Heywood, suggesting his serious demeanour. (Manx National Heritage Centre, Douglas, Isle of Man, reprinted here with permission)

Heywood was 'of rather above middle size', well built with brown hair, and heavily tattooed, a reminder of his time in Tahiti. He probably spoke with a distinct Manx accent, reflecting his family origins and upbringing. According to the writer of his obituary (who claims to have known him well), he had 'a serious cast of countenance, but it brightened up in argument', and among friends his conversation was 'lively and energetic'.[5] His intellectual approach to life is suggested by the fact that during the intensely emotional period as he waited for the verdict of the court martial, Heywood occupied his time by compiling a lengthy Tahitian-English vocabulary for the use of future visitors to the islands.[6]

Advancement in the Royal Navy
Heywood's naval career did not seem to suffer because of his court martial – indeed Lord Howe, the commander of the Channel Fleet, made a point of having him assigned to the fleet flagship, the First Rate *Queen Charlotte* (100), where he served as signal midshipman during the Battle of the Glorious First of June in 1794. A few months after the battle, Heywood was promoted to acting lieutenant, a rank that was confirmed by the Admiralty in March 1795 (despite his lacking the required six years' sea service).[7]

Early in 1796 the newly commissioned officer was appointed third lieutenant of the Fifth Rate frigate *Fox* (32), under Captain Pulteney Malcolm, and was aboard the ship when she sailed to join the East Indies Fleet towards the end of the year. While aboard *Fox*, Heywood moved up from third to first lieutenant, and then joined his commander when Malcolm moved to the ship of the line, the Third Rate *Suffolk* (74) in 1798. The master of *Suffolk*, Duncan Weir, was an able marine surveyor who took Heywood under his wing, so that he soon became a skilled hydrographer. Heywood and Weir used their time aboard *Suffolk* to chart some of the key anchorages used by the ships of the East Indies Fleet, such as the vast natural harbour at Trincomalee, Ceylon (Sri Lanka).[8]

In August 1800 Peter Heywood was appointed to command the bomb vessel *Vulcan* (10), stationed at Amboyna (Ambon), one of the Spice Islands captured from the Dutch in 1796. Even while a passenger on his way to take up his command, Heywood spent his free time measuring and recording, using a pair of chronometers to determine the meridian distance (difference in longitude) between Bombay and his destination of Amboyna. He probably owned one of these expensive instruments, an indication of his commitment to the idea of scientific navigation.

He continued this surveying work around Amboyna until ordered to escort a convoy to Madras, using an unusual route south of Timor and Java, rather than the customary northerly track through the Java Sea. The southern route

A marine chronometer made by Thomas Arnold, like the ones that Heywood used.
(Science Museum, London)

was poorly charted and beset by contrary currents and shoals, forcing Heywood and his charges to make a long loop south before turning west towards India. However, the wind was against them, and the convoy was slowly pushed eastwards, encountering the dangerous islands and shoals off the northwest coast of New Holland (Australia). It took Heywood more than a month to overcome the contrary winds and avoid the many hazards before he got his convoy out into the deep waters of the Indian Ocean on their way to Madras. Throughout this ordeal, he collected information, making meticulous observations of water depth and coastal topography, annotating existing charts for the use of future mariners, and even painting a watercolour of the appearance of the Australian islands from the sea. A modern analysis has revealed that despite all the difficulties he encountered, Heywood's observations were very close to the locations given on modern charts, testifying to his skill as a hydrographer.[9]

Vice-Admiral Peter Rainier, commanding the East Indies station, recognised Heywood's talents and promoted him, first to commander in 1801, and then in

1803 to the all-important rank of post-captain. During this time he commanded several ships, undertaking routine naval duties, including cruising to capture enemy warships and privateers, and escorting convoys. Occasionally he was given the task of making surveys of areas such as the eastern coast of Ceylon and the Malabar (western) coast of India. Heywood also used his voyages

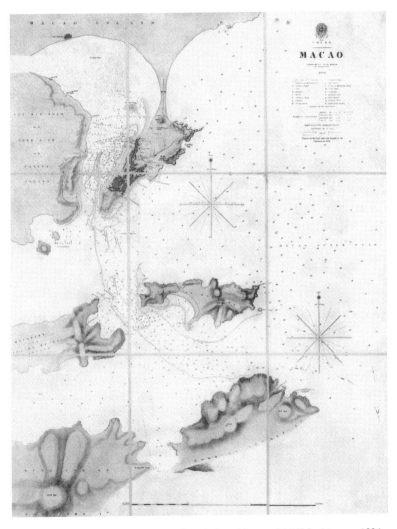

Admiralty Chart of Macao, surveyed by Captain Peter Heywood, HMS *Dedaigneuse*, 1804, published 1840, correction to 1858. (GetArchive, LLC, public domain)

around the Indian Ocean to make accurate measurements of various locations, fixing the longitude using the chronometers he carried. When his ship, the Fifth Rate frigate *Dedaigneuse* (36), was dismasted in a typhoon and had to put into the Portuguese port of Macao (Macau) to refit, her captain took the opportunity to make a comprehensive survey of the Typa, the protected anchorage near Macao where the merchant ships of the East India Company gathered. During his eight years in the eastern seas he undertook about twenty surveys, accurately locating about 350 places around the Indian Ocean.[10]

In January 1805 Heywood successfully applied to the admiral to resign his command of *Dedaigneuse* and return to England (he had been absent for eight years) to attend to urgent family matters resulting from the death of his elder brother. In addition, his health was suffering from the rigours of the eastern climate. The captain travelled home on the East Indiaman *Cirencester*, which also happened to be carrying James Horsburgh of the East India Company, a noted hydrographer. Naturally, over the course of the voyage the two men discussed the challenges of charting the eastern seas, and compared the charts they had prepared and used during their time in those waters. This was to be the beginning of a long and close friendship, in which Horsburgh ensured that the new information that Heywood had discovered was incorporated into the charts published by the East India Company, for which he eventually became the official hydrographer. In an interesting sidelight revealing the enthusiasm of the two men for exploring the natural world, when *Cirencester* reached St Helena, Horsburgh and Heywood set out to walk around the circumference of the island in one day, a gruelling twenty-mile hike over rugged topography.[11]

Scientific achievements

Over the next few years, Heywood commanded several warships, carrying out his naval duties in exemplary fashion, while still finding time to collect information on the places and phenomena that he encountered. His private journal for this period reveals how he combined these two activities. Entitled *Nautical Remarks & Memoranda of Occurrences on board His Majesty's Ships Polyphemus, Donegal and Nereus*,[12] the work goes beyond the scope suggested by its title to range over a variety of topics. For instance, in it Heywood analysed the best sea route to reach the Cape of Good Hope, discussed the people and agricultural prospects of what is now Uruguay, and proposed a kind of nautical Trojan horse to destroy the French ships anchored in Basque Roads in 1809.

The journal seems to have been written up almost every day, but this version may be a copy of the original, since the entries are very neatly written, with almost no changes of pen or ink evident, and very few corrections or additions

A typical page from Heywood's journal.
(McGill University Library, Montreal, reprinted here with permission)

after the fact. Some later hand (possibly biographer Edward Tagart) has added a few marks and written the year at the top of each page. Rather than naming the day of the week, Heywood has accompanied each day's entry with the astronomical symbol denoting that day; an occasional skull and crossbones marks the passing of a crewman, whose name and circumstances of death are always recorded. Heywood regularly noted the barometric pressure and temperature, along with his best estimates of latitude and longitude. The entries for some days were brief and to the point, reading like those of a captain's log, while for others he wrote more extensive and discursive accounts of matters of interest. Because this was a private journal, recording information that the writer thought worth keeping for future reference, it reveals the thinking of the man as he seeks to measure and understand aspects of the world around him.

Several of the earliest entries in the journal deal with Heywood's interest in marine chronometers as tools for navigation. While preparing his ship, the Third Rate *Polyphemus* (64) for service abroad in late 1806, he applied to the Admiralty for the loan of several of these instruments. Since such expensive timekeepers were supplied only to officers going on foreign stations who would be likely to use them effectively, it is a measure of Heywood's growing reputation as a surveyor that a few days later he received two timekeepers made by John Arnold. Between voyages, these had been kept at the Royal Naval Academy in Portsmouth under the supervision of William Bayly, who had been an astronomer on two of Cook's voyages, and was now headmaster of this school for prospective naval officers.[13]

The invention of the marine chronometer in the late eighteenth century had made the determination of a ship's longitude at sea a far more straightforward (though not foolproof) process than it had been previously. These timekeepers were intended to keep Greenwich Mean Time throughout the voyage. At sea or on reaching distant landfalls, this standard time would provide a benchmark to compare to local time, measured by noting when the sun reached its maximum height in the sky, which defined noon. The resulting time difference between local noon and the chronometer's noon was a direct measure of the ship's longitude east or west of Greenwich. For each timekeeper, Bayly provided details of their measured 'rates of going' – the small amount of time that the chronometer gained or lost each day. The rate of going would be factored into calculation of the difference between the time kept by the instrument and the local time.

Heywood also collected his own chronometer, newly cleaned and checked after its long service in East Indian waters. The three chronometers would act as a check on one another, since individual rates of going could vary as the ship encountered changing weather conditions. The importance of understanding the accuracy of each instrument is evident in that Heywood consulted both Alexander Dalrymple, the official East India Company hydrographer, and Duncan Weir, his old mentor from *Suffolk*, about their experience with the particular timekeepers in his charge.[14] Even before his voyage began, the captain was taking measurements at Portsmouth to assess the accuracy of his instruments. He recorded the results in a special 'rate book', measuring these changes over many months whenever he reached a location whose longitude was firmly established.

Polyphemus, accompanied by several other ships, travelled south to Cape Town, reaching the port on 12 March 1807. Heywood soon took to his journal, spending several thousand words to describe the navigation, weather and general topography of Cape Town and Table Bay in detail, even though he noted that the location was already well-known to seamen. His explanation was that:

> … whatever comes within the scope of ones observation in any foreign place of anchorage had always be better remarked than passed by in silence, for however trifling and uninteresting many little occurrences may appear to ourselves at the time they happen, yet the account of them may at a future day chance to be acceptable, & perhaps even useful to those <u>perfect strangers</u> who come after us.[15]

At the Cape, *Polyphemus* and her consorts picked up a number of troop transports destined for the River Plate to reinforce the British troops already there. On 15 June the convoy reached Montevideo on the north side of the River Plate, anchoring off the town, which the British had captured in February. The troops on the transports were prepared for a second assault on Buenos Aires, the first one having been defeated in 1806 by its Spanish and colonial defenders. This new attack was also unsuccessful, and Heywood recorded details of how the defenders had reinforced individual homes and streets to make it impossible for the British to retake the city. As British troops withdrew under the terms of a treaty made with the victorious Spanish, and naval activities wound down, Heywood decided that the River Plate should be better surveyed, especially since a warship had recently grounded on an improperly charted shoal. Nelson's famed Third Rate, *Agamemnon*, would wreck in the same area in 1809.

Rather than offering his own services, Heywood recommended that Commander Francis Beaufort of the store ship *Woolwich* be ordered to determine the correct location of various navigational hazards in the area. Heywood explained in his journal that Beaufort was 'more competent, from his thorough scientific knowledge of his profession than any other naval officer in the River' (presumably including himself).[16] This comment suggests that a small group of scientific officers was developing within the navy, forming an informal community that shared information and techniques.

When Beaufort returned from this task, he and Heywood undertook to accurately locate the town of Montevideo, still (temporarily) held by the British. They collaborated on 'taking some angles' from the tallest hill in the town (the site of a disused lighthouse), and from the top of St Philip's Church, in an effort to provide accurate landmarks for mariners approaching the city. This seems to have been a completely unofficial initiative, a result of the two officers' zeal to document their surroundings.[17]

On 15 September *Polyphemus*, with several other warships and a convoy of troopships, departed Montevideo to return the defeated soldiers to Britain. The ships of the convoy were slow and unco-operative, and the weather was often bad. One of the transports was leaking so much that her troops and stores were transferred to other ships. The only other notable event was the sighting of a comet. Naturally, Heywood did not just mention the sighting in his journal; on two nights he recorded the specific location of the apparition, triangulating it in the sky using several astronomical points of reference.[18]

While attending to his duties as captain of the ship, Heywood was also making regular observations of the movements of his marine barometer. His friend James Horsburgh had alerted him to the fact that within the tropics, the height of mercury in a barometer would fluctuate in an apparently regular manner, unrelated to the normal variation in air pressure resulting from changes in the weather. Heywood wrote, 'As I was determined to ascertain this fact without trusting to any second agent, I examined the Mercury & registered it myself.' He admitted, 'I have found [this] to be an employment of much fatigue, the registering during that time of the Height of the mercury in the Barometer every hour both night and day,' over a period of twenty-eight days.[19] Sailors were used to a pattern of four hours on watch and four hours off, but waking every hour to check the mercury level seems astonishingly dedicated, even for a scientific sailor! In the spirit of scientific enquiry, Heywood recorded information in his journal about the make, location and method of suspension of the particular marine barometer on which he made these observations, before listing his detailed results from both the southern and northern hemispheres. These confirmed Horsburgh's suggestion that between the tropics of Capricorn and Cancer the atmospheric pressure fluctuated regularly every six hours.

He then went on to speculate why this might be, suggesting the phenomena might be a result of the intense sunlight in the tropics, and the distance from land when on the open ocean. We now know that these regular changes in air pressure are caused by complicated 'atmospheric tides' generated by the heat of the sun reaching the earth. Rather than being solely a tropical phenomenon, regular barometric movements are also present in temperate latitudes, but are swamped by the irregular pressure fluctuations resulting from the much more variable weather in this area. Nevertheless, Heywood's approach to observe, measure, record and then hypothesise is a clear indication of his scientific approach to understanding the world around him.

Bad weather slowed the voyage, so that it was mid January 1808 before the convoy reached its final destination, Portsmouth. On arrival at this accurately defined location, Heywood checked his chronometers to find out how well they had kept time (and thus indicated the ship's position) over the previous six months. He concluded that their cumulative error was very small and advised:

> These two chronometers, <u>if kept together</u>, would be more invaluable & ought not to be separated; because their rates are equal, though one gains and the other loses; & each is differently affected by heat & by cold, so that [while] they may, on a passage, measure distance widely different, the mean of them both is always very near the true longitude.[20]

Despite his recommendation, he was soon ordered to return one of the chronometers to the Admiralty for use elsewhere.

Within a few months a new captain was appointed to *Polyphemus*, leaving Peter Heywood on the beach without a ship. Finding that there were few prospects of immediate employment, and rather than becoming an 'Idle useless drone', he undertook to prepare several charts to accompany a set of sailing directions for the Indian seas that James Horsburgh was compiling. He combined what he modestly called 'the little experience I had been myself able to acquire in those seas' with Horsburgh's own written descriptions to create accurate guides to sailing those waters. This work was interrupted by an offer to take temporary command of Captain Pulteney Malcolm's ship, the Third Rate *Donegal* (74) while Malcolm was on leave.[21]

There followed six months of active service, during which Heywood and the *Donegal*s were part of the British force blockading ports on the west coast of France. Apparently this duty allowed Heywood little opportunity to pursue his scientific researches, since the journal is solely concerned with the normal matters of commanding and navigating his ship, and fighting the French. However, even officers recognised for their skill at surveying needed to ensure they impressed their lordships as fighting sailors, which Heywood did very successfully whilst commanding *Donegal*.

In June 1809 he received orders to take up a very desirable post: captain of the newly built Fifth Rate frigate, *Nereus* (32). The next few months were occupied with routine matters – completing the ship's complement, loading the necessary stores and cruising in the North Sea. In September the ship was ordered to the Mediterranean to join Admiral Lord Collingwood's fleet off the French base at Toulon. Even though the passage south to Gibraltar was a familiar route for Royal Navy ships, Heywood made detailed navigational notes and used his chronometers to check the positions of places against the co-ordinates on the official Admiralty chart. These observations continued as *Nereus*, loaded with naval stores for the fleet, travelled from Gibraltar to Collingwood's station off the French coast. Heywood spent the next few months in the dangerous and occasionally exciting work of watching the French fleet at Toulon.

After returning to Britain where *Nereus* received some urgent repairs, Captain Heywood received orders for Brazil. Once again, he applied to the Admiralty for a chronometer, and Captain Thomas Hurd, the official hydrographer, promptly offered him the choice of two Arnold instruments.[22] He selected one, and used it in combination with his own pocket chronometer throughout the commission to South America. During the voyage out, Heywood touched at Madeira, making the usual detailed observations and comparing his measurements of the longitude of these isles with those of earlier mariners, including those of his friend James Horsburgh. He reached Rio de Janeiro at the beginning of November 1810. This was the beginning of a thirty-month sojourn on the South American coast, in which naval duties were punctuated with careful and detailed navigational observations and measurements. His journal ends as it began, with observations of longitude based on the information provided by his much-valued chronometers.

One of Heywood's more important scientific achievements in this period was his survey of several remote South Atlantic islands, including Tristan da Cunha and Gough's Island, in order to establish accurate co-ordinates for their location. Naturally, he also collected detailed information on the topography, weather and wildlife of the islands, which were the breeding places of elephant seals. These animals attracted American sealers to harvest the blubber and skins, and Heywood spent several pages of his journal discussing the sealers' techniques, and their prospects for making a living off this grim trade.[23] Moving on to Benguela on the African coast, Heywood gave this Portuguese outpost his standard treatment, surveying the anchorage and compiling detailed information on the town and its inhabitants.

During *Nereus'* time on the South American station, her captain was closely involved with various complicated political and trade conflicts resulting from the growing disputes between the Spanish government and its South American colonies. Again, naval duties prevented Heywood carrying out full surveys, but the observations he made during this period (combined with material from his earlier time in the area) enabled him to create a chart of the River Plate (published in 1817), and to compile sailing directions for the area. These were published in 1813, and were of considerable use to the growing number of merchant ships trading between Britain and the newly independent countries of Argentina and Uruguay.[24]

Somewhat to his regret, Heywood had now become too senior to continue commanding a frigate, but he was fortunate enough to be transferred to the Third Rate *Montagu* (74), which returned to Britain in October 1813. When Napoleon escaped from Elba to reclaim the throne of France, Heywood and *Montagu* were ordered to the Mediterranean, to join the fleet under Admiral Lord Exmouth. While he participated in the admiral's first mission to Algiers to free the Christian prisoners of the Dey, Heywood was not present when Exmouth bombarded the city in August of 1816, his ship having been paid off at Chatham the month before. In a tribute to Heywood's benevolent style of leadership, his departing crew presented him with a poem 'The Seamen's Farewell to HMS *Montagu*', including the lines: 'The seamen who served thee, would serve *thee* for ever / Who sway'd but ne'er fetter'd, the hearts of the brave.'[25]

Heywood's retirement

This was the end of Peter Heywood's active service, though according to his wife, Frances, a widow whom he had married in 1816, Heywood turned down the post of Hydrographer to the Admiralty twice, once in 1823 and then again in 1829.[26] On the latter occasion, he recommended his friend Francis Beaufort as the best person to fill the position. Beaufort went on to hold the post successfully for twenty-six years, supervising dozens of Royal Navy surveys around the world, and publishing the resulting accurate charts. While Heywood may well have felt Beaufort was better qualified for the post, he (Heywood) was also by this time not in the best of health, which would also have deterred him from taking on this demanding position.

However, even during his retirement on half-pay, this scientific sailor maintained an active involvement in the growing community of naval explorers and surveyors who were probing the unknown parts of the planet. In 1816 he apparently advised the Hydrographer to the Admiralty, Captain Thomas Hurd, on setting up a formal surveying service to replace the ad hoc arrangements that had used up to that point.[27] A few years later, he spent time in the Hydrographic Office at the Admiralty, drafting charts of some of the surveys he had made earlier in his career.[28] Heywood closely followed the progress of expeditions sent out to find the Northwest Passage, a major focus of attention for the Admiralty. In the aftermath of the expeditions of John Ross and Edward Parry, Heywood published a book entitled *The Impracticability of a North-West passage for Ships, Impartially Considered*, using the pseudonym 'Scrutator' (investigator).[29]

In nearly two hundred pages of closely argued text, he reviews the evidence various authors had advanced in favour of such a passage, analyses the results of the various expeditions over the past few years, and comes to the conclusion that while a sea connection probably exists across the top of North America, the prevalence of thick, multi-year ice will make it impossible for ships to navigate. With considerable insight, he noted that by framing these voyages as searches for the elusive passage, rather than as scientific expeditions to better understand the Arctic, their proponents had raised expectations that made it difficult to abandon the premise that such a passage existed. His conclusion that the Northwest Passage was not practicable (essentially correct until the recent advent of icebreaking ships and climate change) illustrates Heywood's scientific approach to this and many other problems. He amassed the evidence, reviewed it dispassionately, and came to a conclusion based on the material at hand. Presumably, the reason he did not publish this book under his own name was to avoid a public disagreement with his naval colleagues, who were convinced of the existence of a viable Northwest Passage, despite the evidence that Heywood had marshalled.[30]

In his retirement, Heywood lived in Highgate, a suburb of London, with his wife and stepdaughter, and enjoyed lively discussions with a group of naval, scientific and artistic friends. His political beliefs were liberal – he sided with the Whigs in their approach to the independence of former Spanish colonies in South America, and supported the relief from the legal restrictions imposed upon Roman Catholics. Always religious, in his later years he became a strong adherent of the American Unitarian minister William Ellery Channing. Towards the end of his life he and his small family moved to Cumberland Terrace, just east of Regent's Park, where he died in 1831. Those who laid him out for burial must have been surprised to see the tattoos that covered much of his body.

Though the rest of his life story never matched the high drama of the *Bounty* mutiny, Peter Heywood became a distinguished officer with a fine record during the Anglo-French wars of 1793–1815. Throughout his service, he was never content just to observe something and move on, 'without desiring to investigate into its properties or cause of existence'.[31] The author of his entry in the *Oxford Dictionary of National Biography* accurately sums up his importance: 'he formed one of a group of more scientific naval officers devoted to improvements in charting and surveying an expanding empire and to wider intellectual and liberal concerns.'[32]

Captain Peter Heywood, see colour plate 3

Fighting Instructions, Signal Books and the Line of Battle: The Evolution of Sailing Tactics in the Royal Navy, 1740–1815

Andrew Venn

Throughout the eighteenth century and into the early nineteenth century, the Royal Navy experienced various favoured command styles. From Hawke's daring pursuit of the French into Quiberon Bay, to Rodney's breaking of the line at the Saintes, to Nelson and his band of brothers' heroics at the Nile and Trafalgar, each admiral had his own way of commanding in battle. At the forefront of these varying tactical ideals were fighting instructions, signal books and various tactical memoranda, each conveying new developments on how to control and command a fleet. First issued in 1653, the fighting instructions and the various additional instructions sporadically circulated by admirals provide us with an important insight into how the tactical discourse in the Royal Navy shifted throughout the eighteenth century. This article will focus on additional instructions, signal books and tactical memoranda issued between 1740 and 1815 in order to explore the favoured command style throughout the period and piece together how certain admirals, such as Nelson, contributed to a shift in thinking.

Decentralisation of command in the mid eighteenth century

Perhaps the first admiral to introduce ideas of decentralisation of command in battle to the Royal Navy was Edward Vernon in the 1740s. The admiral believed strongly in the study of tactics, focusing on the matter in considerably more detail than his contemporaries.[1] Recognising that complete centralised command of a fleet by an admiral from his flagship was impractical and near impossible, Vernon instead placed a large amount of faith in his subordinates to use their initiative when the situation permitted.[2] Vernon issued additional instructions, dated circa 1740, which provided some flexibility to the current fighting instructions and provided explanation for various signals.[3] One such additional instruction stipulated that smaller ships in the fleet should break away from the main line of battle in order to form a reserve squadron, providing that the enemy fleet was inferior in number.[4] The rationale was that this reserve squadron could then help other ships in the line of battle and provide general support where needed. This is a tactic that Nelson later echoed in his much revered memoranda of the early nineteenth century. The key principle of this tactic focused on captains mutually supporting each other, using their initiative to decide when and where to help their comrades.

Although Vernon strongly believed in decentralisation, he was also cautious about signals being clearly displayed for all ships to see, suggesting a continued reliance on signals from the flagship to control a fleet.[5] For that reason, he also stated in his instructions that signals should be hoisted higher on the topgallant shrouds when in battle in order to improve visibility, and that every ship should appoint someone to specifically observe signals.[6] This highlights that although Vernon allowed decentralisation and individual thought, this was only part of a wider strategy which revolved around signalling and the admiral maintaining control of his fleet.

Another admiral who made great strides in tactics and control during the 1740s was Lord Anson, who published his own additional instructions, dated circa 1747.[7] Anson was said to have first practised a new system revolving around a line of bearing, allowing ships to tack on the same compass bearing in unison. This can be seen in his additional instruction, which mentioned hoisting different flags and pennants in order to distinguish compass bearings for the line of battle.[8] Like Vernon, Anson was also willing to depart the formality of the line of battle if the circumstances permitted it, such as at Cape Finisterre in May 1747 when he ordered a general chase that led to the capture of a French squadron. In 1758, when in command of the Channel Fleet, Anson issued another instruction stating that when the signal was given, all ships should drift out of the line of battle and attempt to engage the enemy as closely as possible.[9] This was similar to Vernon's second instruction from circa 1740, in which he advocated the need for close action, stating that the admiral would signal when he wished the fleet to move closer to the enemy. N A M Rodger summarised this line of thinking by suggesting that both Vernon and Anson spent much time instilling the importance of close action into their fleets, stressing its importance in achieving a decisive result in battle.[10] Again, Nelson would later echo this idea during his preparation for the Battle of Trafalgar in 1805. As the line of battle was not the solution to every problem, sometimes alternative decentralised tactics would prove to be more effective in order to achieve a decisive victory over the enemy.

Admiral Hawke, who succeeded the ill-fated Admiral Byng in the Mediterranean in 1756, also issued additional instructions, designed to prevent a recurrence of the events that led to the loss of Menorca to the French in that same year. Byng had become separated from the main part of his fleet, limiting his ability to command his fleet effectively and causing heavy casualties to his vanguard. To counteract this, Hawke made provisions to ensure that his fleet

Vice-Admiral Sir Edward Vernon. A print from a painting c1790,
by Henry Singleton (1766–1839). (US Naval History and Heritage Command, NH695)

could come into action with the enemy in unison. He referenced a specific signal for the leading ship to alter her course towards the enemy, with the other ships subsequently following.[11] Later on in the memorandum, Hawke also echoed the thoughts of Vernon and Anson, by ordering to steer towards the closest enemy ship and engage her if the signal was given.[12] Again, this highlights the need for different tactics for different scenarios and the importance of close action.

Despite the best efforts of individuals like Vernon, Anson and Hawke to push towards decentralisation, many other individuals in positions of power in the navy were reluctant to accept this approach. Michael A Palmer has cited this reluctance as the main difficulty facing the Royal Navy during the period, as the consensus by the authorities was still very much centred around tightly centralised command and control.[13] Michael Duffy added that, 'Commanders who could manage to contain the drift to "bottom-upwards" leadership were then in a position to use their fleets positively.'[14] Despite this, the developing trend towards the last few decades of the eighteenth century was a rejection of decentralisation in favour of improved signalling and centralised control from the flagship.

Signalling reforms and the American War of Independence

Following the end of the Seven Years War, the Royal Navy quickly shifted tactical focus away from a decentralised approach in favour of improved signalling systems, which by nature favoured a more centralised and controlled approach. This shift came with considerable French influence, and multiple French strategic and tactical texts were translated during the time of peace following the conflict. One of the leading figures in this tactical shift was Lord Howe, who was at the forefront of implementing a new centralised system that tended to limit the initiative of captains under his command. Taking command of the American station in July 1776, Howe issued a new system of signals and instructions which, albeit unofficially, displaced the traditional fighting instructions.[15] Howe followed up with another set of instructions issued in 1782 when he was in command of the Channel Fleet.[16] Both of these give a valuable insight into Howe's new style of command and how he sought to centralise fleet control.

Admiral Lord Richard Howe (1726–1799), by John Singleton Copley (1738–1815), 1794.
(© National Maritime Museum, Greenwich, London, BHC2790)

In the first pages of the 1782 instructions, Howe referred to an instruction for forming the line of battle, with reference to obeying signals from the flagship.[17] Howe also stated: 'In line of battle, the flag of the admiral commanding in chief is always to be considered as the point of direction to the whole fleet, for forming and preserving the line.'[18] Of course, this poses a potential problem if the conditions of battle obscure other ships' views of the flagship. In another article in the same set of instructions, Howe stated: 'no ship is to separate in time of action from the body of the fleet, in pursuit of any small number of the enemy's ships beaten out of the line', while acknowledging that ships may assist other ships if they were in danger, but only if the admiral first granted permission.[19] Howe followed this up by later reinforcing that captains could act independently only if signalled to do so by the admiral.[20] This is very much a contrast to the style of Vernon and Anson, who encouraged initiative and mutual support where possible.

Howe had served under Hawke as a junior officer during the Battle of Quiberon Bay, but took the astounding victory not as showing the merits of decentralisation, but rather demonstrating the need for a more centralised and rigid control system.[21] As Palmer has argued, the problem with Howe's tactics was that they placed virtually all decision-making capability solely with the fleet's commander-in-chief, which could pose problems if the signals were not visible or were interpreted in a different manner than intended.[22] Of course, further problems could arise if the commander was tactically inept or lacked the ability to effectively control his fleet. With such a system stifling free tactical thinking, captains in a fleet would be less likely to act on initiative, in turn reducing the chances of victory if a battle was to turn unconventional.

Another individual at the forefront of the push for centralisation during the American War of Independence was Admiral Kempenfelt. Like Howe, Kempenfelt's tactics revolved heavily around the use of signalling systems with French influence, but unlike his counterpart, Kempenfelt had little interest in providing his captains with the opportunity to use initiative. A set of instructions issued by Sir Charles Hardy to the Channel Fleet in 1780 has been attributed to Kempenfelt, who was serving as Hardy's chief of staff at the time.[23] These instructions include a number of preparatory signals, to prepare captains for different actions, along with a complicated system of arranging an order of retreat.[24] They also feature the idea of splitting a fleet into separate divisions, as well as a signal for doubling up to attack specific parts of an enemy's fleet.[25]

Howe and Kempenfelt also collaborated on a set of instructions that were issued to the Channel Fleet at some point during 1781/2.[26] Howe was given command of the Channel Fleet following Kempenfelt's death during the sinking of his flagship, the First Rate *Royal George* (100) in 1782 and made several alterations to a set of instructions that Kempenfelt had previously worked on.[27] This set of instructions bears similarities to Howe's 1782 instructions mentioned previously, and it can be difficult to figure out which parts can be attributed to each admiral. It features an article stating that any number of ships separated from the main squadron were still at liberty to obey signals during their separation.[28] This is another example of centralised control, which again could pose problems. What if the separated ships could not see the signals from the flagship? The reliance on signals to prepare captains of the fleet for manoeuvres also could pose problems if these signals were misinterpreted or missed completely.

Admiral George Rodney also played a large part in the shift from decentralisation to centralised, signalled control, albeit in a different manner from Howe and Kempenfelt. Although he favoured centralisation, Rodney was not influenced by the French systems and did not necessarily follow his peers. He tended to rely heavily on signalling in battle and to treat his captains poorly, demanding obedience from them.[29] He fought an indecisive action on 17 April 1780 at the Battle of Martinique, during which there was much confusion with signals and an overall lack of explanation, from which Rodney shirked much of the blame.[30] He did later win a decisive victory at the Battle of the Saintes in 1782, but nevertheless debate continued as to what he could have achieved had he controlled his fleet less. He issued a set of instructions in 1782, referring to signalling.[31] An example of Rodney exercising his authority is evident in article sixteen of these instructions, which stated that the leading ship should inform the admiral when it is possible to weather the enemy, through the use of signals repeated down the line by each ship.[32] This seems a lengthy process and would certainly slow down any fleet manoeuvres.

Rather than letting the leading ship use initiative and simply make the decision, the captain instead would have to wait for his signal first to reach the admiral and then wait for the admiral's response, by which time the opportunity could well be over. This also brings in the factor of individual error, with the meaning of a signal being potentially lost or misinterpreted down the line. One thing that is clear, however, is that despite the potential shortcomings, Howe, Kempenfelt and Rodney all saw the merits of signalling and felt that the control it provided outweighed the negatives and potential for misinterpretation.

In 1790 Lord Howe published a new signal book, which would be reprinted several times throughout the next twenty years with extra additions.[33] In particular, the 1799 edition featured different signals for use during the day, at night and in the fog, along with scenarios for breaking the enemy line.[34] The signal for breaking through the enemy line featured a plan to penetrate in line abreast at various points, engaging the enemy on the opposite side and bringing both broadsides into play.[35]

Howe's explanatory instructions that accompany the signal book also display a few differences from his earlier efforts. Specifically, article XI stated that should the fleet be engaged with an enemy inferior in number, the surplus ships should leave the line of battle without waiting for a signal and proceed to help out where needed.[36] This highlights a slight shift back towards ideas of decentralisation and allowing subordinates to exercise initiative. However, there are also articles that state that ships should not leave the line of battle if they are 'hard pressed' or if they wish to pursue the enemy, without prior permission from the admiral, harkening back to Howe's 1782 instructions.[37] Howe was trying to find the right balance of a centralised signalling system while providing opportunities for individual thought, showing that he was learning from and adapting the ideas of his contemporaries, no doubt in part due to his own battle experiences.

Further advancements in signalling came during the early nineteenth century, through Sir Home Popham's visual telegraph system. Popham's system included letters, words and common phrases, increasing the breadth of expression available to an admiral.[38] It also enabled two-way communication, allowing ships to communicate with each other in a much easier manner.[39] The Battle of Trafalgar of 1805 took place under Popham's system. Increasing the extent of communication and options available for an admiral quelled the problem of misinterpretation. Nevertheless, the potential for mishaps in signalling and miscommunication was still very much a factor.

Throughout the period surrounding the American War of Independence and the years following, there were no clear examples of a Hawke or Anson, showing that the default command style was a more centralised approach, despite Howe's best efforts to include elements of both styles.[40] However, this would soon change as Nelson stepped to the forefront of naval tactics during the turn of the nineteenth century.

Nelson's tactical revolution

Nelson has long been seen by historians as a revolutionary figure who changed naval tactics through his many innovations. Despite this, he developed many of his ideas through studying the systems of old and learning from the mistakes and experience of his predecessors. Nelson strongly believed that an admiral could never fully control his fleet in battle and was fully aware of the shortfalls of signals.[41] As Sam Willis has stated, controlling a large fleet could be very difficult, with smaller squadrons proving much easier to handle.[42] This principle rested at the core of Nelson's tactics that he developed over the course of multiple battles.

The Battle of Cape St Vincent in 1797 proved to be Nelson's first true taste of fleet battle. He witnessed Admiral Jervis struggling to control his fleet

The Battle of the Nile, 1 August 1798, by Nicholas Pocock (1740–1821), 1808.
(© National Maritime Museum, Greenwich, London, BHC0513)

through signals, which further reinforced his own mistrust of the signalling system.[43] Although Jervis did appreciate the value of letting his subordinates use their initiative, he failed to do so during the early stages of the battle.[44] Nelson proceeded to use his own initiative to wear out of the line of battle and head towards the enemy, eventually leading to the capture of two enemy ships in a much-heralded manoeuvre. Colin White suggested that this experience had a profound effect on Nelson, using Jervis's failings to craft his own system to ensure success in his future engagements with the French and Spanish navies.[45]

Nelson's first taste of fleet command came at the Battle of the Nile in 1798, during which he devised a plan of separate squadrons with devolved command. David Davies argued that Captain Foley's famous manoeuvre to get between the French ships and the shoreline to catch them off guard came not only due to his own initiative, but also because Nelson's principles of battle had been laid out in prior meetings.[46] Later at the Battle of Copenhagen in 1801, Nelson planned to focus on one part of the enemy line in order to overwhelm it, an idea previously used not only by himself at the Nile, but also by previous commanders such as Rodney at the Saintes.[47] Nelson was not only innovating his own style of command; he was also borrowing or developing the tactics of his predecessors, shaping them in his own way.

Nelson issued two separate memoranda during his tenure as commander-in-chief of the Mediterranean Fleet in the lead-up to the Battle of Trafalgar, one dated to 1803 and the other a few weeks before the battle in 1805.[48] It was in these documents that the ideas he had developed throughout years of experience and experimentation came to fruition. The key elements were a pair of squadrons featuring captains who could mutually support each other, along with a reserve squadron, as well as a focus on overwhelming part of the enemy fleet, overarched by the idea of the 'Nelson Touch'.[49] In the 1803 memorandum, he explored the idea of close action, stating that there should be as little manoeuvring as possible and that signals would not be required.[50] This is a far cry from the tactical systems employed in the decades prior, harking back to the style favoured by Vernon, Anson and Hawke. It is in the 1805 memorandum that Nelson goes into more detail of his ultimate plan for the battle. He suggested that in order to avoid confusion and wasted time, the order of sailing should be the order of battle, reducing the amount of manoeuvring needed to get into position before battle.[51]

Nelson also revealed his intentions to divide the fleet into three squadrons, with Admiral Collingwood, his second in command, having direct control of his line.[52] Finally, Nelson explained that he wished to cut off part of the enemy fleet by dividing it into three sections and concentrating the attack on two of those sections.[53] Marianne Czisnik argued that the independent role of the second in command was a new aspect to naval tactics and that the overall plan ensured minimal reliance on signals.[54] Again, the idea of eliminating the need for signals was one of the key points of Nelson's overall plan, a dramatic shift from the days of Howe and Kempenfelt during the American War of Independence. Despite this, the elements of breaking the enemy line, concentrating fire and bringing both broadsides to bear do resemble the tactics of old, particularly those of Howe and Rodney.

The whole essence of Nelson's tactics at Trafalgar, although not completely unique to him, was revolutionary and marked the culmination of years of development through various systems. The origins of this evolution can be traced as far as the American War of Independence, finally peaking at Trafalgar. Nelson borrowed ideas from various sources to shape his own masterpiece which sought to transform naval tactics. Palmer sums up Nelson's mindset by suggesting, 'While others sought to bring order to the chaos of battle, Nelson sought to bring chaos to the order of battle.'[55] Discarding the uniformity of the line of battle, Nelson played to the strengths of his fleet in order to gain an advantage. However, somewhat ironically, Nelson's resounding victory at Trafalgar may have done more harm than good in the long run for the development of Britain's naval strategy.

Shifts in command style

David Syrett stated that 'the years 1776 through 1805 were ones in which the Royal Navy's fleet tactics were perfected to a point that was not surpassed during the age of sail.'[56] Culminating at Trafalgar, Nelson found the almost perfect balance between centralisation and decentralisation, something that commanders had been striving to achieve for decades. However, as Trafalgar would prove to be the last major fleet action for over twenty years, any momentum gained towards this new school of tactics quickly diminished.[57] As a result, the default command style continued to revolve around signalling and formalised central control.[58] In fact, linear tactical formations and signal books would prove to reign supreme throughout the nineteenth century.[59]

Of course, there were several more instructions issued after the Battle of Trafalgar, most notably by admirals Gambier and Collingwood, who both borrowed the ideas of a split attack and divisional control from Nelson.[60] Opinions were divided on Nelson's tactics, with some wanting to learn from them and use them in their own developments, and some seeing Nelson's memorandum as sacred, due to his death.[61] Another signal book was produced in 1816 utilising Sir Popham's signalling code, but it was still largely based around the idea of the line of battle and centralised signalling.[62] It did prove to make use of some of Nelson's tactical concepts, but as James J Tritten suggested, 'the style of warfare practiced at Trafalgar was the correct style for a particular set of circumstances and under a unique charismatic leader whose essence could never be "bottled."'[63] Some even misinterpreted Nelson's tactics to advocate a 'go straight at them' approach, with a complete disregard of tactical nuances.[64]

Overall, it is apparent that throughout the course of the eighteenth century, the role of fighting instructions in naval tactics shifted, eventually becoming displaced by signal books. It is also clear that the favoured command style of admirals in the Royal Navy shifted, and this is mirrored in the fighting instructions and doctrines analysed in this article. The decentralised approach of admirals such as Vernon, Anson and Hawke in the mid eighteenth century was replaced by the centralised, signal-focused system of Howe, Kempenfelt and Rodney. Nelson's approach in the early nineteenth century was an amalgamation of these ideas and schools of thought, borrowing ideas from various sources and experiences. After all, that was one of the intended purposes of the fighting instructions, to collate the knowledge and tactics for future use.

From analysing several iterations of these instructions, it is easy to find correlation between the ideas of Vernon right through to those of Nelson. For example, the idea of having a reserve squadron appears in the early works of Vernon, circa 1740, and in Nelson's 1805 memorandum, some sixty-five years apart. Similarly, both Hawke and Nelson emphasised the advantage of close action. The works of Howe and Rodney paralleled those of Nelson, all featuring the idea of breaking the line and concentration on part of the enemy fleet. Although commanders over the course of the eighteenth and early nineteenth centuries may have had contrasting views on issues such as the merits of signalling, it is clear that there were also some mutual shared concepts, such as those mentioned above.

Palmer stated that the focus by historians on fighting instructions and signal books is misplaced, suggesting that these issues come second to the notion of command and control, the absence of which leads to failure.[65] Similarly, Duffy contended that 'effective naval leadership required moral courage: to be prepared to risk failure to achieve positive results.'[66] Willis adds that the role of the individual is also another key factor in fleet performance, disproving the myth of a top-down power structure.[67]

In particular, the 'bottom-up' approach to naval tactics required admirals to explain their thinking, examples of which include Hawke gathering his captains in 1756 after taking over from Byng, Howe gathering his captains before sailing to relieve Gibraltar in 1782 and, of course, Nelson's pre-Trafalgar dinners with his officers in 1805.[68] Therefore, it is apparent that the notion that fighting instructions and signalling systems ruled naval tactics and strategy is misguided. Instead, these written doctrines played only a part in the overall scheme of things, alongside notions of command and control, individuality and performance, and many other indeterminable factors. It is hoped that this article has made it clear that the fighting instructions and signal books issued in the eighteenth and early nineteenth centuries can be put into a wider context to be fully understood. It should not be a debate of which style of command is right and which was wrong, but rather we should see the development of tactics throughout the period as a result of combining command styles, tactics, experience and strategy.

Lord Nelson briefs his officers prior to Trafalgar, see colour plate 4

Advances in Shipboard Care in Nelson's Navy

Linda Collison

Britain engaged in many military conflicts throughout the eighteenth and early nineteenth centuries and many of the scientific and technological advancements made during this time, such as the marine chronometer, copper sheathing and carronades, benefited Royal Naval operations. Yet throughout the Georgian era and beyond, more British seamen died from disease than from battle wounds. The causes of illness were misunderstood, and the treatments of the day were ineffectual at best. With typical scathing wit, Voltaire quipped, 'Doctors pour drugs of which they know little, to cure diseases of which they know less, into human beings of whom they know nothing.'[1]

The field of medicine saw precious little enlightenment during the reign of the Kings George until the twentieth century; with a few notable exceptions, there was little science involved in the practice. The mainstay of treatment consisted of blood-letting, counter-irritation, and purging with strong laxatives to balance the humours. Surgery was often successful, but would have been

Pewter bleeding bowl, seventeenth to eighteenth century. (Wikicommons)

more so if it had not been for a high rate of post-operative infection. Not to mention, until ether was first used as a general anaesthetic, the only relief for a patient about to go under the knife was an oral dose of alcohol and opium. This paper examines major advances in naval medicine during the Georgian era, covering treatment of scurvy, shipboard surgery, supportive care, and reforms in shipboard healthcare.

While eighteenth-century scientists Edmund Halley, John Hadley and Thomas Godfrey were developing precision octants and better telescopes to observe and compute astronomical sizes and distances, contemporary physicians were prescribing ineffective and often noxious treatments and physicks based on faulty deductions. Captain James Cook's shipboard astronomer, Charles Green, observed and recorded the transit of Venus in Tahiti as part of his effort to compute the Earth's distance from the sun. Although the theory was sound, the results weren't precise and the Royal Society was disappointed. Such is science. Yet even while the Cook party was using state-of-the-art technology, doctors and surgeons were bleeding, purging and blistering their patients in a vain effort to balance four bodily 'humours' believed responsible for life and well-being. Infectious diseases were thought to be caused by miasmas – poisonous vapours emanating from decomposing matter. Human anatomy was known, at least on a macro level, but physiology

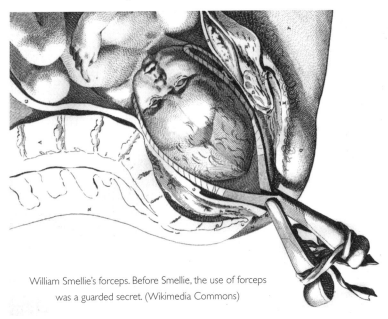

William Smellie's forceps. Before Smellie, the use of forceps was a guarded secret. (Wikimedia Commons)

– the way the body worked to stay alive – wasn't understood or even studied in a systematic, scientific manner.

Yet there was progress in naval healthcare during the eighteenth and early nineteenth centuries, and some attempt at improving treatments by the scientific process of observation and controlled trials. William Smellie (1697–1763), a Scottish naval surgeon aboard Second Rate HMS *Sandwich* (90) for two years, retired to establish his own medical practice specialising in obstetrics. Smellie improved the obstetric forceps in use at the time, reducing infant mortality rates. The travelling Englishwoman Lady Wortley Montagu (1689–1762) was among those who promoted the practice of smallpox inoculation as used in Asia. By the end of the century, British physician and scientist Edward Jenner (1749–1823) discovered a less threatening procedure using a similar, less virulent virus, cowpox. Jenner's paper describing his experiment and twelve subsequent trials was rejected by the Royal Society, but Parliament later rewarded him with a large purse. American Thomas Jefferson wrote to Jenner in 1806, 'You have erased from the calendar of human afflictions one of its greatest.'[2] Yet global eradication would take another 169 years.

Advances in treating scurvy

Scurvy was an affliction that mariners who spent long periods at sea were particularly susceptible to. It had been suspected for some time that diet played a role in this debilitating, eventually deadly disorder – a deficiency we now know is caused by a lack of ascorbic acid, an essential co-enzyme humans need to make collagen. Cook believed in the importance of fresh, local meat, fish, fruits and vegetables. He resupplied his ship whenever possible and encouraged the ship's company to eat a varied diet:

> Few men have introduced into their Ships more novelties in the way of victuals and drink than I have done; indeed few men have had the same opportunity or been driven to the same necessity. It has however in a great measure been owing to such little innovations that I have always kept my people generally speaking free from that dreadful distemper the Scurvy.[3]

Citrus fruits had long been thought by some to cure the symptoms of scurvy. Vasco da Gama wrote that when his sailors were suffering from scurvy in 1498, he sent a boat on shore for oranges. Sir Richard Hawkins, in 1593, when sailing offshore of southern Brazil, reported that oranges and lemons seemed to recover the symptoms of scurvy. John Woodall, surgeon-general of the East India Company, reported on the antiscorbutic properties of lemons in his 1617 book, *The Surgeon's Mate*, recommending a good quantity of juice of lemons to be

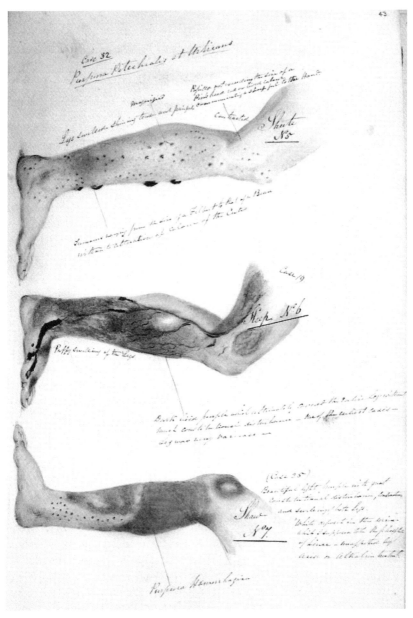

Page from the journal of Henry Walsh Mahon showing the effects of scurvy, from his time aboard HM Convict Ship *Barrosa* (c1841). (TNA and Wikipedia, public domain)

sent in each ship. It would take more than a century – almost two – until the Admiralty listened.[4]

Many naval practitioners kept records of their observations and results of treatments. The surgeon Scot James Lind (1716–1794) conducted one of the earliest known clinical trials for the treatment of scurvy, a disease that crippled more fleets than any naval battle. As ship surgeon aboard the Fourth Rate HMS *Salisbury* (50), Lind selected twelve seamen ill with telltale signs of scurvy and compared various treatments for their efficacy: cider, elixir of vitriol, vinegar, sea water, oranges and lemons, and a purgative. By the end of the month, the men assigned citrus fruit were almost recovered. One had returned to duty and the second helped nurse the others.[5]

Lind's *A treatise on the scurvy* was published in 1753. His observations flew in the face of Cockburn's *Sea Diseases*, in which scurvy was attributed to bad air, congenital laziness and indigestible food.[6] Cockburn was senior physician at Greenwich Hospital at this time. Yet it would be decades before changes reflected Lind's study and recommendations. A naval surgeon, Lind's status was not high. In the same year that Lind's treatise was published, Dr Anthony Addington (1713–1790), the father of the future prime minister, recommended the liberal use of seawater and bloodletting. Lind did have a disciple – the French physician Poissonière who, in 1767, published a book on the diseases of seamen, citing Lind's study.[7]

It would take half a century, more costly wars, a threat of invasion and two mutinies to reconsider the value of a seaman's health and the worth of a good ship surgeon. Sir Gilbert Blane (1749–1834) and Dr Thomas Trotter (1760–1832), both Scotsmen, are credited with pushing through reforms, including the Admiralty issue of lemon juice in 1795.[8] (Incidentally, lemons provide more vitamin C than limes, but the co-enzymes we know as vitamins wouldn't be identified until the twentieth century.)

Shipboard surgery

A good eighteenth-century ship surgeon was skilled and effective, if not university educated. Surgical training wasn't standardised, and apprenticeships were common. Pay for naval surgeons was never generous, and surgeons had to supply their own instruments. At that time naval surgeons were warranted, not commissioned.[9] At sea, surgeons functioned as physicians as well, diagnosing ailments and prescribing medicaments, which they supplied at their own expense until the early nineteenth century. Loblollies served as nurses, assisting the surgeons and making sure the sick were nourished.

Physicians, if not gentlemen born, were scholars with university degrees and therefore higher in pay and social status. Physicians were assigned to fleets, to hospitals, and to hospital ships. Some surgeons later took their medical degrees, becoming physicians. Thomas Trotter, for example, joined the navy as a surgeon's mate in 1779. He later earned his medical degree at Edinburgh, then rejoined the service. In 1805, when there was an increase in half-pay for naval surgeons, Trotter applied for an increase in his pension, but the Admiralty refused him.

Throughout the Georgian era, the mainstay of medical treatment was based on the principles of what is now called the 'heroic depletion' theory of disease. The basis of medicine for nearly two thousand years, it centred around a belief in four bodily humours – blood, phlegm, black bile and yellow bile – the balance of which was thought to be necessary for health. Like Claudius

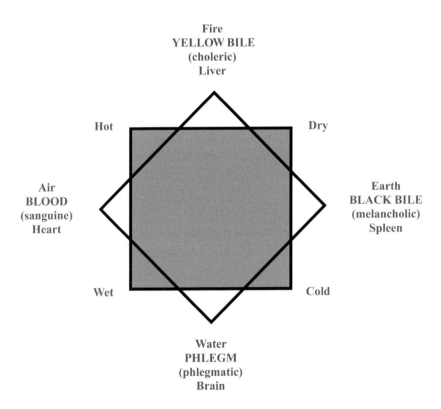

Humoural theory: Galen's metaphysical concept of a balance of the body's humours remained the basis of eighteenth and early nineteenth-century medicine. (Creative Commons)

Galenus, of the first century AD, eighteenth-century naval ship surgeons bled, purged, blistered and dosed the ship's company in a mistaken attempt to balance the humours (see illustration).[10] Only the strong survived the malady – and the treatment, the strong and the lucky. Sometimes even the strong did not survive. As Sir Gilbert Blanc observed after tracking the number of deaths in the fleets and hospitals, 'Disease was still more destructive than the sword.'[11]

Surgeries, more grounded in anatomy and mechanics, were often successful – especially lifesaving amputation – but many patients died from post-operative infection. In this pre-Lister era, sterile technique was unheard of. A surgeon was good if he had a strong arm, a quick and steady hand. He may also have been only as good as his assistants in battle. Good surgeons cut and stitched quickly and effectively. They set bones, trepanned skulls, removed stones from ureters and bladders, amputated limbs to prevent further tissue necrosis. And in action, they made split-second triage decisions and directed others in first aid. Ship surgeons saved as many lives as possible with limited supplies, with little, if any assistance, on a moving platform in dark, cramped quarters amid deafening noise and the cries for help.

In 1782 Turnbull and Blane advocated early intervention by non-medical crew during battle. This eighteenth century version of 'first aid' or 'first responder' action might have helped to reduce death rates. Blane suggested that officers carry tourniquets during battle and Turnbull thought all seamen should be taught how to use a field tourniquet. 'He need not be a medical officer; and the only instruction necessary would be to point out to him the situation of the great artery in the thigh and arm, since with this interest alone, the blood might be stopped by a handkerchief tied tight.'[12]

The use of tourniquets was not new to the eighteenth century, and there are recorded instances of army officers using field straps or makeshift tourniquet devices in battle on land.[13] The surgeon used a Petit screw tourniquet, developed by the French surgeon Jean Louis Petit (1674–1750), to adjust the degree of compression during an amputation.

Despite the conservative nature of the Admiralty and the entrenchment of medicine in the antiquated and unsubstantiated humoral theory, the Napoleonic Wars brought about advances in naval medicine and healthcare. These advances were not the result of improved technology, but in allocating more resources to the seamen's well-being, including pay, victualling, and accommodation for the sick and injured. The decision to spend more on the seaman was a result of the naval mutinies of 1797. To ensure Britain's supremacy at sea, the Admiralty had to concede that the fighting men who sailed the ships were as important as the vessels themselves, and all the armament they carried. Equally important were the naval hospitals and hospital ships, and those who served them.

Supportive care

Let us not forget the rest of the healthcare team, as we might call it today. Physicians and surgeons don't work alone, then or now. The surgeon's mate, the loblolly, the nurse, the dispenser, the apothecary: all played a role. The surgeon does his work and if the seaman doesn't return immediately to duty, he must recuperate either on board, ashore in hospital, or aboard a hospital ship. Recuperation calls for nursing care, then as now. Physicians examine and prescribe medication, surgeons operate, but the sole reason for hospitalisation is for nursing care. In the age of Nelson, nursing was not the organised profession it would later become, yet it was still important for the recovery of hospitalised seamen. It isn't always high-tech gadgets or patented drugs that save lives, but speedy intervention followed by supportive care during the recuperative process.

Although the nineteenth century brought some important medical discoveries, it wasn't until the twentieth century that real progress in healthcare was made. Germ theory finally replaced heroic depletion and miasmic theory. Antiseptic technique and antibiotics replaced bleeding, blistering and purging as the mainstay. Significant improvements were made in shipboard health of British ships during the late eighteenth and became more widespread in the early nineteenth centuries. These improvements were not due to any technological invention or scientific discovery but came about in part because of the Spithead and Nore mutinies, and an increased awareness of the living conditions of British seamen: not to soothe Britain's social conscience, but to protect the home shores from invasion and to dominate sea trade.

Besides the quick action of the ship surgeon in splinting a broken bone or removing a mangled limb, it was supportive care that made a difference. Supportive care included preventative measures such as a separate, well-ventilated sick berth, and removal to hospital, where nursing care mattered. Aboard ship, it was loblollies who saw that recuperating men were nourished, and may have helped them perform other necessary activities, providing important care, especially in an age where the cure often did more harm than the disease.

Naval hospitals ashore depended on female nurses to deliver medications, change dressings and maintain cleanliness, and in general, care for the men. At Haslar, the first official nursing matron was appointed in 1756. The number of nurses was based on the patient population; generally, one nurse per ten patients. The nurses were involved in disputes regarding pay and working conditions, complaining of being 'confined and imprisoned, and never eat a hot meal, and are served the scraps left by the seamen, and badly paid by only having a trifle of the wages at a time when three or four months are due.'[14]

Reforms in shipboard healthcare

Shipboard health did begin to improve, especially at the beginning of the nineteenth century. This had nothing to do with scientific discoveries or engineering advancements, and it was not due to any one brilliant man's invention. Instead, it was due to naval reforms, long called for, and at last implemented. The mortality rate from illness dropped from one in eight, in 1780, to one in thirty in 1812.[15] Accommodation for the sick improved, both on board and ashore, and a better medical department was evolving.

Throughout the Georgian era, the practice of medicine by physicians remained stuck in the past. Although the ship surgeons weren't as highly educated as physicians, it scarcely mattered, since the physician's medical training was not science-based, with the exception, perhaps, of anatomy. And anatomy is one subject the shipboard surgeon learned first hand, particularly during action, when presented with mutilating battle wounds. These may have been the ship surgeons' finest hours, working as quickly as they could under horrendous conditions with little help, and long after the engagement was over.

In 1802 all officers except surgeons and chaplains had their pay raised. Two years later, the Sick and Hurt Board was asked to draw up a plan based on the army's medical department 'to induce well-qualified and respectable persons to enter the service'. Finally, in 1805 the Admiralty put into effect further reforms, including pay raises for surgeons and assistant surgeons.[16]

If it wasn't for the Napoleonic threat of invasion – and the mutinies of Britain's own seamen – the reforms might not have happened when they did. The changes were made to retain and preserve the most important component of Britain's naval defence: the officers and the seamen, and the surgeons and assistants who tended them.

'Amputation', satire, see colour plate 5

The Navy's Naturalist and Polymath: Sir Joseph Banks (1743–1820)

Tom D Fremantle

It is perhaps surprising to find an article in the *Trafalgar Chronicle* about someone who was not a leader within the Royal Navy. Sir Joseph Banks's illustrious career was, however, significantly boosted through his relationships with the navy and, as his knowledge and influence grew, he became increasingly influential with the Admiralty, the Navy Board and the officers who were given commissions in distant and unexplored lands.

Early years

Banks was born into a well-off family in Lincolnshire at Revesby Abbey, which his great-grandfather had owned. The estate provided him a countryside environment that framed his early years. He was sent to school at Harrow at the age of nine, and to Eton four years later. There he began to show a great interest in botany and zoology, and by the time he left he had already amassed a considerable herbarium. His education continued at Christchurch Oxford where his enthusiasm for botany was further encouraged. This was an era of exceptional interest in the pursuit of knowledge and exploration, and Banks was fortunate that his natural aptitude fitted well with the times, despite frequent complaints by his tutors that he should spend more time learning ancient Greek. His father William died when the young Banks was only eighteen and it was three years before he could take possession of his inheritance at Revesby. During those three years his mother lived in a house close to the Chelsea Physic Garden,[1] which was an important focus for the study of botany, and clearly a useful neighbour for Banks.

Whilst at Eton, Banks had met Constantine Phipps, heir to extensive estates in Yorkshire, who shared his interest in botany and exploration. When Phipps was on half-pay as a naval lieutenant in 1766, he persuaded Banks to join him on a trip to Newfoundland as passengers aboard the Fifth Rate frigate HMS *Niger* (32), commanded by Captain Sir Thomas Adams RN. It was not only Phipps who facilitated the voyage, but also Lord Sandwich, First Lord of the Admiralty, whom Banks had met previously. Banks's decision to go also rested on the recommendations of the renowned botanist Dr Solander. On this voyage Banks and Phipps covered many miles on Newfoundland, noting the details of

Portrait of Sir Joseph Banks, 1772, by Sir Joshua Reynolds (1723–1792).
(National Portrait Gallery, London)

species of plants, fish, birds and animals. Here he began to create a reputation as a naturalist and explorer, well connected and self-supporting. Though he was away for only eight months, he had laid the foundations of his herbarium, which was later to become famous, collecting some 340 different species. In his absence he found that he had been elected a Fellow of the Royal Society, a supremely prestigious body dedicated to the advancement of science and knowledge.

With Cook for the transit of Venus

In February 1768 the Royal Society initiated the project to observe the transit of Venus across the sun in a 'memorial' to King George III. This would involve, amongst other things, the commissioning of a suitable ship and the necessary observers and astronomers to go to a suitable South Sea island. The Admiralty, under Lord Hawke, moved with commendable speed despite the preoccupation with the Seven Years War, appointed James Cook to lead the project, and acquired and fitted out HM Bark *Endeavour* (6). Cook's was clearly an inspired, though slightly curious, appointment, although he had secured a good reputation as a surveyor and cartographer through his work in Newfoundland and on the St Lawrence River during the Seven Years War. It was unusual for a master to be promoted as a commissioned officer, but on 5 May 1768 Cook was appointed lieutenant and commissioned to command *Endeavour*. The Royal Society arranged for Banks to accompany the expedition, 'a gentleman of large fortune, well versed in natural history'. He took with him a considerable entourage comprising the renowned Dr Solander, who had volunteered his services, and seven others, including a draughtsman/secretary, an artist, a watchmaker and four servants, not to mention two dogs. On 25 August 1768 the wind set fair from Plymouth and the *Endeavour* sailed.

Cook's *Endeavour* expedition is well documented, and it is not the intention to repeat the details of the voyage. The transit of Venus was duly observed and after a three-month stay, during which Banks was able to collect and record many species, the ship's company left Tahiti on 13 July 1769 and sailed on to New Zealand. The ship was variously welcomed and threatened as the passengers and crew explored the coastline and Banks observed the people, plants and animals. From there they explored the eastern seaboard of New Holland and followed it northwards. At the end of April 1770, the wind turned against them and they entered a bay which became known as Botany Bay, where they stayed for nine days. This visit eventually became the basis upon which the British government decided seventeen years later to establish a convict colony.

As *Endeavour* sailed northwards, Cook spotted an entrance which was named Port Jackson, which we now know as Sydney Harbour, but he did not venture to explore within. Banks and his naturalists continued to collect specimens whenever they could land. On 10 June *Endeavour* grounded on a reef, and for forty-eight hours they feared losing the ship altogether. Cook succeeded in repairing the ship and after more frightening experiences they made their way through the Torres Strait to Batavia, which they reached in October. There, Dutch shipwrights repaired the ship more thoroughly, while the crew suffered from endemic fevers and many of them perished. Even after they sailed in January 1771, the infections remained with them and several more died. Banks, amongst others, was seriously ill. *Endeavour* reached England on 12 July 1771 and Banks almost immediately became a celebrity, stealing the limelight from Cook, no doubt because of his prestigious connections with the Royal Society and some senior politicians. What was particularly important from Banks's point of view was that the voyage gave him first-hand experience of being at sea under naval command, of visiting both New Zealand and what later became New South Wales, and understanding the risks of shipwreck and the fear it induced.

A few weeks after *Endeavour*'s return, the newspapers were reporting that the government was about to provide ships, men and money for another voyage to the South Seas. Cook was promoted and by November 1771 was given command of two ships, HM Sloop *Resolution* (12) and HM Bark *Adventure* (10), and began to work on the preparations for a second voyage, with the assumption that Banks would accompany him again. For various reasons, Banks procrastinated and then demanded alterations to *Resolution*. The Navy Board reluctantly ordered the alterations, but as soon as the ship set sail it was apparent that the alterations were more than the hull could bear. The vessel was no longer seaworthy and she was returned to her former dimensions. When the Admiralty refused to consider providing a frigate, Banks backed out of the whole project, accusing the Admiralty and Navy Board of high-handedness. Lord Sandwich, the First Lord of the Admiralty, wrote, but never sent, a withering response, pointing out that Banks had effectively demanded to be placed in full command of the expedition, the commanding officers and the ships, with which the Admiralty could not possibly agree.[2] From that moment Banks seems to have abandoned any intention to join Cook's second voyage and he soon set off to visit Iceland and then the Netherlands. In 1773 he was in contact with his old school friend and Newfoundland companion Captain Phipps, who was about to embark on an expedition to the North Pole.[3]

Banks's developing influence

Two particular developments, originating in 1773, had a profound impact on Banks's ability to influence government. The first was his increasingly close relationship with the King, George III – Farmer George. Banks began working closely with the superintendent at Kew Gardens, which had been established primarily as a leisure garden for the King and his family, but gradually became a fully botanic garden, actively supplied with new species by Banks's growing network of collectors around the world. The King evidently appreciated Banks, especially for the active interest he took in farming matters on his own estate at Revesby, and was keen to share experience, especially when it came later to improving the breeding of sheep for wool production.

The second development was Banks's election to the Council of the Royal Society, where he took much trouble to attend all its meetings and play an active part in all its decisions and contacts. In 1778 the then president, who was over seventy and had fallen out with the King, decided not to seek re-election and after much discussion amongst fellows, Banks was elected president in November of that year, giving him an unchallenged position of influence and a guarantee of the ear of government in almost any matter.

Botany Bay and New South Wales

After the American Declaration of Independence, it became clear that the American colonies would no longer accept transportees from England's gaols. In 1779 Banks wrote a memorandum for Lord Sydney, Secretary of State for Home Affairs, which proposed Botany Bay as a suitable destination, but no action was taken. Several expeditions to other places were commissioned to find a new destination for transportees, but none emerged as a viable or attractive option. In 1786 Banks was consulted by Evan Nepean,[4] then Secretary at the Home Department, and it is likely that the decision by Secretary of State Lord Sydney to send convicts to Botany Bay owed much to Banks's positive indications and advice. The detailed plan came together extraordinarily quickly, no doubt partly because of the pressure from the over-crowded gaols and prison hulks. Captain Arthur Phillip was appointed to lead the expedition in August 1786, with the original intention of sailing before the end of the year. Difficulties emerged during the following months, so that it was May 1787 before the little fleet left Spithead.

Captain Phillip, first governor of New South Wales, had met Banks before leaving London, for one of his first letters sent from Tenerife on 5 June 1787[5] thanked Banks 'for his very friendly & polite attention', and went on to assure him that he will ask about plants they must have discussed, when he reaches Rio and the Cape. A postscript begs 'to make my complements acceptable to the Ladies of your family', showing clearly that Phillip had visited Banks at Soho Square. The next letter written in September from Rio informs Banks of the despatch of some specimen plants, and after arriving in New South Wales in 1788, Phillip continues his correspondence with Banks, sending him samples and seeds. Letters followed at the rate of about four a year throughout Phillip's governorship, frequently referring to seeds and specimens, including an aboriginal head, boxed up for the voyage. When the second governor, Captain Hunter, took up the governorship, a new correspondence began, though rather less frequent. Hunter's performance as governor was seen in London to be less than successful and he was recalled. His final letter to Banks, written after his return home, pleaded for his support. Hunter was succeeded by Governor King, who was charged with restoring order, achieving progress and reducing the costs to government.

Governor Philip Gidley King

After the First Fleet, under Captain Phillip, arrived in New South Wales, Lieutenant King was despatched to Norfolk Island with a small group of convicts and marines to take the island for Britain and establish a settlement there.[6] King's first journal (1788–90) makes no mention of correspondence with Banks, but when he returned to London in 1790 he must have visited Soho Square. His first letter from the island in May 1792, after his return, was written in a much more relaxed style than his formal reports to the Secretary of State.[7]

Banks had become an interested friend. King informed him of a stone hatchet indicating the presence of some earlier inhabitants on the island; he asked for details on growing indigo and cotton, and for 'smallpox matter' to inoculate the young children on the island. He commented on the crops of maize and sugar cane, and asked Banks to send some quickthorn hedge plants. He asked Banks to act as editor of his first journal, which was about to be published with that of Captain Hunter, evidently against King's wishes, for he described Hunter's as 'being only a plain incorrect & unornamented being'. In a later letter he describes it as 'what I may safely call my ill wrote but faithfull journal, with that bundle of jaundiced detraction [Hunter's Journal] which preceeds it.'

The importance of the relationship begins to emerge after the mutiny that King had experienced on the island, for which his actions had been called into question by the acting governor: 'I must request you & all my friends to suspend their judgement until it is cleared up. Thank God we are now perfectly quiet.' Clearly, he was concerned that other reports would reach London, unjustifiably placing King in a poor light; the assumption was that Banks had sufficient influence to ensure that the facts were fully known before judgements were made.

King left Norfolk Island on the grounds of ill health and arrived back in London in May 1797 having recovered considerably, but the correspondence continued. In October 1797 King wrote a sad and appealing letter to Banks bemoaning the fact that the navy had more or less rejected him after nine years of colonial service and asking effectively for Banks to put in a good word for him, so that he could secure employment. Banks had clearly become King's patron and sponsor. In May 1798 King was awarded a dormant commission as governor of New South Wales and planning began for his return in a new vessel, a store ship specially commissioned for colonial service. Banks influenced the design to allow the best possible chance of plants and specimens surviving the nine-month voyage through the tropics.

Sir Joseph Banks, by James Gillray (1756–1815), 1795. 'The great South Sea caterpillar transformed into a Bath Butterfly. Description of the New Bath Butterfly – taken from the "Philosophical Transactions of 1795" – This insect first crawl'd into notice from among the Weeds and Mud on the Banks of the South Sea; & being afterwards placed in a Warm Situation by the Royal Society, was changed by the heat of the Sun into its present form – it is notic'd & valued solely on account of the beautiful Red which encircles its Body & the shining Spot on its Breast; a distinction which never fails to render Caterpillars valuable.' (National Portrait Gallery, London)

Months passed and King became increasingly anxious, until finally in February 1799 the store ship *Porpoise* was ready to sail from the Thames to Portsmouth. She met a westerly gale and proved to be impossible to handle and dangerously unseaworthy. King, who had moved to Portsmouth with his family, ready to embark, wrote tirelessly to try to sort out the mess. The solution turned out to require the removal of most of Banks's special requirements. Even then, when *Porpoise* did sail in September, she had only reached Torbay when the rudder broke; she returned to Portsmouth and was subjected to further extensive rebuilding. Banks's intervention in ship design was not a success. King and his family transhipped to a whaler, which was ready to leave, and sailed with little further delay.

In September 1800 King assumed the role of governor in New South Wales. He was immediately faced with a raft of major problems which his predecessor, Captain Hunter, had failed to address. The first uprising by Irishmen took place within days, drunkenness was rife, and the army and some civil officers were exploiting the situation for personal gain. King must have been ordered by the government in London to get a grip of the issues, and to reduce the cost of the colony to the Exchequer. He knew that the actions necessary would make him very unpopular, and so it proved. His letters to Banks reveal his need for reassurance. In his letter of 21 August 1802 Banks wrote, 'I give you joy of the better state of the colony & of the credit you have obtained by bringing it into its present condition.'[8] King's response was one of real gratitude at receiving such recognition,[9] which clearly gave a significant boost to his morale.

Banks sent King detailed instructions about how to use the HM Armed Survey Vessel *Lady Nelson*, which was designed with a drop keel very suitable for inshore exploration.[10] Banks strongly emphasised the need to chart the coastline and rivers, to record as many plants as possible, and to observe any local inhabitants who might be found. The vessel eventually arrived in Port Jackson (Sydney) early in 1801. King first sent her to explore the coal-producing area around what is now Newcastle, north of Sydney, and later south into the Bass Strait. On this voyage, Lieutenant Murray found Port Phillip and the Murray River, where Melbourne now stands. King later organised settlements to be established on Van Diemen's Land (Tasmania), on the Derwent River (Hobart), and Port Dalrymple. After this southern exploration, King reported to London and wrote to Banks that Port Phillip at the entrance to the Murray River would be an ideal place for a new settlement, but that he had no one equal to such a project. Banks was then clearly instrumental in the appointment of Colonel David Collins to lead a new expedition of settlers and convicts from England to establish such a settlement.[11]

The letters from Banks to King which have survived are few in number –

and extremely difficult to read, as his handwriting is appalling, his punctuation erratic and most appear to have been written intermittently between Banks's many other meetings and commitments. Nevertheless, they were generally approving of King's actions and recognised the difficulties under which he laboured. King has often been accused of being too severe in his punishments of those who transgressed, but such was not Banks's attitude. On 29 August 1804 Banks wrote at the end of his long letter which contains approval and compliments for King's success: 'There is only one part of your conduct as governor which I do not think right that is your frequent reprieves.'[12]

Sadly for King, by the time he returned home, a sick man, in 1807, Banks seemed to have lost interest in him and did nothing to help King secure a reasonable pension and recognition for his hard years of service. Banks surely had enough influence to secure a reasonable level of payment (his successor received twice as much) and save King's widow from the penury into which she was forced.

Captain Matthew Flinders

In 1795 Banks had spotted and recommended a young Lincolnshire man named Matthew Flinders to sail with Captain Bligh on his second voyage to carry breadfruit from Tahiti to the West Indies in HM Sloop *Providence* (12), and had then been instrumental in his appointment to the discovery vessel *Reliance* in 1795, which was to take Governor Hunter to Port Jackson as a passenger. Whilst officially aboard *Reliance*, Flinders had been ordered to take command of a little 35ft, locally built vessel, *Norfolk*, and with surgeon George Bass explore the north of Van Diemen's Land and, if possible, to circumnavigate the island and return to Port Jackson. The mission was accomplished with great skill and the strait, named after Bass, secured Flinders's reputation.

Duck-billed Platypus, *Ornithorhynchus anatinus*, 1801, by Ferdinand Bauer (1760–1826), the artist accompanying Flinders. (Natural History Museum, London)

Even before Flinders arrived home in *Reliance*, he had written a letter to Banks, as a result of which Banks wrote to the King and Earl Spencer, First Lord of the Admiralty, recommending the urgent equipping of an expedition to circumnavigate New Holland and the appointment of Flinders as its commander. The commission was prepared very quickly and Flinders took command of the survey vessel *Investigator* in January 1801. Banks appointed civilian participants: a naturalist, two illustrators, an astronomer, a gardener and a mineral specialist. Shortly before departure Flinders was married to the love of his life, but Banks, on hearing of it, advised him very strongly against taking her with him, threatening that the command of the survey would be handed to someone else. It was with enormous sadness that Flinders and his new wife parted at Spithead; they would not meet again for ten years.

Flinders[13] began his survey of the Australian coastline late in 1801, starting in the southwest at what is now Albany, working along the whole south coast and reaching Port Jackson in May 1802. After a few weeks of repairs and restocking he sailed to complete the circumnavigation of the remainder of Australia. On his return to Port Jackson he was anxious to take his precious charts home, but *Investigator* was no longer seaworthy. So he sailed in another ship, which subsequently was wrecked at the southern end of the Barrier Reef. He returned to Port Jackson in an open boat and was then allowed to take another small vessel for the voyage home. He stopped for water and victuals at Isle de France (Mauritius) which, unbeknown to Flinders, had been handed back to the French in 1803. Flinders was interned there until March 1810. During the frustrating years of Flinders's internment, Banks, who was not only president of the Royal Society but a member of its very select counterpart in France, *L'Institut National*, had been working behind the scenes trying to persuade the French scientific authorities to secure Flinders's release despite the war between Britain and France.[14]

When Flinders eventually reached England late in 1810, apart from renewing his acquaintance with his wife, his priority was to publish his charts and his journal, for which Banks provided much guidance and evidently succeeded in opening various doors. It is of some interest that although Flinders had been commissioned to carry out the survey of the coastline, he was required to fund the printing of the charts himself, a cost of nearly £1,000, when his pay – half-pay as he was not being carried onboard a ship – amounted to only £250.

Captain William Bligh

One of Banks's most celebrated pupils was William Bligh. During the 1790s Banks sought to exploit a perceived opportunity for growing breadfruit, a native of the East Indies and Polynesia, and persuaded the government to fund an expedition for that purpose. He was clearly influential in the appointment of William Bligh, previously a master, in command of the *Bounty*, to fulfil the purpose. Bligh's story of mutiny and heroic navigation across 3,000 miles in an open boat is well known and opinions about his character and capability vary widely. There was a high degree of personal chemistry between these two men which, despite all the criticisms of Captain Bligh, led to the second, more successful breadfruit voyage (mentioned above in relation to Flinders) and subsequently to Bligh's disastrous appointment as the fourth and final naval governor of New South Wales.

The tone of Bligh's letters to Banks was far more confident than that of letters from King. On 13 September 1805, shortly before his departure, Bligh wrote that he was 'harrassed by attending on my equipment and by disappointments', as if this was something over which Banks might have some influence. In this letter, he was openly critical of Lord Barham, the First Lord of the Admiralty, for not giving him total command of all naval vessels in the vicinity of New South Wales. Banks's reply of 17 September[15] made it clear that Lord Camden, previous Secretary of State for the Home Department, had specifically consulted Banks about a 'fit and proper person' to assume the governorship. He advised Bligh to call on Evan Nepean, by then Secretary to the Admiralty, to show him Banks's letter, and ask 'his advice on how to proceed'.

Once in post, Bligh immediately began to change the atmosphere in the colony which King had so assiduously cultivated. Despite their earlier criticisms of King, the colonists resented even more many of Bligh's actions, which were considered high-handed and dictatorial. Nonetheless, the scientific relationship between the governor and Banks continued and a letter from Bligh to Banks in November 1807[16] was entirely devoted to discussion of plants and specimens, describing some very fine lilies, samples of which he was sending home with seeds and, amongst other things, a preserved Maori chief's head. There is no indication here that Bligh was beginning to find life particularly challenging. The last letter in this series was dated 13 August 1811,[17] in which Bligh expressed concern for the witnesses who came from New South Wales to testify in his defence, who had been given less than a week's notice to re-embark for their return voyage. He refers 'to that notorious bad man McArthur' who had, at least to some extent, been the architect of his downfall.[18] There is no evidence of Banks's further intervention in the matter.

The final reckoning

As he aged, Banks suffered increasingly from gout and other ailments. One final and significant connection between Banks and the sea concerned the Board of Longitude, on which he had served for many years. He had fallen out with

Portrait of Sir Joseph Banks, 1810,
by Thomas Phillip (1770–1845).
(National Portrait Gallery, London)

the Astronomer Royal, Dr Nevil Maskelyne, over the merits and demerits of a certain chronometer, and it was only after Maskelyne's death that Banks achieved one of his last triumphs, securing for the Royal Society the right to elect five suitable fellows to the Board of Longitude. He remained president of the Royal Society until his death in 1820.

Banks lived a full life and contributed much to botanical, zoological and anthropological knowledge of his time. He had great influence over the establishment and development of the new colony in New South Wales, collecting and analysing samples of plants, animals and minerals, and doing his best to ensure that plants were introduced which would have a positive impact on the colony's well-being. He positively encouraged the naval governors and other naval officers to contribute actively and consistently to knowledge, not only about the sea and coastlines but also the flora and fauna they might encounter inland.

Banksia integrifolia, see colour plate 6
His Majesty's Armed Survey Vessel *Lady Nelson*, see colour plate 7

Family Tradition in the Life of Sir Harry Neale: A Clarification

Barry Jolly

Editors' note: This article is a follow-on to the article that Mr Jolly published in the 2021 Trafalgar Chronicle, New Series 6, titled 'Political Admiral and Royal Favourite: The Career of Sir Harry Neale, Baronet GCB'.

Admiral Sir Harry Neale (1765–1840) did not take part in any major fleet actions, but he was a charming and dauntless officer who commanded the respect and loyalty of his crews. His varied career encompassed sitting in Parliament as a member for the family pocket borough of Lymington, where he was also a burgess and mayor, serving as a Lord Commissioner of the Admiralty, commanding the two royal yachts for the best part of a decade, and engaging in valuable reconnaissance work off the coast of Brittany.

His epitaph can be found across the Lymington River at Walhampton on a magnificent monument, known as the Burrard Neale Monument. Three recent articles provide a reappraisal of his career.[1] This article examines the posthumous change of name from Neale to Burrard Neale and its interaction with historic and contemporary links with Canada.

Born Harry Burrard in 1764, he inherited a baronetcy and estate from his uncle, Sir Harry Burrard, 1st Baronet, in 1791. In 1795 he took the name of Neale in marriage in order to fulfil the conditions of the will of his wife's grandfather, Robert Neale of Shaw House, Wiltshire. The will stipulated that the name would replace rather than be added to his original surname, a detail overlooked by all who have enquired into the matter since.[2]

Admiral Sir Harry Neale, by John Bryant Lane (1788–1868), published by Thomas Cadell the Younger, after William Evans, after Sir William Beechey. (National Portrait Gallery)

Throughout the remaining forty-five years of his life, he was punctilious in using the name 'Neale'. The name appeared not only in personal correspondence: all naval correspondence – to, from or about him – referred simply to Sir Harry Neale. So, too, did parliamentary papers, records of Lymington Corporation, and of the Admiralty. It was only when he died that he became a Burrard once more.

A posthumous name change

The *eminence grise* of this posthumous name change was his brother and heir, Revd Sir George Burrard, 3rd Baronet, who engineered the change of name in spite of local opposition. After testing the water with an obituary in the *Hampshire Advertiser* – the name 'Burrard' was placed strategically in brackets – the evidence points to George arranging a carefully orchestrated public meeting held on 25 February 1840, seven days after Neale's funeral. The purpose of the meeting was to decide how to honour Neale with a monument, and what the epitaph on the monument should say. The various proposals had been circulated prior to the meeting, and the principal speaker was chosen carefully.

This speaker was Captain (later Rear-Admiral) Sir David Dunn, a serving officer. Dunn's origins are obscure, apparently born in Ireland with a brother, Robert, who was a surgeon RN.[3] His naval service was by no means undistinguished. He served under Nelson in the chase to the West Indies, missed Trafalgar, but served as a midshipman at Duckworth's victory at San Domingo in 1806. Dunn was in action at the famous battle at Lissa in 1811, when a small British force routed a Franco-Venetian fleet with double the number of guns and three times the number of men. Captain William Hoste, under whom he served as first lieutenant, described him as 'a zealous, brave and intelligent officer; and his exertions, though wounded, in repairing our damage, is [*sic*] as praiseworthy as his action in the battle', an accolade which resulted in promotion to commander. Made post in 1814, he was knighted in 1835 and KCH two years later.[4]

Dunn had married for the second time on 16 April 1838, his bride being Louisa Henrietta Montagu. The wedding took place in the rather obscure location of Chesterton, Cambridgeshire, in spite of Louisa being from a notable Norfolk family.[5] He does not appear in any censuses for Lymington, nor in a much reprinted local guide throughout the preceding decade and a half.[6] His arrival was probably occasioned by his new wife being the sister of Mrs Hockings, for whom see below. Indeed, his sojourn was brief, as he moved to Devon by the late 1840s, probably after Mrs Hockings died in 1848 and in order to be near to another of Lady Dunn's sisters, Mrs Ensor.[7] He was the only speaker to call Sir Harry by the name Burrard Neale. As a serving officer, he would have been aware that Sir Harry was only ever known, or referred to, in the navy and in Admiralty papers as Sir Harry Neale. The suggestion is that he was persuaded by Revd Sir George that the proper name to use was Burrard Neale; as an outsider, he would not have been in a position to demur.

The newspaper report of the meeting on 25 February was accompanied by a sanitised résumé detailing the eight motions with their proposers and seconders.[8] Dunn's motion, the erection of a monument in honour of Sir Harry Burrard Neale, was shown as seconded by F R West Esq. West, though, carefully qualified this by referring specifically and pointedly to Sir Harry Neale (without the addition of 'Burrard').

The others who spoke at the meeting were the mayor, Dr William Towsey, and Revd Thomas Robinson (vicar of nearby Milford) who both carefully avoided referring to Sir Harry by name. All other speakers – James Monro, Captain R Hockings RN, and Major C M Roberts (all of whom were appointed to the old Lymington Corporation in 1830 when Sir Harry held sway),[9] James Brown (another burgess), and Captain W A Willis RN – referred meaningfully to 'Sir Harry Neale' without any mention of 'Burrard'.

The Organising Committee elected on 25 February 1840

H C Compton MP
Captain Sir David Dunn RN KCH
Lieutenant Colonel D'Arcy KSL
F R West Esq
James Monro Esq
Captain Hockings RN
Charles St Barbe Esq
Captain T E Symonds RN
Captain W A Willis RN
Rev T Robinson
William Towse Esq MD Mayor
Colonel H T Roberts CB
Edward Hicks Esq
J H Stephen Esq
William Bartlett Esq

Honorary members:

Admirals:
Sir Thomas Williams GCB
Sir Thomas Byam Martin GCB
Right Hon Sir George Cockburn GCB
Sir George Moore GCB GCMG

The Organising Committee elected on 25 February 1840.

All these speakers were gentlemen of independent means, well able to speak their minds. Robert Hockings had served as Neale's signal lieutenant in 1810 at the attack in the Basque Roads. He was promoted following command of a fire-ship in that action, the cause of the infamous spat between Admiral Gambier and Lord Cochrane, and had given evidence at Gambier's court martial.[10] He had been the last mayor of Lymington before the changes wrought by the Municipal Corporations Act of 1835, which deprived the Burrards of their control of the parliamentary seats at Lymington.

James Monro, a local banker, had also served as mayor, both before and after the act.[11] J R Stephen was a local resident of literary interests.[12] William Bartlett, the designer and manager of the Lymington Sea Water Baths, for which Neale had laid the foundation stone in 1833, as well as managing the Archery Grounds, also owned the land on which the new Poor Law Union workhouse had been built.[13]

Frederick West was a grandson of the 2nd Earl de la Warr and a former MP for Denbigh Boroughs. His father-in-law was the late Captain John Whitby RN, and his mother-in-law, Mrs M A T Whitby, came from the Symonds dynasty of naval officers. William Willis, born in 1799, was rather younger, and had served as flag lieutenant to Sir George Cockburn in the West Indies. He was still only a commander at this juncture, and not the reported rank of captain (to which he was promoted in 1844), but claimed to be 'an inhabitant of several years standing in this neighbourhood [and] a near neighbour [of Sir Harry]'. His house, Vicar's Hill Cottage, was indeed very close to Walhampton, and he had probably lived in the area since his marriage in 1827.[14]

All of these men (bar Major C M Roberts) were included in the Organising Committee established by the meeting on 25 February, which comprised the great and good of the area.

Of those not mentioned previously, H C Compton was the MP for South Hampshire, for whom Neale had canvassed in the 1832 election, thereby attracting the ire of the First Lord of the Admiralty, Sir James Graham, and the withdrawal of the offer of the position of Port Admiral, Portsmouth.[15] Captain (later Admiral) Thomas Symonds was a brother of Mrs Whitby. He was made post in 1814 after extensive active service, but remained on half-pay, thereafter engaging largely in civic affairs. St Barbe was a banker and Hicks a lawyer. Colonel and Major Roberts were brothers from an army family. Colonel D'Arcy lived variously at Milford House, Priestlands (in Pennington) and Holme Mead (in Lymington), all substantial houses in the area. He had a distinguished army service, and served as aide-de-camp to the Lord Lieutenant of Ireland, the Marquess of Wellesley.[16]

Despite the evident wishes of this array of worthy gentlemen, the report of the meeting headed 'Public Memorial to Sir Harry Burrard Neale Bart GCB', was published in the *Hampshire Advertiser* on 29 February 1840, together with the sanitised advertisement summarising the outcome of the meeting and the resolutions in full. This advertisement was then published more widely: in the *Morning Post* of 2 March 1840 and the *London Evening Standard* of 3 March 1840. The message was well and truly hammered home. It would appear that Neale's friends resisted the change of name in death, but to no avail.

Tensions remained, however, for a short while longer. A report in a more obscure newspaper, *The Era*, on 29 March stated:

It appears it is not yet decided where the monument to the memory of the late Admiral Sir Harry Neale is to be placed; some say at the entrance of the Lymington river, as being nearer to the element his valuable professional life was spent upon, and also as the place of the greatest public utility to mariners entering the Needles passage from sea. Others say it is to be erected on an elevated spot on the Walhampton estate, known by the name of 'Mount Pleasant,' and opposite to the town of Leamington [*sic*].[17]

The use of the name 'Sir Harry Neale' without 'Burrard' being inserted is clear evidence that Revd Sir George Burrard was not behind this report. As the offer of land at Mount Pleasant on the Walhampton estate can only have been (and, indeed, was) made by Sir George, it is apparent that the more prominently positioned alternative suggestion of proximity to the sea came from the naval contingent. There is an interesting parallel here in that five years later, in 1845, a monument to Cuthbert Collingwood was erected at Tynemouth, rather than Collingwood's home city of Newcastle, and 'deliberately sited to be seen from the sea and the river'.[18]

The memorial

A similar situation arose with the memorial itself. The committee approached William Railton, whose proposal for Nelson's Column had been accepted the year before. Railton proposed a design based on the Great Obelisk at Thebes, and the accompanying notes refer clearly to 'Admiral Sir Harry Neale'.[19] Again, this would not have suited the agenda of Revd Sir George Burrard, and it seems likely that it was he who then approached the eventual architect, George Draper of Chichester, for a design incorporating the name, 'Sir Harry Burrard Neale'.

The debate continued for some months, with the announcement of Mount Pleasant being the chosen site not made until late July. Another suggestion, reported in the *Morning Herald*, had been mooted in the interim:

It was at first suggested that the sum subscribed should be appropriated to the erection of an eleemosynary asylum, to be appelled the 'Neale Almshouses,' but the majority of subscribers were of opinion that an obelisk erected to the late gallant baronet's memory would be more in character with the circumstance, and better befitting the occasion.[20]

This alternative suggestion, in keeping with Neale's concerns for the poor and with the obvious appeal of (and to) Christian charity, came from a sufficiently significant source for it not to be ignored completely. The use, again, of the correct name of 'Neale' in 'Neale's Almshouses' indicates another person from outside Sir George's camp, in this instance possibly Neale's widow, who was otherwise noticeably absent from Lymington.

The high-flown phraseology of the *Morning Herald* report, including the use of the obscure word 'eleemosynary' – synonyms for which include charitable, philanthropic, benevolent and altruistic – masked the strength and the attractiveness of the suggestion. It took 'the majority of subscribers' – who totalled 208, although it is difficult to believe that the majority of these were actually consulted – to express a preference for an obelisk, and for the suggestion of the almshouses to be rejected.

The site chosen was indeed Mount Pleasant, in full view of the High Street in Lymington, as a reminder of the power of the Burrard family, and conveniently positioned *vis-à-vis* the Burrard residence at Walhampton, agreeably visible from the terrace. The architect, George Draper, referred later to the monument as a useful seamark, but this was a piece of window dressing for his audience, the Royal Institute of British Architects, as the dichotomy expressed in *The Era* makes plain.[21]

Although there is an element of speculation in the foregoing about Sir George Burrard's activities, the final piece of evidence is overwhelming. Revd Sir George held another card: as an honorary chaplain to George III and

The Burrard Neale Monument at Walhampton, 1840; obelisk by G Draper, builder G Banks.
(Courtesy of Peter Stone, The Friends of Sir Harry)

subsequent monarchs including Queen Victoria, he could communicate directly with Princess Augusta, one of the remaining daughters of the late George III. In an extravagantly worded letter to Revd Sir George, she wrote:

> I cannot let any other pen than my own, return my most sincere thanks to Sir George Burrard for the very melancholy but most interesting paper containing all that I truly feel respecting the character of my most excellent and worthy friend, the late Sir Harry Burrard Neale.

Continuing at length in like vein, she approved his suggested wording for the proposed memorial, including the name 'Sir Harry Burrard Neale'.[22]

Although studiously avoiding being a member of the organising committee for the memorial, Revd Sir George had succeeded in establishing the agenda. Once Princess Augusta's letter had been received, there was no going back: the great and good of the area had been bounced into a decision before having a chance to discuss it. Sir George Burrard had succeeded in reclaiming his brother from the clutches of the Neale family dynasty, and the name 'Burrard Neale' became enshrined in the Lymington psyche for the next 180 years.

Three enigmas in Canada – now resolved

Although Neale never visited Canada, his association with that country had its roots in his early naval service and has resulted in three enigmas which can now be resolved. The first concerns the naming of the Burrard Inlet on the Pacific coast, the other two relate to artefacts in the possession of Vancouver Maritime Museum: a telescope and a naval officer's sword.

After the Nootka Sound crisis of 1790,[23] the British government sent Captain George Vancouver to Canada to chart the Pacific coast. In June 1792 he named one bay Burrard Inlet, after Sir Harry Burrard. The received wisdom was that this was Sir Harry Neale, with whom Vancouver had served in the Fourth Rate HMS *Europa* (50) in the West Indies in the 1780s. However, in 1946 Sir Gerald Burrard, 8th Baronet, queried this, reasoning that the bay must have been named after Sir Harry Burrard, 1st Baronet, who was still alive when Vancouver left England. Earlier, there had been suggestions that it was named after Sir Harry's father, Lieutenant-Colonel William Burrard, an even less likely possibility.

Nonetheless, Vancouver was quite clear that he had named the bay 'after Sir Harry Burrard of the navy', although it must have been inconvenient to learn that the latter had changed his name to Neale in the interim. It was too late to change the name to 'Neale Inlet', and it is an historical idiosyncrasy that the bay was named after someone who no longer bore the name himself. A descendant of Revd Sir George Burrard, David Burrard Smith, has discussed this matter in detail, concluding that Sir Harry Neale was the man thus honoured.[24]

Today, Vancouver has a Burrard Bridge, Burrard Street and Burrard Hotel. Conversely, the Vancouver name has become embedded in the Burrard consciousness. So much so, that two descendants of Neale's brother, Revd Sir George Burrard, have made gifts of Neale memorabilia to the Vancouver museums.

The second enigma concerns a telescope which had been a Burrard family heirloom. Sir Gerald Burrard, 8th Baronet, donated to the Vancouver Museum the telescope which, according to family legend, Nelson had given to Neale when the latter took command of the Second Rate HMS *London* (90) in 1805. A formal ceremony handing over the gift took place in London on 13 June 1943, the 151st anniversary of the discovery of Burrard Inlet.[25]

David Burrard Smith, who has charted much of the Burrard family history, noted later that the Vancouver city archivist and the museum curator were divided on the question of provenance.[26] There were indeed good reasons for doubt.

The first, and quite straightforward, reason is that Nelson was in England only briefly in 1805, having been at sea for well over two years. His visit lasted from 18 August to 15 September. He spent some time at Merton with Lady Hamilton before being summoned to London, where he met with Pitt, Sidmouth, Castlereagh and Barham, as well as, supposedly, having a chance encounter with the future Duke of Wellington. No opportunities arose to meet Neale, who was in attendance on George III at Weymouth throughout the summer as captain of the royal yacht, *Royal Sovereign*. By the time Neale took command of *London* on 28 November, Nelson had been dead for more than five weeks.

The second reason is that, in his will, Nelson left all his telescopes to Captain Hardy, a collection assembled over time and apparently not dissipated by occasional gifts.

Finally, there is only minimal evidence of Nelson and Neale ever meeting. For Neale to have been the worthy recipient of a valuable telescope, he would have featured strongly in Nelson's correspondence. Yet Neale is mentioned only twice in the seven volumes of Nelson's papers published by Nicholas in 1844/5, and then only because he was carrying despatches between Nelson and Hood in 1794.[27]

There was an intriguing epilogue to this in 1863. Nelson's great-nephew, Rear-Admiral Maurice Horatio Nelson, married Emily Burrard, a daughter of Admiral Sir Charles Burrard. Burrard was the son of Neale's cousin, and served as Neale's flag captain in the Mediterranean from 1823 to 1826. Nonetheless, this posthumous event cannot have involved Neale himself and the telescope was passed down through Sir George Burrard's descendants, rather than those of Sir Charles Burrard. Provenance from Neale is very possible, indeed quite likely, but it is quite apparent that the telescope now in Vancouver could not have been a gift from Nelson.

Maurice Rooke Kingsford gave this story an added twist when writing about the novelist, W H G Kingston, a grandson of Neale's sister, Harriet. He claimed that Nelson gave Neale a sword shortly before Trafalgar. This claim was by no means frivolous, being made in an Oxford BLitt (Bachelor of Letters) dissertation in 1947.[28] However, as with the telescope, it ignores the movements of the two men at the time. The confusion of the telescope and a sword is a reminder of how family legends become distorted as they pass down from

Naval officer's sword, Vancouver Maritime Museum Collection.
(Photo Vancouver Maritime Museum, M973.476.1a-c)

generation to generation, and beyond. There was a sword, though, which is the subject of the third enigma.

The naval pattern sword in the Vancouver Maritime Museum was donated in 1957 by Commander Burrard A Smith RN, of Nelson, British Columbia – another descendant of Revd Sir George Burrard – which leads back to Neale's posthumous change of name. The Vancouver Maritime Museum has labelled it as a naval dress sword of c1837, and noted the engraving on the scabbard: 'HBN June 1797'.[29] That this sword has been passed down through the generations of the Burrard family is not in doubt. On the other hand, the engraving most certainly is.

June 1797 was the occasion when Neale was trapped at The Nore by the

Oil painting by Nicholas Pocock (1740–1821):'HIS MAJESTYS Ships St Fiorenzo Capt Sir H. Neale Bart & the Amelia, the Hon Capt Herbert. Engaging three French Frigates & a Gun vessel; Close in with Belleisle Road – April 9th 1799.' San Fiorenzo is to the left. (Wikipedia Commons)

infamous eponymous mutiny. Neale was able to flee, having, as the Walhampton Monument asserts, 'retained the loyalty of his crew'. His reputation in Lymington today rests on that claim, but there were other exploits more deserving of lasting fame.

It is worth recalling Cornwallis's retreat in 1795 with respect to the incident at The Nore. Then, Cornwallis's small squadron escaped from the French Brest fleet, without the loss of a single life, through skilful seamanship and courage. Cornwallis was offered the Order of the Bath (ie, a knighthood), but declined it; fleeing from the enemy was not, in his opinion, worthy of an honour.[30] Neale's escape from the clutches of a mutinous British fleet was small beer in contrast, as Neale himself would have known.

Indeed, his wife clearly thought so too, commissioning a painting from Nicholas Pocock depicting his capture of two French frigates in March of the same year, a far more worthy achievement. Two of Pocock's original sketches are now in the National Maritime Museum in Greenwich, and include a note identifying Lady Neale as the person commissioning the painting.[31]

Nonetheless, it is the flight from The Nore that the sword commemorates. The initials 'HBN' can refer only to Neale, even though he would not have recognised them himself. A thorough trawl through contemporary and more modern databases and navy lists has failed to find a single naval officer in the Georgian navy with these initials, so they must be assumed to refer to Neale under his posthumous name of Harry Burrard Neale. The engraving on the sword reveals that it was made by E & E Emanuel of Portsmouth, Cutlers to Her Majesty – ie, Queen Victoria – a firm established only in 1830.

Quite clearly, the sword was new at the time of Neale's death in 1840, and probably purchased to be borne on his coffin at the funeral. The engraving on the scabbard, with the initials of Neale's posthumous name displayed for posterity, is of a piece, therefore, with the stage management of the planning for the Walhampton Monument.

Both the Neale and the Burrard families claimed a lineage dating back to the Norman Conquest. Investigation of the Burrard claims has shown that they are quite unsustainable, and the origins of the Neales' wealth in trade scarcely indicates the landed family that would have the necessary muniments and other records to substantiate such a pedigree. Nevertheless, the claims are indicative of families seeking to emphasise their longevity and social standing.

Robert Neale, the grandfather of Sir Harry Neale's wife Grace, had been beset by bereavement. His son, also named Robert, had died in 1774 aged just thirty-seven, having followed his own infant son, another Robert (actually the sixth in succession to bear this name), to the grave. For Robert Neale, the grandfather, this potentially presaged the end of the Neale dynasty. The situation was worsened by his daughter-in-law remarrying the year after she was widowed, with Robert deprived prospectively of any control over, and possibly even contact with, his two granddaughters.

His reaction was to complain of 'the great disaffection indiscretion and ingratitude which Mrs Grace Neale widow of my said late deceased son the said Robert Neale has shown and given ample testimony of', and to stipulate in his will that his daughter-in-law should not have any contact with her daughters on pain of their losing their bequests under his will. (Unsurprisingly, this stipulation was overturned in court in 1778.)

He went on to stipulate that any future husband of a female beneficiary under his will would have to take the name of Neale instead of his own. This went rather further than the more usual requirement for a name to be taken as an addition. Furthermore, the provision was to continue for a period of no less than five hundred years.[32]

Sir Harry Neale was the most eminent member of the Burrard family, but one difficult for them to celebrate as such because of his enforced change of name. That he died childless proved in one respect, for the Burrards, to be a welcome blessing. At the same time, Lady Neale's inheritance reverted to her when Sir Harry died, and would pass to other members of the wider Neale family on her own decease, thereby removing from the Burrards any vestigial financial self-interest in the Neale name.

Thus the way was open for the Burrards to reclaim Sir Harry Neale for their own. In 1840, through some remarkably adroit machinations, Revd Sir George did indeed succeed in regaining Sir Harry for the Burrard family, and the name 'Harry Burrard Neale' is the one still recognised in Lymington today.

Plate 1. Jan Verbruggen's boring machine at his shop, a camera obscura drawing by Pieter Vergruggen (1778). Jan Verbruggen was born in the Netherlands. In 1770 he moved to the UK where he was appointed Master Gun Founder of the Royal Arsenal in Greenwich. (Flickr, commercial use authorised)

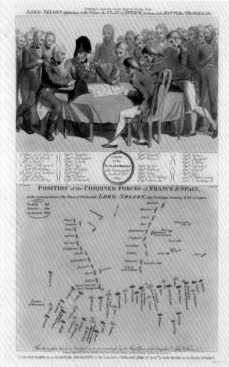

Plate 2 (above). 'The Yankey Torpedo', etching by W Elmes, 1813. (British Cartoon Prints Collection, Library of Congress, public domain)

Plate 3 (right). Captain Peter Heywood, c1822, by John Simpson (1782–1847). (© National Maritime Museum, Greenwich, London, BHC2766)

Plate 4 (left) Lord Nelson briefs his officers prior to Trafalgar, by James Godby (printmaker, active 1790–1820), 1806, for Williams Marshall Craig and Edward Orme. (© National Maritime Museum, Greenwich, London, PAG9025)

Plate 5 (overleaf) 'Amputation', satire by Thomas Rowlandson (1756–1827), coloured etching, 1793. (Wikimedia Commmons. Wellcome Library, London, M0011783)

E SURGERY.

T. Rowlandson. 1793

LIST of EXAMINED and APPROVED SURGEONS

Sir Dreary Dropsical
Doctor GLISTERPIPE.
Doc^R S
Sir Iaundice Jollop
BALLOON THICKSKULL Esqr
BENJAMIN BOWELLES
PAUL PURGE
DAVID PUKE
Doct
Nic. NERVOUS
Scurvy Scrubgu
Twistum Trul

Sir VALIANT VENERY
Doctor Peter Putrid
Abraham Abcess
Doct. GLEET
Launcelot. Slashmuscle
Gabriel Clands
Frederick Fistula
Cristopher Cutgutt
Samuel Sawbone
Tor Scrotum
r Proudflesh
Roger Rowell

Plate 6 (above). 'Banksia integrifolia', by Sidney Parkinson, 1770, published in Banks's Florilegium. (Natural History Museum, London)

Plate 7 (opposite above). His Majesty's Armed Survey Vessel Lady Nelson, undated, artist unknown. 'View of the Lady Nelson in the Thames ...', reproduced in The Narrative of a Voyage of Discovery, performed in His Majesty's Vessel the Lady Nelson ... to New South Wales, by James Grant, published in London in 1803. (Mitchell Library, State Library of New South Wales)

Plate 8 (opposite below). 'Rendition of the unfortunate demise of the Frigate Falster on June 3rd 1753'. Contemporary illustration showing two stages of the frigate on fire, first in the middle of the Safia roadstead and then closer to the beach where the ship exploded. The other ships are from left to right: Friderich & Louise, Docquen, Christiansborg, Blaae Hejren and Neptunus. (Frederik 5's Atlas, Royal Library, Copenhagen)

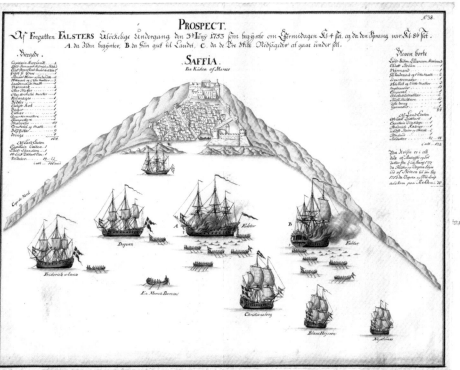

PROSPECT.

Af Fregatten **FALSTERS** Ulÿckelige Undergang den 3:de Iunÿ 1753 som begÿnte om Eftermidagen Kl: 4 slet. og da den Sprang var Kl: 8½ slet.
A. da Ilden begÿnter, B da Siin guk til Landet, C. da de Tre slik Redssegeder at gaae under sil.

SAFFIA.
En Kiøbm: of Maroco

Plate 9. Contemporary sketch showing the rigging of the Danish frigate *Blaae Hejren* (Blue Heron), one of the other vessels in the Danish squadron in 1753. (National Museum of Denmark)

George Matcham (1753–1833): A Biography of Lord Nelson's Inventor Brother-in-law

Lily Style

George Matcham was born on 30 November 1753 in Britain's fortified colony at Bombay. He achieved adulthood with a single lung and an adventurous spirit. When his restlessness was stilled through happy marriage to Lord Nelson's youngest sister, his lively curiosity turned to sedate problem-solving and resulted in his patenting two inventions of benefit to the Royal Navy. Although biographies of Nelson and Lady Hamilton mention him often, no biography has so far focused on George himself.

Bombay had been under British control for the best part of a century. The island was a fortified garrison that the East India Company rented from the British monarchy for £10 a year. A 1754 watercolour depicts the fortified island as predominantly rural. Rolling, scrub-covered hills rise behind blocky

King's Topographical Collection: 'BOMBAY on the Malabar Coast; BOMBAY sur la Cote de Malabar'. (British Library, public domain)

European buildings clustering on the shore. A two-storey, grey stone warehouse dominates the left-hand side of the image with a pier protruding into the sea. Behind it peeks St Thomas's Cathedral looking every bit like an English rural parish church. A red-roofed building beside it is likely the theatre.

George's parents were born in England. His mother, Elizabeth Peirce Bidwell, came from a devout Presbyterian family. Her father had been lured to Bombay by job opportunities in the predominantly Presbyterian East India Company. She wed Captain Simon Matcham in 1751. They named their first child Simon, and George was born soon after. Elizabeth filled their garrison home with exotic knick-knacks[1] and her husband brought home equally exotic tales from his patrols of the Indian Ocean: one being about frequent sightings of shoaling mermaids with long, glossy hair, pug noses and fins in place of forearms, which were hacked up by Mombasa fishermen and tasted like fishy pork.[2]

The Matcham brothers are described as 'pasty-faced' in a pair of Indian miniature portraits, depicting them in 'precocious dress of velvet coat, laced waistcoat, frills and velvet ribbon'.[3] Simon died aged six. A second brother, Charles, baptised in 1761, lived only until age two. No causes of death are recorded, but contemporary travellers reported 'deadly illnesses in Bombay'.[4]

Employment with the East India Company 1771–1783
George was sent to board at Charterhouse, near Smithfield in London. He was a fee-paying boarder in the house of the headmaster. The school's archives hold no record of his arrival, though boarders as young as eight were admitted. Their records, however, tell us he left in December 1769.[5] He spent a year in the East India Company's graduate school in Haileybury, Hertfordshire,[6] and joined the Company as a senior merchant in 1771.[7] This was the highest rank in their commercial service (the hierarchy being senior merchant, junior merchant, factor, writer).[8] The East India Company, whose original name had been the Company of Merchants of London Trading into the East-Indies[9] was at heart a merchants' club with a private militia. Their 1757 victory at Plassey over the allied native and French forces paved their way for domination of Bengal.[10] When the Mughal emperor ceded to them in 1765, the East India Company became 'the effective rulers of Bengal. An international corporation was transforming itself into an aggressive colonial power.'[11]

George was one of fifty-eight senior merchants listed in Bombay in 1771. Part of their remit was the administration of outlying factories (trading offices) in places such as Surat (the most important port for exporting textiles from Gujarat, north of Bombay). A contemporary account from Bengal tells of a lowly free merchant rising to Resident (governor) within ten years.[12] George, however, didn't need to work his way up the ranks. The East India Company was not a meritocracy, and posts were awarded on a 'who you knew' basis. His father had been promoted to 'Master Attendant of the Honble [*sic*] Company's Marine Officers' by 1765[13] and eighteen-year-old George was known to the right people when he graduated from their school in England. He was quickly made their Resident at Baroche [Bharuch],[14] charged with ensuring the profitability of native calico production, which required the hard labour of thousands of locals.[15] Though young and privileged, George was deeply moved by 'the misery of the people, and waste of fine agricultural land' and filled journals with ambitious improvement plans.[16]

His father's career peaked in 1774 when, aged sixty-four, he was made Superintendent Marine of the Honourable East India Company (the equivalent of admiral)[17] and Senior Member of the Council of Bombay.[18] Simon Matcham had little time to enjoy these pinnacles of Company success for he was buried in Bombay on 22 June 1776.[19] George's widowed mother set sail for England in the next year, never to return.[20]

Twenty-three-year-old George decided to follow the overland caravan trail from Basra to Aleppo instead. The route was of keen interest to the East India Company, who wanted to transport merchandise and communication as swiftly as possible between Asia and England. Several British expeditions had previously explored the route in that century. George's decision to attempt it in

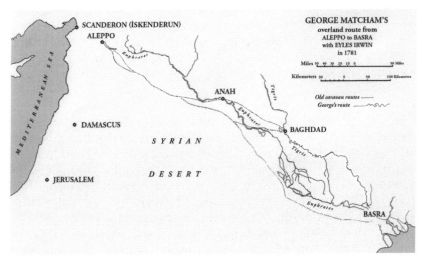

Map based on Eyles Irwin's account and 'The Great Desert Caravan Route, Aleppo to Basra', from *The Geographical Journal*, vol 52, no 3 (September 1918). (Author's own work)

1777 coincided with the Company's increased interest in further exploration. James Capper, who travelled the route from west to east in 1778, published 'various land and sea-routes to India, with their qualifications'. Lieutenant Samuel Evers led a party in 1779. And in 1780,[21] Eyles Irwin, an Irish poet and writer two years older than George[22] 'rode from Aleppo to Ana, and thence passed to Baghdad, Basra and India' in the company of several Englishmen, of whom one was George Matcham.[23] Irwin documented his travels in the Mideast in two published volumes, one in 1778 and one in 1780/81.

George's friends were horrified by his intention to travel overland because he was seriously ill with a damaged lung, but a doctor pronounced his health already so bad it would make no difference if he went. George indeed went and, in his own words, was 'compelled to ride on untam'd horses at a rate of sixty or seventy miles a day, sometimes exposed to a burning sun, sometimes to the cutting air of the mountains, and often obliged to sleep in the open air.' He had a small Persian rug to sleep on and subsisted entirely on mare's milk. These privations apparently agreed with him, for his lung healed during the journey (although it never entirely recovered).[24]

The East India Company's cordial relations with the Iraqi port of Basra were lost between 1773 and 1779 because of plague and Persian occupation. So it is unlikely George landed there in 1777.[25] Detouring into Egypt, he was dismayed to find 'the wretched Egyptians ... sadly oppressed by an aristocracy, and there is no security in the Government.' The ruins of Alexandria caused him to reflect:

We cannot sufficiently regret these despicable tyrants chacing [sic] away from this happy country the arts, sciences and commerce; for what it still remains of the latter may be compared to the sweeping of a great warehouse, their merchants couldn't even raise enough money to purchase the Italian cargoes ...

He enjoyed visiting Egyptian merchants on donkey back (horses being prohibited to Christians). He then dawdled his way through Europe, where he studied 'the height of civilisation in contrast to the East', before joining his mother in her country home at Charlton Place, near Canterbury in Kent.[26] He toured England and Ireland, making Indian-style sketches 'for his mother's amusement', and wrote pragmatically to friends, 'if the bulk of our fortune should come home safe, I mean to buy an estate jointly with my mother. I shall then marry and have three principal sources of amusement; my wife, farming and hunting. If our fortune should not be happily remitted, I must again betake myself to Bombay.'[27]

He wrote to his mother from Brussels at the start of his second overland journey in September 1780.[28] Irwin's account helpfully describes Matcham's journey as well as his own. On 11 March 1781 Irwin was surprised to be joined in Aleppo by 'Mr. Matcham ... whom we had left at Venice, looking for a passage to Scanderon [İskenderun, southeast Turkey]'.[29] They departed the comforts of Aleppo on 19 March 1781 with a party of Arab guides,[30] but after five hours, they had travelled only thirteen miles. Their camels' slow pace of 'two and a half miles an hour' frustrated Irwin, George, and their friend, Smyth, who eventually found horses, so that the three could ride 'the whole stage'.[31] Their route loosely followed the Euphrates, which provided vital drinking water. On the morning of 2 April, exactly two weeks after departing Aleppo, the party passed an abundance of ancient riverside aqueducts as they approached Anah. The ancient city was in a sorry state with 'forsaken mosques and towers ... a broken bridge and surrounding ruins'. Food there, however, was sumptuous: 'good mutton and fish, which were carp from the Euphrates, of a size, that, perhaps, no table in Europe could boast. The milk was excellent, and fruit was brought to us in abundance.' Irwin calculated that Anah was exactly 338 miles from Aleppo.[32]

A week, and 200 miles later, they at last approached Bagdad. Irwin wrote:

Messieurs Smyth, Matcham and myself remounted our horses, and, accompanied by our servants and seven Arabs well-armed, we bid our friends adieu, and pushed on for the city, in order to hasten preparations for our journey down the Tygris ... What crowned our satisfaction, on having so happily finished our arduous journey by land, was to find from our host that a boat was engaged to carry us directly to Busrah [*sic*],[33] [but] Rude materials and ruder workmanship marked the only vessel in Bagdad, that was to be procured for money. [Baghdad comprised] narrow and dirty streets, ill-built and worse designed houses, deserted market-places, with more than half the city lying level with the ground.[34]

The party languished until 21 April. Their Tigris voyage was frequently delayed by the necessity to evade hostile tribes. Irwin left George at Basra on 7 May, headed for a ship expected to arrive at Bombay.[35]

George 'retired from service' in 1783 when the Baroche was ceded to the Mahrattas.[36] The Mahrattas were an indigenous warrior culture whose subcontinental empire had displaced the Mughals, and were then displaced by Europeans.[37] Negotiation with Mahratta leader Sindia, who held several British hostages, culminated in the Company granting him Baroche in June 1782, though formal acceptance was delayed until March the next year.[38]

George embarked on his final overland journey after August 1784.[39] His travels took him through 'Persia, Arabia, Egypt, Asia Minor, Turkey, Greece, the Greek Islands'.[40] He also went to 'Hungary, and almost all the countries and courts included in the usual continental tour. Attended only by an Arab suite, he performed a journey from Baghdad to Pera [probably Pera Magroon in northwest Iraq] ... and traversing the wild regions of the Kurds'.[41]

Matcham's marriage and family life

Gilbert Stuart, creator of George Washington's one-dollar bill portrait, painted Matcham's portrait circa 1785.[42] Shortly thereafter, at last ready to realise his English country gentleman idyll, Matcham headed to Bath, one of the best places to meet an eligible young lady. There, he met Catherine Nelson at a ball in the winter of 1786/7 and fell in love at first sight.[43] They were married by his nineteen-year-old bride's father, Revd Edmund Nelson, at Walcot Church, Bath, on 26 February 1787.[44] She was the youngest sister of Horatio Nelson. Her not-yet-famous brother was a witness to their marriage settlement. This eighteenth-century precursor to prenuptial agreements transferred the groom's estate[45] to named executors as insurance for the bride and future children.[46] George 'assigned and transferred ... one thousand six hundred and sixty-six pounds thirteen shillings and four pence bank annuities unto the executors',[47] namely Kitty's father and brother, the Reverends Edmund and William Nelson, and her uncle, William Suckling.

Their first home, Barton Hall, was a grand red brick building on Barton Broad.[48] According to their great-granddaughter, 'At Barton ... "We walkt on the broad," [Kitty] writes in May, "the water was calm and of a deep blue, corresponding to the

George Matcham, Esq, by Gilbert Stewart, c1785. Author's rendition based on several low resolution versions. Original in a private collection.

Barton Hall, George Matcham's first marital home. (Author's photo, 2017)

etherial arch. How beautiful did the scenery round present itself.'"[49] It was here that the first children were born. George Nelson Matcham was born on 7 November 1789,[50] and Henry Savage Matcham was baptised on 4 February 1791.[51]

George and Kitty toured southern England in the summer of 1790, seeking land to manifest George's country idyll. 'They passed by Bath, Stonehenge and Salisbury with the object of seeing a property near Ringwood in Hampshire … what could please them better than building [a house] and planting the grounds with woods.'[52] Building commenced in 1791, and their new home, Shepherd's Spring, was completed in 1793.[53] A 2017 *New Forest* magazine article stated, 'George Matcham … borrowed capital to do so, annually paying off the interest. His creditors were Nelson's father and brother, Edmund and William, and an uncle, William Suckling.'[54] The story appears to stem from an essay held by Ringwood Meeting House & History Centre, interpreting a 1791 legal document as a court order for George and his wife to promptly repay money to her father, brother and uncle.[55] The writ's date coincides with the start of building (see facsimile) so seems to be a consent for land purchase.

Many visitors 'flocked to them undaunted by the abominable roads which led from Bath'.[56] But George realised his children's education needs would be better met in Bath.[57] He was reluctant to leave Shepherd's Spring until, in the early months of 1798, his infant daughter, Mary Anne, died there. They moved to No. 19 Kensington Place, Bath, their home for many years. Their eighth-born, Harriet, was baptised in the newly extended parish church of Walcot St

---

Roll 87
    Trinity Term 31st K Geo 3rd: 1791

*C*y [county] *of Southampton Edmund Nelson clerk William Nelson*
    clerk & William Sucking Esq. Plts [plaintiffs]
    George Matcham Esq. & Catherine his wife
    Defens [defendants] *- of one thousand two hundred*
    acres of forage and heath [,] *one hundred acres of*
    moor [,] *common of pasture for all manner of*
    cattle [,] *common of turbary* [the common right to
    cut turf for fuel in the New Forest] *& common of*
    estovers [the right to have wood from the New Forest
    for fuel] *with the appurts* [appurtenances: property
    assets] *in Barren*[?] *Field otherwise Barn Field in*
    the parish of Christchurch Twyneham & in the
    New Forest[.] *Before Sr. Henry Gould Knt* [Knight]
    *one of the Justices of the Common Bench 27 Aug*t
    *31*st *K Geo 3* [King George 3]

Returnable from the day of the Holy Trinity in 3 weeks

Examined with the entry of the Kings Silver
Office Elm Court Temple March 11th 1801

        *W*m *Archer*

        *Depu*y *Clk* [clerk] *Kings Silver*

Author's facsimile of the Matcham writ held by Ringwood Meeting House and History Centre.

Swithin in September 1799. The city's growing popularity as a spa and social hub had prompted a spate of grand, neoclassical redevelopment using gold-toned Bath rock.

George's brother-in-law, Horatio Nelson, wrote to his wife, Fanny, in July 1797, 'I never saw Sheppards Spring nor do I fancy if it was within our purse it would suit us.' Although Fanny and her elderly father-in-law were frequent winter visitors to Bath, the Matchams hadn't seen Horatio for several years. He finally joined them in Bath in September 1797 after the loss of his right arm at Tenerife in July. 'Sorrow was mixed with rejoicings … for he was in a miserable state of suffering.'[58]

George and his father-in-law befriended the British Consul to the Balearics, Henry Stanyford Blanckley (known as HSB). They had much in common. Both had been born abroad and spent most of their lives in warmer climates. Both had settled around English game-lands in the late 1780s (although HSB had been employed as a gamekeeper, rather than employing one). And both were family-orientated men with many children.

In January 1798 '[a] happy family party gathered at Bath, its pleasures enhanced by the Admiral's presence in renewed health and spirits.'[59] Later that year, when news reached them of Nelson's pivotal Nile victory, 'there was much national and family rejoicing at the news.'[60] Nelson finally arrived home on 6 November 1800 with Sir William Hamilton and his wife, Emma. Nelson had been England's hero since his Nile victory, but Emma had already been famous as an 'influencer' who had instigated the entire 'Jane Austen' fashion revolution. It became apparent that Britain's two national treasures were amorously involved, despite being married to different people. The winter of 1800 saw Fanny subjected to a succession of public slights by Nelson in favour of Emma. He eventually walked out on her during a dinner and went to the Hamiltons, with whom he then permanently stayed.[61] Nelson biographer, Sugden, notes George 'alone remained uncomfortable with the family's treatment of Fanny.'[62]

On 3 December 1800 George attended an elegant London dinner[63] hosted by the East India Company for the 'Rt. Hon. Lord Nelson, for his service to his country'.[64] George took advantage of the event to secure grants of Australian land for people he was helping to emigrate.[65]

In 1801, at Nelson's behest, Emma bought Merton Place in Surrey. Nelson felt guilty that it was partly financed by £4,000 loaned from George's marriage settlement.[66] 'Mrs Matcham and her eight children', as well as her siblings, Susannah Bolton and Reverend William Nelson, with their families[67] spent Christmas there with Emma, but there is no record of George's attendance.

Inventions for the Royal Navy

Now settled into city life without the distraction of land management, George applied himself to solving problems besetting the navy. On 29 January 1803, aided by his friend James Oliver,[68] a patent was recorded for:

GEORGE MATCHAM, of the city of Bath, Esquire; for a principle or mechanical power for raising great weights, in preventing ships from sinking, in raising ships when sunk, in rendering ships which are disproportioned to shallow-water capable of entering rivers, passing bars, or shoals, or otherwise moving in shallow water; and for a variety of other useful purposes.[69]

A breakwater, completed in 1814, to protect Plymouth's naval harbour[70] may have been 'based on work when he was in India', but George learnt his design had been purloined only when a friend urged him to claim recognition, but credit had already gone elsewhere. His great-granddaughter noted that his design to transform wetlands into 'the pleasure grounds of St James' Park was officially recognised'[71] (although sole credit seems to have been given to James Nash).[72]

The Matcham family's relationship with Nelson, Emma Hamilton and Horatia

George's mother was buried at Bathford on 9 April 1803. She bequeathed most of her estate to George.[73] He purchased a family residence at 2 Portland Place, Bath:[74] an 'elegant house [with] all necessary fixtures … substantially built, in a decent state of repair … and from the size of the principal rooms, well adapted for a large family.'[75]

When Nelson departed Britain for the last time on 13 September 1805, the last person he spoke to was George Matcham. Nelson had publicly acknowledged paternity of his and Emma's four-year-old daughter, Horatia (but continued to pretend she was Emma's ward for fear of misogynistic backlash). 'Nelson expressed regret that he had not yet been able to repay the £4,000 George had lent him.'[76] Horatia's biographer, Gérin, suggests 'it is not improbable that in these last moments' Nelson asked George to protect Horatia if he died at sea.[77]

When news of Nelson's death reached them in November, George and Kitty stayed in Merton to comfort Emma.[78] Nelson's siblings were gifted generous grants by the British government. William Nelson received £120,000 and an earldom worth £5,000 a year; Kitty and her sister Susannah received £10,000, later increased to £15,000.[79] George re-embraced his country idyll by

George Matcham's mother's sarcophagus in Bathford churchyard with Ann Nelson's sarcophagus beside it. (Author's photo, 2018)

purchasing Ashfold Lodge,[80] in Surrey, thirty-five miles due south of Merton.

By 1808, debt forced Emma to give up Merton.[81] Nelson's only dying wish – that Emma and Horatia receive state pensions – had been systematically denied. Perhaps worse, the jointure of £800 a year he had bequeathed her was administered by William Nelson, who paid her nothing until 1808,[82] and was then consistently tardy.[83]

Biographer Kate Williams described George as a man 'of energy, but not much money ... always looking for help with [his pack] of children'[84] who, after Nelson's death, 'inundated her with begging letters. Emma handed over more cash she did not have.'[85] Is there truth to this portrayal of George as a scrounger? The Matchams repeatedly aided Emma after Nelson's death. For example, George lent her £100 in 1811, which she spent celebrating her forty-sixth birthday.[86]

Postcard showing Ashfold Lodge, c1900. (Author's collection)

Correspondence from George's grandson, Major-General Montgomery Moore, is included in a reprint of Sichel's 1891 *Memoirs of Emma, Lady Hamilton*: 'Lady Hamilton was a frequent visitor at my grandfather's (Mr Matcham) place, Ashfold Lodge, Sussex, for years after Lord Nelson's death, and my mother always spoke of her periodical visits to them as gala days, which the children of the family always looked forward to.'[87] On learning that Horatia had developed whooping cough in the winter of 1812/13, Kitty urged them to come to Ashfold.[88] The Matchams, at that time, were unaware Emma was confined to debtor's jail.[89] It was at this time that William Nelson had ceased all payments of her jointure.[90] George wrote to Emma in November:[91]

We will supply you with potatoes all the winter, and send you a turkey by the first opportunity. If you find it impossible to pay us a visit, Mrs M. and I shall be tempted to go to Temple Place [the debtor's prison] before the close of winter and pass a day with you.

cemetery till 1810. The ground was shortly ~~~
time used as a timber yard, and all vestiges of the graves
it contained were swept gradually away. On the news of
the decease of Lady Hamilton reaching England, a Mr. H. *Not so*
Cadogan and Earl Nelson went over to Calais, where the
former paid the funeral expenses of the deceased, which
amounted to £28 10s., and on his return brought her
daughter Horatia back to her native land with him.
Earl Nelson, as one of the trustees of Horatia, also probably thought it incumbent on him to see her safely back
in England after the decease of her mother. On her
arrival with Mr. Cadogan she was transferred to the care
of Mrs. Matcham (Lord Nelson's sister) in accordance with
the last wishes of Lady Hamilton. With Mrs. Matcham
she remained for two years, and afterwards resided with
Mr. Bolton (Lord Nelson's brother-in-law) until February,
1822, when she became the wife of the Rev. Philip Ward,
sometime Vicar of Tenterden in Kent. By him she had
a large family, and died in the 81st year of her age, March
6, 1881.

Mr. Matcham, not Earl Nelson, went over to Calais, & brought back Horatia to England, dressed in Boy: Clothes!

George Matcham's great-grandson William Eyre Matcham's handwritten corrections to Sichel's account of Horatia's rescue from Calais. (Author's photo, 2017)

They invited her to tour Europe with them, but had no immediate plans to leave, and Emma was in a hurry to escape her debtors.[92] Emma quietly sailed from London for Calais with Horatia on 2 July 1814.[93] When Emma died there on 15 January 1815, Horatia was stranded. Sichel's account is refuted by another descendant, William Eyre Matcham. On page 313 of his copy of Sichel's *Memoirs*, he underlined 'Earl Nelson went to Calais', writing 'Not so' in the margin, and, at the foot, 'Mr. Matcham, not Earl Nelson, went over to Calais, and brought back Horatia to England dressed in boy's clothes.'[94]

According to Gérin:

At Ashfold Horatia found her five girl cousins (ranging in ages from twenty-three to eleven) and none of them as yet engaged, and the four boys whose education was mostly given at home. Tolerance, good-breeding and kindness were the family's characteristics. The Matchams' world, like the world of their contemporary Jane Austen, was conditioned by rural surroundings and limited society; its occupations and interests derived from the country pursuits and its pleasures were dependent on good neighbourliness ... Their balls and parties were mostly impromptu affairs, organised between neighbours.[95]

George Matcham was keen to travel as soon as the Napoleonic wars ended.[96] Gérin wrote: 'Horatia's surviving correspondence tells us something about the family's trip abroad in 1816, which lasted from May to October. Lisbon was the objective, and there Mr Matcham established connections with wine, fruit and vegetable exporters'.[97]

Matcham's later years

The family returned to England in early 1817 for the wedding of their eldest, George, to Harriet Eyre, heiress of the New House estate in Wiltshire.[98] George and Kitty gifted them an estate adjoining Ashfold Lodge.[99] Returning to Europe, HSB helped them find a house at Boulogne-sur-Seine, for the annual rent of £116, and a carriage into central Paris for £5 a week.[100]

A succession of marriages for their daughters followed. The first was Harriet, who married HSB's son, Lieutenant Edward Blanckley RN, on 24 April 1819 in Naples.[101] For George and Kitty, now nearing seventy and fifty-five respectively, '[h]alf settled in Paris, half spent in visits to England, a good many years passed away.'[102] Meeting again with Nelson's spurned wife, they were 'not sorry to renew old acquaintanceships.'[103]

According to their great-granddaughter:

At last, Paris abandoned and Ashfold Lodge sold, a house in Holland Street, Kensington, became their final home. From thence, long yearly visits were paid to George (Jr) and his wife, each equally devoted to the old couple. By the grandchildren they were adored ... Full as ever of his hobbies, G. M. would potter about on his long-tailed pony, with a stream of little grandchildren running or riding after him, to whom he was a perpetual delight and playfellow ... He would have his own workmen; and carry on improvements to his heart's desire. A large pond was dug one year. Planting and cottage building absorbed him. Stories of him and his factotum, one Noyce, still linger in the family.

George Matcham died, aged seventy-nine, in his and Kitty's house at Holland Park in Kensington.[104]

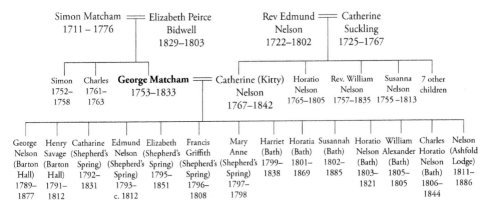

Matcham's family tree as developed by author.

Constitution versus *Guerriere*:
The Lost Historical Significance of the
Single Ship Actions of the War of 1812

Nicholas James Kaizer

The War of 1812 is chiefly known in the United Kingdom for its dramatic single ship actions. The three most famous occurred in the first six months of the war, when three British Fifth Rate frigates, *Guerriere*, *Macedonian* and *Java*, were captured or destroyed by the heavy frigates USS *Constitution* and *United States*. Their losses were traumatic for the Royal Navy and the British nation – during the Napoleonic period, the navy won virtually every action it fought against the French, Spanish and Dutch. The British were not accustomed to defeat at sea, and the culture of the Royal Navy, to say nothing of its fighting ethos, had been shaped by the victories of titanic figures such as Lord Nelson. Yet the year 1812 concluded with Britain losing three frigates and two sloops to the fledgling and outnumbered United States Navy.

In Canada and the United States, these actions hold an outsized place in the historical memory. They were all-consuming events at the time, even as Britain and her colonies were largely preoccupied by the war waging in Europe; after all, it was a global war. Even Lord Wellington, commander of the Anglo-Portuguese army in the Peninsular War, was concerned by these frigate losses.[1] In the historiography of the Royal Navy, however, these actions are largely dismissed as unequal contests of little note; giants such as N A M Rodger or Andrew Lambert remind readers that *Guerriere*, *Macedonian* and *Java* were outclassed by their rivals, and thus had no real hope of success. That was also the public understanding at the time, in Britain and here in Nova Scotia, the home of the Royal Navy's North American station. However, this historiographical understanding ignores several key aspects of historical significance, one of which will be explored herein.

That the British ships were hopelessly outgunned by America's heavy frigates was immediately apparent to the public, and continues to be the de facto argument of many British (and Canadian) naval history buffs – the obvious explanation for these defeats in the context of an ever-victorious Royal Navy. One would expect that each of the British captains, who faced a court martial on the loss of their ship, and a verdict that would determine their future service

Constitution crossing *Guerriere*'s bow: *Not the Little Belt*, by Elizabetha Tsitrin, oil on canvas. (Courtesy of Blue Nautilus Art)

and reputation, would have clung to this defence. Captain James Dacres of *Guerriere*, however, proclaimed the opposite in his court-martial defence.

The prevailing views of the British contemporary public and modern history community that define the understanding and importance of the single ship actions of the War of 1812 clashes with that of the contemporary serving officers of the Royal Navy. For many, including James Dacres, these actions were not hopeless contests, where British defeats were sufficiently explained by a disparity in broadside weight. Instead, the prevailing view of the Royal Navy itself was that, with the right tactics and right conditions, a British Fifth Rate frigate could, and indeed should, defeat even the heavy American frigates. This view resulted in a determined, and at times reckless, quest by Royal Navy captains to seek engagements with the American frigates, even when expressly ordered otherwise. It highlights how the Nelsonic naval culture, refined by two decades of triumph, was affected by some of the most shocking losses of the Napoleonic period.

Prevailing views: historiographical and contemporary

In British historiography of the War of 1812, single ship actions are hardly presented as significant. British historians today tend to focus on the unequal nature of the three contests: USS *Constitution* and her sister *United States* were vastly heavier and better-armed ships than their opponents. In particular, the disparity in broadside weight (the contemporary measurement of a vessel's firepower) between the American heavy frigates and Britain's Fifth Rates was considerable. The standard British Fifth Rate – and *Guerriere*, *Macedonian* and *Java* were all Fifth Rates – carried a main battery of 18pdr guns and a total armament of about forty-eight guns and carronades in total. The American heavy frigates, by contrast, were armed with main batteries of 24pdr guns and a total armament of approximately fifty-four to fifty-six guns and carronades in all. Another advantage for the Americans was that the gun decks sat higher in the ships' hulls. Taking the *Constitution–Guerriere* action (19 August 1812) as an example, the difference in broadside weight between the American heavy frigate (approximately 700lbs) and the British Fifth Rate (approximately 500lbs) constituted a 50 per cent advantage for the Americans.[2] Further, the American ships were larger and had thicker planking, and could withstand more punishment than their British counterparts (hence *Constitution*'s nickname 'Old Ironsides'). They had been designed to be powerful enough to defeat any frigate, yet swift enough to run from enemy ships of the line. Power and speed were badly needed, for the United States Navy was small and underfunded and could never hope to fight an enemy battle line.

Some will have noticed an anomaly. Famously, *Constitution* and her sisters are rated as 44-gun ships; *Guerriere* and her fellow British were rated as 38-gun ships. A curiosity of rating of frigates of the period is that by the early 1800s, almost no frigate in the British or American navies appears to have carried the number of weapons they were rated for. A 38-gun Fifth Rate typically carried about forty-eight weapons in total, and an American 44-gun carried well over fifty. This strange trend had come about with the invention and adoption of carronades in the 1770s. Carronades were initially considered only supplementary guns, not intended to replace a warship's primary guns, which made up its official rate. But over the decades, ships began swapping out their weather deck mounted long guns for carronades, and it was not until 1817 that the Royal Navy began to count every carronade towards a ship's official rate. Further, a ship's armament was fluid, and captains frequently shifted and swapped guns. A 38-gun frigate remained a 38-gun frigate even if the captain removed or added a handful. However, while not a good indication of the exact number of shipboard weapons, the official rate was usually a good indication of strength in relation to other frigates.

As a result of this disparity in force, modern naval historians have largely dismissed the importance of the actions, as their outcomes were not in doubt. Andrew Lambert, who has written extensively on the War of 1812, highlights that the American victories were against 'smaller, less powerful British opponents'.[3] The prevailing British perspective was summarised by N A M Rodger, who argued that: 'in the case of 18pdr frigates in action with 24pdr ships, the disparity in force is a sufficient explanation. The actions between opponents were vastly unequal and therefore of little historical importance.'[4] Many histories of the British navy of the period dismiss the actions as unimportant; many others ignore them or the whole naval War of 1812 altogether.[5]

Contemporary British views on the actions were similar. The popular press, Members of Parliament, and the lawyer-turned-naval-historian William James highlighted the same disparity in force when discussing the dramatic losses of 1812. The navy and the nation were unused to naval defeats during the period, and many clung to this explanation as it justified their sense of British naval superiority: the American victories were not fair, hence they were not a stain on the honour of the Royal Navy, its officers and sailors. These arguments were ubiquitous in the popular press in Britain and in Halifax.[6]

The Admiralty agreed and took substantive policy steps to avoid further single ship losses in the war; first by requiring frigates to sail in company with other warships whenever possible, then by prohibiting British captains from engaging any of America's heavy frigates alone. The First Lord of the Admiralty even wrote to Admiral Warren (Commander-in-Chief of the North American station) to state that British frigate captains should be aware that they were:

> not only not expected to attack those large American Ships, but that their voluntarily engaging in such an encounter would be considered here in the same light as if they did not avoid an action with a Line of Battle Ship.[7]

This statement was followed by an order issued on 10 July, in which the Admiralty stated that under no circumstances should any frigate captains 'attempt to engage, single handed, the larger Class of American Ships, which though they may be called Frigates, are of a size, Complement and weight of Metal much beyond that Class, and more resembling Line of Battle Ships'.[8] In material terms, the losses were not substantial, as the number of ships assigned to the North American station alone vastly outnumbered the United States Navy. However, they wounded British morale. Worse for the Admiralty, many in the press scapegoated them for the losses.[9]

In this they agreed with the prevailing public sentiment: the American heavy frigates were dangerous. They must be, or the great heroes of the Royal Navy could not have been defeated by them! As such, these one-sided contests must be avoided at all costs. This argument is still made in history works today, and can even be found in the discussions of British (and typically Canadian) historians and history buffs whenever the subject of the USS *Constitution* arises. That the single ship actions of the War of 1812 were unfair contests was, and still is, a ubiquitous understanding for the British, except the serving officers of the Royal Navy during the war.

Prevailing views: serving naval officers

Many officers of the Royal Navy rejected the notion that the American heavy frigates were inherently too dangerous for a Fifth Rate. They believed that, under the right conditions and with the right tactics, an 18pdr British frigate had the ability to tackle and defeat a 24pdr adversary at close action. Even with American victories suggesting otherwise, they remained confident in their abilities, and were eager for action.[10] Chief among them was James Dacres, the captain of *Guerriere* when she was defeated by *Constitution* on 19 August 1812. Dacres' report of the loss did not hinge on the obvious (from the public and historiographical perspective, anyway) defence that his ship was vastly outgunned. In fact, his report highlighted everything except for the disparity in firepower:

> I hope, in considering the circumstances, you will think the ship entrusted to my charge was properly defended; the unfortunate loss of our masts, the absence of the third lieutenant, second lieutenant of marines, three midshipmen, and twenty-four men considerably weakened our crew, and We only mustered at quarters two hundred and forty-four men, and nineteen boys, on coming into action; the enemy had such an advantage from his marines and riflemen, when Close, and his superior sailing enabled him to choose his distance.[11]

He emphasised the enemy's superiority in crew size, small arms fire, and fewer mounting casualties compared to *Guerriere*, and the enemy's superior sailing qualities, but does not ascribe the loss to the superiority in gunnery and broadside weight. Dacres made a similar argument in his court-martial testimony, attributing the defeat more to ill fortune than to the inherent advantage in firepower of the heavier American frigate. His concluding remarks were particularly bold:

Notwithstanding the unlucky issue of the affair such confidence have I in the exertions of the officers and men who belonged to the *Guerriere*, and I am so aware that the success of my opponent was owing to fortune, that it is my earnest wish, and would be the happiest period of my life, to be once more opposed to the *Constitution*, with them under my command, in a frigate of similar force to the *Guerriere*.[12]

According to Dacres, the enemy could have been overcome if not for the whims of fortune, and as such, Dacres describes an earnest wish for a rematch with the *Constitution* in another 18pdr frigate.

This statement could be genuine, or designed to appeal to the zeal of the court's presiding officers, whose verdict would determine Dacres' fate. Either is difficult to prove or disprove, but both explanations suggest that this sort of confidence was common and expected of officers of the Royal Navy, and that the bold assertions would have appealed to the members of the court. Whether out of genuine sentiments, deliberate manipulation, or a combination of both, Dacres' speech enshrines the Royal Navy's fighting spirit, bred over two decades of unparalleled success at sea.

Other officers discussed their thoughts in published and private accounts. Captain William Tremlett, a frigate captain whose career was cut short by the sinking of his ship after a very successful cruise, wrote to the *Chronicle* to set the record straight:

'Captain Richard Dacres, HMS *Guerriere*' (1906), unknown artist. (*Harper's Encyclopedia of United States History*, via Wikipedia.org)

> Much has been said about their superior weight of metal, and size of the vessels, but in my opinion more than is necessary; although it certainly assists; but every naval officer must know, that in action one good active seaman is at least equal to three landsmen, or such poor creatures as are to be found in every one of our men of war.[13]

For Tremlett, the superior broadsides of the American frigates were only assisting factors in the losses; seamanship mattered far more. The larger and better trained crews of the American navy were the decisive advantage, giving the Americans an edge in sailing, manoeuvring, gunnery and small-arms fire.[14]

The personal journal of Henry Edward Napier, a lieutenant on board the Fifth Rate HMS *Nymphe* (38) during her blockading cruise off New England in 1814, expresses this sentiment as well. One entry examines the importance of crew size in depth, and he explains that, whereas the complement of *Nymphe* was only 300, the complement of the similarly armed USS *Congress* (38) was upwards of 400. This advantage, he explained, allowed the Americans to deploy a much larger body of disposable men in action. In his view, this advantage is sufficient to explain the losses in 1812: 'I say when this is considered … people perhaps may cease to wonder at the Americans having captured so many of our ships, as, the *Java* excepted, none of those ships had even 300 men and officers.'[15]

Captain Sir William Dillon, in his published narrative, emphasised the importance of the size and skill of the American crews:

> Accustomed as our Navy had been to triumph on all occasions where a foe was met on anything like equal terms – and sometimes when he was vastly superior – these measures were necessary … But the American frigates were far superior in every respect: the hulls were larger, and they had heavier metal, with crews of at least 500 picked men – no boys – whereas the crew of one of our 46-gun frigates never exceeded 285, including boys. Consequently, we were obliged to improve the size of our ships and increase the number of their crews.[16]

Dillon considered heavier armament one of several advantages held by the Americans, but he also acknowledged that the Royal Navy had triumphed against enemies with 'vastly superior' armament before. What the Americans had that their French counterparts did not were exceptionally trained, 'picked' crews, manning ships superior both in size and armaments. In fact, some members of the American crews were British trained.

The views of these, and many other officers, clashed with the prevailing public sentiment developing in the wake of the 1812 actions. One notable officer, however, does highlight the superiority in broadside weight as a factor to explain his loss. Captain John Carden, in his report following the loss of HMS *Macedonian* (38) to USS *United States* (44), highlighted not only the larger American crew – which contained, he made sure to add, a number of British veterans – but also the much heavier broadside, saying that he had:

> ceased to wonder at the result of the Battle; the *United States* is built with the scantline of a seventy four gun Ship, mounting thirty long twenty four pounders on her Main Deck, and twenty two forty two pounders, Carronades, with two long twenty four pounders on her Quarter Deck and Forecastle. Howitzer Guns in her Tops, and a travelling Carronade on her upper Deck, with a Complement of Four hundred and seventy-eight pick'd Men.[17]

Whereas Dacres had ignored the superior broadside and size of his opponent entirely, Carden emphasised the fact, linking it with the size and skill of the enemy's 'pick'd Men'.

He does not argue that the superior broadside was the sole justification for defeat, but presents it as a nonetheless important factor in the action. As such, it was not, in Carden's mind, a defeat that robbed Britain of prestige or reputation. 'My country has lost a ship but I consequentially feel that is all she was lost; Victory over such a superiority of force could not be obtained.'[18] This defence sounded far more like that printed in the popular press than that of Dacres. Carden and his officers were to be exonerated because they faced a vastly superior force, whereas Dacres made it clear he thought the enemy's superior force to be of little consequence.

Carden's opinion, however, was in the minority at his court martial. His own First Lieutenant David Hope believed that a different tactical approach may have resulted in a British victory. He was critical of his captain's reluctance to bring his ship into close action in the first phase of the fight. *Macedonian* had stood off at a distance whilst trying to maintain the weather gauge over *United States*. Hope's view was that a more aggressive approach would have enabled *Macedonian* to cross the enemy's bow at close range and inflict raking fire on *United States*, and that his priority would have been to engage 'close alongside of the enemy'.[19] The court agreed, and Carden was questioned on this extensively, as highlighted in the verdict:

> … previous to the commencement of the action, from an over anxiety to keep the weather gage an opportunity was lost at closing with the enemy,

and that owing to this circumstance the *Macedonian* was unable to bring the *United States* to close action until she had received material damage ... [20]

Despite the advantage in broadside weight that Carden had emphasised, the court was clear in their view: *Macedonian* could still have triumphed had she engaged her opponent at close range. Carden's defeat was not blamed on his ship's inferiority in guns and men, but on failing to bring about a close action.

What sets Carden apart from his fellow captains, and even his own first lieutenant? Carden's entry into the navy was peculiar. His father was an army officer, and he joined the navy at seventeen, only after being privately educated ashore at the Royal Naval Academy. He had no familial ties to the Royal Navy and had spent half of his life ashore, whereas Dacres and most other naval officers had served at sea from a young age, having been immersed in the navy and its culture for the whole of their adult lives, and for a good portion of their childhoods as well. As such, the traditions of odds-defying confidence that Dacres demonstrated may not have been as hard-set in Carden's psyche, which may suggest why he was more willing to emphasise the enemy's superiority in firepower in his report.

The inherent problem with studying the mindset of historical figures is that, with few exceptions, personal accounts do not survive. The mood and views of the serving officers of the Royal Navy can only be explored through a handful of accounts, as well as how others reacted to them. Dacres' bold proclamation to the court may have been a genuine reflection of his views on his defeat, or they may have been exaggerated. Either way, they suggest that his sentiments – that he expected that victory was still attainable and sought a rematch with the same crew and a similar frigate to *Guerriere* – were prevalent in the Royal Navy. It reflected zeal and boldness on Dacres' part, and a Nelsonic determination to seek action at all costs. When a different set of captains tried John Carden, they expressed a similar sentiment, rejecting his more logical, but insipid, defence.

We see also that a number of Royal Navy captains sought to avenge the navy's honour by seeking action with the enemy. Whereas the public had accepted the losses as unfair contests, Royal Navy captains were not satisfied. Several of them published public statements in British and Haligonian newspapers expressing their desire to seek out the American heavy frigates and avenge the losses. An account of a speech given by Captain Alexander Kerr of the Fifth Rate HMS *Acasta* (40) highlighted the determination of that officer and his crew to avenge the loss of *Guerriere*, and accounts supposedly written by the crews of Captains Pigot and Hickey in a Halifax paper did the same.[21]

Like Dacres' account, these may have expressed a genuine urge for vengeance, or inflated accounts designed to highlight the zeal and gallantry of the respective captains and their crews, thereby highlighting the wider naval culture they were appealing to. The navy, far from accepting the losses, was demanding revenge.

Captain Philip Broke of the Fifth Rate HMS *Shannon* (38) highlighted this view in a letters to his wife, Louisa. Broke's accounts are especially useful, as they were never intended for publication, and are thus likely to be a more genuine representation of his opinions. They are not influenced by a desire to appeal to wider naval culture; instead, they are a reflection of Broke's own deep-set beliefs. They depict a naval captain obsessed with revenge, inflamed by the mood of his fellow captains of the North American station. On more than one occasion, he explained to Louisa that 'now the unlucky events of *Guerriere* and *Frolic*'s actions bind us all to the service until we have restored the splendour of our flag.'[22] It was to that end, restoring the honour of the British flag, that Broke engineered a two-on-two fight off Boston in early 1813.

The majority of the British blockading squadron off Boston, including its two ships of the line, were dispatched to Cape Sable, Nova Scotia, and Broke remained with two Fifth Rate frigates. He sent word ashore via Boston fishermen, inviting two American frigates in the port – the Fifth Rate USS *Congress* (38) and the heavy frigate *President* (44) (a sister of *Constitution* and *United States*) to come out and fight. The two American frigates, having missions to accomplish, instead took advantage of the inadequate blockading force and slipped away in the fog. The news of *President* escaping sent waves of panic throughout the Admiralty. In his quest to restore the honour of the Royal Navy, Broke had violated his orders – to

Captain Philip Bowes Vere Broke, HMS *Shannon*, unknown artist, unknown date. (William Greatbach Library and Archives Canada)

153

blockade the port – and wider Admiralty instructions to avoid action with the American heavy frigates. His career was very likely saved from a growing call for an inquiry by his later challenging of the frigate USS *Chesapeak* (38), a Fifth Rate of similar armament to Broke's *Shannon*. Broke tried the same gamble twice, and dispatching his companion Captain Hyde Parker of the Fifth Rate HMS *Tenedos* (38) back to Halifax, he invited *Chesapeake* to single combat. Her captain, James Lawrence, was so eager for action that he had weighed anchor before the invitation arrived in port. In an action of just eleven minutes, *Chesapeake* was engaged, boarded and taken by Broke's superbly trained crew.[23]

British naval culture

The most famous single ship actions of the War of 1812 – the three losses in 1812 itself, and Philip Broke's victory in 1813 – reveal much about how the contemporary Royal Navy thought about itself and its sense of honour. Where modern historians concluded that a disparity in force between America's heavy frigates and Britain's Fifth Rates made the result of any action inevitable, Royal Navy officers highlighted other factors – superior seamanship, larger crews, even luck – rather than admit that the American frigates were too much for them to handle. Britain's naval culture, defined by the victories of Nelson and his contemporaries, was not compatible with this seeming objective reality. They could not rationalise their defeats in the same way as the public and historians have done to this day. British naval culture and British naval honour were tied to the determination of Royal Navy captains and sailors to seek battle against all odds. Even when the strategic thinkers sought to limit one-on-one action with the enemy, more than one captain sought it. These actions are steeped in the Nelsonic naval culture, defined by zeal and determination, and perhaps too much pride. They tell a tale of hubris, traumatic defeat and vindication, but they are not the whole story of the Royal Navy's experience in the War of 1812. It is not even the whole story of the single ship actions of the conflict.

A Futile Danish Expedition to Morocco – and its Perspectives

Jakob Seerup

Editors' Note: This article is based on a paper that Dr Seerup presented to the Biannual McMullen Naval History Symposium, Annapolis, Maryland, September 2021. His paper was sponsored by The 1805 Club.

On the afternoon of 3 June 1753 there should have been a festive gathering on board the Danish flagship *Christiansborg*, a Sixth Rate frigate of 24 guns. The ship lay at anchor off the Moroccan port city of Safia. At half past three in the afternoon, officers from the other Danish ships were in an unusually cheerful mood because an agreement had finally been reached for the release of forty-five Danish prisoners who had been held captive by the Moroccans since 1751. But the joy ended abruptly at half past four that afternoon.

Suddenly the men on board the *Christiansborg* noticed smoke rising from the Fith Rate frigate *Falster* (30) a little further out on the roadstead. Shouts of alarm were heard from the ship, and immediately after, they observed distress signals from the frigate. The flag was tied in a wheft, cannons were firing in slow cadence, and trumpets were sounding. Likewise, men were jumping overboard.

Without doubt, the ship was in danger. *Falster*'s captain, Commander Hooglandt, on board the *Christiansborg*, was immediately rowed over to his ship. He was followed by every available boat from the other Danish ships at anchor in the Safia roadstead. They brought buckets, pumps and fire hoses. But as they approached the burning ship, everything was chaos. People splashed around in the water. The boats picked up some of them. As many as three other Danish ships were near *Falster*, namely *Blaa Heyren*, *Neptunus* and *Christiansborg*, all making an effort to come to the rescue. But they were to the leeward of the burning ship and could not risk embers blowing over into their rigging and setting them on fire. An additional problem was that most of the cannons on the *Falster* were loaded. As the fire reached each cannon, it went off, cannonballs hurtling in all directions. The other ships found it most prudent to weigh anchor and sail away from the inferno.

After an hour, the remaining people on board the burning ship could see that their ship could not be rescued. They cut their anchor and let themselves be driven by the wind towards the beach. The fire had not yet reached the rigging, and brave sailors entered aloft and set two mainsails and the jib, so that the ship could move faster to the beach. Then there was hope that the sailors could survive the relatively short swim inland. On board the *Christiansborg*, it was noted at six o'clock that the flagship returned and approached the burning ship. From here they could see the *Falster* burning near the beach.

At seven o'clock in the evening *Christiansborg* was again in the same position as she had been when *Falster* initially caught fire. The men on board could only stand idly by and watch as the frigate met her fate. At eight o'clock the inevitable happened: a thunderous explosion followed by a pillar of fire and smoke showed that the fire had reached *Falster*'s magazines.

It was later found that the cause of the fire and subsequent destruction of the Falster was a simple accident. A boy in the carpenter's shop had fumbled with a lit candle which caused the fire.

An attractive project

Denmark's loss at the Safia roadstead that fateful day in 1753 was not only a frigate and 132 dead sailors. There was, of course, a loss of prestige associated with losing a ship. But the fire was just the last humiliating link in a long chain of misappropriations, defeats and outright foolishness, resulting from a Danish ambition to establish a permanent trading post in Morocco.[1]

It all began in 1749, when a Moroccan Jew named de Paz came to Copenhagen. He entertained Danish merchants with a proposed project for sending a ship with goods to Morocco. The project was realised, and it was an economic success. This whetted the Danish appetite for more. De Paz now presented a more ambitious project to establish a trading post in Morocco. By concluding a trade treaty with the North African country, the Danes could ensure access to a new and interesting market – even without competition from countries such as Great Britain, France and Spain, who did not have treaties with the Barbary States in North Africa. There was the general problem with the Barbary States; they were in the habit of capturing European sailors and holding them for ransom. Denmark found a solution to this in 1746 by concluding a treaty with the Barbary States. The agreement was that the Barbary States left Danish and Norwegian seafarers alone and unharmed. In return, the Danes delivered an annual 'present' to the North African pirates in the form of a gift ship heavily laden with weapons, cannonballs, gunpowder and ropes, with which the Barbary States could equip their ships to capture other countries' sailors. In Copenhagen, it was therefore assumed that there was a basis for expanding the scheme with the projected trading post, which was to be located in Safia. The problem was that the North African partners turned out to be quite unreliable.

In 1751 an entire squadron set out from Copenhagen for this North African adventure. It consisted of two warships, the frigates *Falster* and *Docquen*, and three transport ships. In addition to a cargo of merchandise, the ships also brought a troop contingent to protect and man the new trading post. It consisted of over three hundred soldiers and their officers. All in all, it was planned that Denmark would establish a small colonial fortress in Safia. The ships sailed from Copenhagen in April and arrived at Safia on 5 June. Immediately upon arrival, Lieutenant-Colonel Jean Baptiste de Carriere de Longueville, a French officer in Danish service and chief negotiator for the Danes, went ashore to negotiate the treaty. Negotiations began fairly well. But Longueville became greedy and extended the Danish requirement – in addition to the establishment of the trading post – also to include the collection of customs duties from foreign ships.

However, the Moroccans had no intention of permitting the Danish officers and merchants so much power. Instead, they chose to cut their losses and go for a faster win. They captured Longueville and his entourage of twelve people and another thirty-two Danish sailors who were so unlucky as to be ashore at the time. Recognising that the Danish trading post project was likely now all but dead, the Moroccans estimated that it was safer to extort a ransom from the Danes. De Longueville was an especially high-ranking hostage for whom the Danes would probably pay a lot of money to get out of captivity. Two years of back-and-forth negotiations followed.

A prolonged stay on the Moroccan coast

The Danish warships stayed the rest of the year at the roadstead off Safia hoping to somehow convince the Moroccans to release the hostages. In May of the following year, the Danish officers issued a call for reinforcements from home, and the frigate *Christiansborg* made sail as fast as possible for Morocco. The journey was delayed because Captain Holst died while the ship was under way and the ship called at Portsmouth to bury him at the Isle of Wight.[2] In June all the Danish ships finally met up at the port of Lisbon. On 21 July 1752 the small Danish naval force weighed anchor and left Lisbon. Now the course was set for Morocco and Safia. Already the day before, new procedures for distributing water on board had been introduced. It was not certain that there would be access to fresh drinking water ashore on the enemy coast, so it was best to be on the safe side. One pot of water daily per man to drink: it was not much, just under a litre. However, the daily ration of spirits was not changed.

Four days later, on 25 July the Danish ships cast anchor at the Safia roadstead. In order to demonstrate their peaceful intentions, a white parliamentary flag was immediately hoisted on *Falster*'s foremast. On board

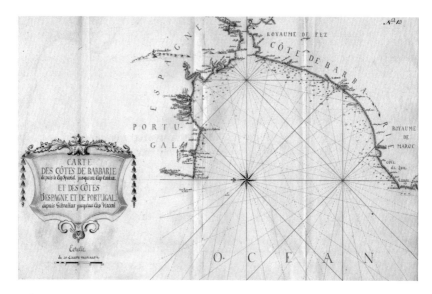

On this contemporary chart, the Moroccan port of Safia is visible in the lower right corner. The map shows the general area where the Danish squadron operated in 1751–53, including the important ports of Cadiz in Spain and Lisbon in Portugal. 'Carte des Côtes de Barbarie depuis le Cap Spartel jusqu'au Cap Contin et des côtes d'Espagne et de Portugal depuis Gibraltar jusqu'au Cap Vincent', map, c1750. (Danish Defence Library)

the Danish ships was a Jew named Zumbel, whom the Moroccans had sent to Copenhagen to negotiate. He was immediately picked up by a local vessel, and the Moroccans greeted the envoy with loud cheering. On that day quite a few other ships were at Safia. There were three Dutchmen, two Frenchmen and an Englishman. And that was, in fact, the crux of the matter. The Danes were far from alone in wanting to trade with the Moroccans, and the Moroccans regarded the Danish demand to collect the customs revenue from the trade as a wild overreach by the Danes. The former might appear cruel and relentless from a Danish perspective, but they were certainly not stupid.

Over the following months, there were courtesy visits and negotiations between the Danish ships and the Moroccans in Safia. On 2 August the envoy Absalem Cande came aboard the frigate *Falster* with salute guns thundering over the roadstead. The shots were, of course, blanks, but people on board were fully aware that the Moroccans could easily attack, so it became a little more cumbersome than usual to render the salutes. The cannons were constantly loaded other than when saluting. Therefore, each shot had to be removed from the gun barrels with much effort and difficulty. And once the salutes were delivered, the guns were loaded all over again. The smaller falconet guns in the stern of the ship were now permanently loaded with grapeshot, and everything was made ready to prepare the ship in the event of an attack by the Moroccans. Such measures were not a regular practice in the Danish navy during the long peace.

If anyone on board the Danish ships doubted the possibility of an actual attack, then the Moroccan artillery exercises on 26 August probably gave cause for reflection. For then, shots suddenly rang out from the cannons of the fortress. They were not aimed directly at the ships, but it was quite clear that the Moroccans were testing whether their heavy 36pdr guns could reach the Danish ships. The impact sent foam spray into the air near the ships. A feeling of insecurity spread among the men.

The negotiations were painfully slow, and the diplomacy was at times on edge. In early September the Moroccan trader Absalem Cande insisted that he could not feel safe on board the Danish ships, so an English merchant ship suddenly became the scene of the negotiations. The two parties arrived with flags flying and visibly ready for all eventualities, with guns loaded and cutlasses at the ready. But these negotiations were also to no avail. After a few hours, the parties separated and rowed back to their respective ships, their issues unresolved.

A few days after these attempted negotiations, the Danish frigates *Falster* and *Docquen* each sent an armed boat close to land to gauge the water depth. If the Moroccans knew the first thing about naval warfare, they must have understood that the Danes were reconnoitring and preparing for an attack on the city from the sea. The Danes concluded that it was indeed possible to sail close enough to the city for their guns to bear on the city, even with the smaller 6pdr guns. But on same day, the Danish officers observed the Moroccan forces ashore on manoeuvres demonstrably preparing for battle. They trained for combat with sabres and guns, and the Danes estimated that about ten thousand men participated in the exercise. These clear indications from both sides had to be seen in the light of the fact that the Danish hostages remained under lock and key on the other side of Safia's fortified city wall.

At long last, the parties reached an agreement. If Denmark paid 18,000 pieces of eight, then the hostages would be released and everyone could sail home again. But the Danish ships did not have that kind of cash with them – and even if they did, they were not authorised by the Danish king to pay such an exorbitant amount. Also, the drinking water and food was nearly exhausted, making it nigh impossible to remain at Safia much longer. So when a letter arrived informing the Danes that more Danish ships were on the way, they decided to leave the uncomfortable anchorage at Safia and head to Lisbon to meet the late Commander Captain Holst's replacement, Commodore Lützow, who was on his way in the frigate *Blaa Heyren*.

On 1 October 1753 *Christiansborg* and *Falster* again anchored near Lisbon to replenish stores of food and fresh water. After a month, Lützow arrived. He had sailed to Cadiz with the frigate *Blaa Heyren*, and then continued overland to Lisbon, while the frigate remained in Cadiz. Lützow now took over the leadership of the squadron. On 3 November he summoned all the officers to a council of war on board *Christiansborg*. Now that the ships were again fully supplied with water and provisions, the question was whether it would be better

Ships waited idly on the roadsteads of Cadiz and Lisbon waiting for instructions from Copenhagen. This watercolour by the master shipbuilder Johan Clemensen Rønneby shows a similar situation in 1757. (National Museum of Denmark)

to return to Safia to put pressure on the Moroccans or not? There was broad agreement that they would not achieve anything by going to Safia at this time. The analysis was that they might even risk exposing the Danish hostages to reprisals. Instead, it was decided that *Falster* and *Christiansborg* should sail to Cadiz to rendezvous with the Danish ships there, and then sail together to Morocco, when the final message came from Copenhagen about what to do next.

On 6 December the two Danish ships weighed anchor and left Lisbon. Now the course was set for Cadiz, where they arrived four days later. In Cadiz the Danish squadron united and settled in for a winter stay in the pleasant city. Both officers and regular sailors thoroughly enjoyed their time in the southern city. They went sightseeing, watched bullfights and marvelled at, to them, exotic Catholic rituals.

Heading for disaster

On 9 May 1753 the Danish ships departed Cadiz and set course for Safia. The small squadron consisted of the frigates *Falster*, *Christiansborg* and *Blaa Heyren*, accompanied by the heavily loaded cargo ship *Friderich og Louise*. The atmosphere on board was not the best. Everyone was aware that no glorious or very honourable ending was in sight. Their mission was to pay off the Moroccans, whom they despised as barbaric pirates. Only then could they set course for home.

On 12 May the Danes arrived at Safia. Negotiations resumed, and on 26 May Mr Zumbel came on board again with a new negotiator, Mr Rey. Zumbel was a Jewish merchant, who said he had been a merchant in France, but after going bankrupt he had fled to Safia. There he had found himself a new life and had become one of the favourites of the Bey. Both men were received with the same honours as ambassadors, including a nine-gun salute. They were on board for only a few hours that afternoon, and the agreement was finalised at long last. To the sound of another nine-gun salute, they sailed ashore again. The next day Zumbel sailed out with a local cargo vessel and the agonising transfer of 'presents' could begin. This first day, fifteen boxes, three kegs and five packages with various contents were transferred. The next day, several local ships returned and this time received fifty-two barrels of gunpowder, 200 12lb roundshot, 300 6lb roundshot, and 300 4lb roundshot.

Joy prevailed on 3 June 1753. At half past ten in the morning, Rey and Zumbel brought the first Danish hostage to *Christiansborg*. It was First Lieutenant Kaas, who together with the other Danes had been a prisoner in Safia for two years. An hour later, the two negotiators sailed back ashore with their big prize in the form of bags and chests containing a total of 18,000 pieces of eight. The large sloop from the *Christiansborg* accompanied the Moroccan vessel. When they reached shore, Colonel Longueville and the other hostages stood on the quay and were ready to be rowed out to the ships. Safia's fortress artillery fired a three-gun salute in honour of Longueville – the man they had kept imprisoned for two years.

To the modern reader, the exchange of chests filled with gold coins appears like something from a pirate movie. But the truth is that the deeply banal exchange could have been conducted by a modern biker gang, Middle Eastern terrorists or Somali pirates. The script will always be the same; a transaction in which human suffering is weighed up against sums of money. In this case it also spelled a resounding defeat for Danish trade policy in Morocco.

Even if the circumstances were humiliating, the joy was still great. The Danish sloop and two Moroccan vessels brought the thirty-two hostages back to the ships. The hostages were received with full honours. Longueville had the status of ambassador and received a welcoming fifteen-gun salute. Then a twenty-four-gun salute was heard from the fortress in Safia. And soon the sloops from the other Danish ships approached *Christiansborg*. The captains of the squadron welcomed and celebrated their long-lost comrades.

Even after this disastrous affair, Denmark still remained active on the Barbary Coast. Danish ships laden with annual 'presents' of guns and gifts returned every year to Tripoli and Algiers until 1846.

Operations far away from home – not all futile

These dramatic events on the North African coast are worth remembering, because they provide an opportunity to look at what the Danish navy actually did during the period known as the 'Long Peace'. The failed adventure in Morocco in 1753 is a good example of the type of operations the navy conducted during the period. The eighty years between the end of the Great Northern War in 1720 and the beginning of the war with Britain with the Battle of Copenhagen in 1801 constituted a heyday for Danish trade on the world's oceans. And although one might have expected that the Danish autocratic state might have wanted to capitalise on the 'peace dividend' and lay up the ships, Denmark actually maintained a large and powerful navy throughout the period. Admittedly, the Danish navy was significantly smaller than the mighty Royal Navy, but still the Danish navy was the world's fifth or sixth largest in the eighteenth century.

Did the Danish navy benefit from the many years of peace? Did the absence of war diminish the navy's capabilities – combat skills and technological advances? These are questions with many surprising answers. There is no doubt that the most formidable enemy that the Danish navy has ever faced was eighty years (1720–1801) without war.[3] This is because the dynamics of war drove the world's navies. Whenever the Royal Navy won another victory at sea, the most successful officers were promoted because of their efforts. With each successive war, the British improved their combat skills, administration, logistics support and shipbuilding capability. But, at the conclusion of these wars, the British sent the sailors home, placed much of their fleet in ordinary, and reduced the financial burden on the King's treasury.

This situation did not exist in the peacetime Danish fleet. This meant that, as something quite unique for Denmark, its navy had to come up with other criteria for promotion, such as education and seniority. The navy also had to keep up with technological developments in completely different ways and went on espionage expeditions instead. And, last but not least, the Danish state had to accept the rather large fixed expenses for the salary and operation of one of the kingdom's largest institutions, without that institution being battle-tested for those many years.

With more than twenty ships of the line and fifteen frigates available, one might think that the Danish navy would regularly deploy their fleet. But that was far from the case. It was expensive to man and deploy ships, and the kingdom always lacked money. Most ships remained in the Fleet Harbour in Copenhagen for most of their existence and were never deployed except for their first test manoeuvres.

In addition to looking neat and impressive in the port and on the international naval statistics, the navy's ships were partly intended for warfare in the Danish immediate area of the Baltic, and partly for a number of other tasks out from local waters. The only fixed rule was that every year three smaller ships were equipped as guard ships in the Great Belt and the Sound, respectively, and on the Copenhagen Roadstead. Aside from these three ships, it differed from year to year how many and which ships were sent to sea. From the 1740s a medium-sized frigate was regularly deployed as a school ship for practical training for the sea cadets. At that time ships began to travel to North Africa every year, partly for diplomatic purposes, partly with the previously mentioned 'presents' to the Barbary States, which ensured free navigation for Danish merchant ships in the Mediterranean. At times it was considered appropriate to have a ship permanently stationed in the West Indies to protect Danish interests in the far flung colonies.

Of the ships that set out on various voyages during the Long Peace period, only very few were ever involved in combat. It did happen, but only rarely. Even as a peacetime navy, the Danish navy maintained a relatively high degree of operational readiness, which was expensive and resource-intensive; for the most part, the Danish fleet was a fleet in being.

In this type of reality, with few ships deployed on regular operations, it was a challenge to maintain a sufficiently high level of experience among both officers and sailors. That meant that deployments like the one to Morocco in 1753 were actually a benefit for the navy. The total cost of equipping and deploying a squadron of warships to Morocco, a huge sum in ransom and, not least, a lost warship, and 132 dead sailors, was the total price for the ambitious plan. But this was only one such deployment, and on other occasions fleet operations did not end so disastrously.

Even though in hindsight the failed Moroccan adventure may seem almost tragicomic and hopelessly naive, in reality it also testifies to a great economic and cultural surplus that the Danish Crown enjoyed during the Long Peace of the eighteenth century. There was an appetite to establish trading posts in distant regions of the globe. There was an ambition to promote trade on the world's oceans to meet the growing demand for exotic goods from other parts of the world back home in peaceful Copenhagen. One of the most important tools in this endeavour was the navy. Not only did it have the ships and the technology that could project Danish power on coasts far from home, it also had a valuable resource of well-trained, well-read and technologically competent naval officers who were masters of the sailing technology of the period. Returning from their voyages, many Danish naval officers communicated their knowledge through art, literature and technological design, and writings back to Copenhagen and the rest of the kingdom. Naval officers became an integral part of the flourishing cultural life in Copenhagen. They translated foreign poems and technical works into Danish, and thus helped to open up the world to the Danes.

'Presentation of the frigate *Falster* on Safia Roadstead as it blew up on June 3rd 1753'. Illustration by F C von Lowenstein, probably one of the embarked Danish soldiers in the squadron. (Royal Library, Denmark)

Contributors' Biographies

Michael Barritt, Captain RN is a former Hydrographer of the Navy, whose sea-going career took him to all the world's oceans. In *Eyes of the Admiralty* (2008) he described wartime hydrographic activity during blockade and patrol duties of the fleet off the French and Spanish coasts in 1799/1800. He has published numerous book chapters, articles and reviews, and is a contributor to the nineteenth-century volume of *The History of Cartography* (in press, University of Chicago). He is working on an account of the emergence of the RN Surveying Service during the wars of 1793–1815. He is Immediate Past President of the Hakluyt Society, which publishes important historic accounts of travel.

Aaron Bright is a Military Professor with the Joint Military Operations Department at the United States Naval War College. As a lieutenant-colonel with the US Army's Field Artillery he came to specialise in the study of both cannon and rocket artillery as well as today's hypersonics, age-of-sail naval guns and First World War history. He has published articles in both *The Journal of the Royal Artillery* and the *Field Artillery Journal*. His overseas assignments include three combat tours to Iraq, one three-year exchange instructor position with the British Army, and one three-year posting in Korea where he commanded the 1st Battalion, 38th Field Artillery Regiment ten miles south of the DMZ. He holds a master's in history from Louisiana State University, as well as both a master's and a graduate certificate in maritime history from the Naval War College.

Anthony Bruce was formerly a director at Universities UK and is now a higher education consultant. His first book (based on his doctorate) was on the purchase system in the British army (1980). It was followed by *An Illustrated Companion to the First World War* (1998) and *The Last Crusade* (2002) on the war in Palestine, 1914–18. His *Encyclopedia of Naval History* (1989) covers the period from the sixteenth century. Revised editions of the *Encyclopedia* and *The Last Crusade* were published in 2020. He is currently working on a biography of Lord Anson.

Linda Collison is an author of historical and contemporary novels. A retired registered nurse, she sailed as voyage crew aboard HM Bark *Endeavour*, the Australian-made replica of Captain James Cook's three-masted ship, on its three-week crossing from Vancouver to Hawaii in 1999. She and her husband Robert Russell have sailed many blue water miles on their sloop *Topaz*, a Luders-36.

Kenneth Flemming joined the RN in 1963 as a marine engineer at a time of modernisation and technical change. He undertook specialist training on modern diesel propulsion and mine clearance work. Joining Her Majesty's Prison Service, he served twenty years as an education officer to help prisoners develop individual learning and work skills before release. As a founding member and life member with The 1805 Club he has held the office of vice president and is a past editor of *The Kedge Anchor*, the club magazine.

Tom Fremantle believes himself fortunate to have two distinguished ancestors who were naval officers in the time of Nelson. Following in their footsteps, he joined the Royal Navy. After ten years he transitioned to a civilian career in the engineering industry. His interest in naval research was stimulated by the 200th anniversary of Trafalgar, at which his forebear Thomas Fremantle captained HMS *Neptune*. He then discovered his other illustrious forebear, Philip Gidley King, who went to Botany Bay with the First Fleet in 1787, becoming the first lieutenant-governor of Norfolk Island and the third governor of New South Wales. In 2020 Mr Fremantle published a novel bringing together Nelson, Fremantle and King; *From Norfolk to Trafalgar* is available from tfremantle@talk21.com. A biography of King is in preparation.

Barry Jolly is a graduate in history, a former lieutenant-commander in the Instructor Branch of the Royal Navy, and a member of the committee of The Friends of Sir Harry (Neale). In 2020 he received a Personal Achievement Award for Local Historians from the British Association for Local History for his work as a trustee of Milford-on-Sea Historical Record Society and as editor of the Society's *Occasional Magazine*, together with his research on the admirals of Milford, which has been published in the *Trafalgar Chronicle* and other journals.

Nicholas Kaizer is a Canadian scholar and teacher who studies the cultural history of the Royal Navy during the War of 1812, in particular analysing Anglo-Canadian responses to single ship losses of that conflict. He has an MA from Dalhousie University and is the author of *Revenge in the Name of Honour*.

He has written for *Warships: IFR*, the *Cool Canadian History* podcast, the *Napoleon Series*, and the *Navy Records Society*. He has an article forthcoming with the *War, Literature, and the Arts* journal. His website is https://nicholasjkaizer.ca/.

Paul Martinovich is a retired museum planner, with many years' experience in creating exhibitions on a variety of subjects for museums in Canada (where he lives), the United States and Ireland. His interest in naval history, particularly that of the French Revolutionary and Napoleonic Wars, dates back many years and began with the Hornblower novels of C S Forester. He has contributed a number of items to the online magazine of the Navy Records Society, of which he is a member, and recently published his biography of Admiral Sir Pulteney Malcolm, titled *The Sea is my Element.*

Christopher Pieczynski is a retired US Navy commander who served twenty-four years as a surface warfare officer. He has master's degrees from Old Dominion University and the US Naval War College. Currently an assistant professor with the University of Maryland Global Campus teaching a variety of history classes, he has received several grants from the Virginia Beach Historic Preservation Commission and has documented numerous little known aspects of the area's history. His research specialty is the War of 1812 and maritime history under sail.

Dr Jakob Seerup is a museum curator and researcher currently employed at Bornholms Museum, Denmark. He has previously worked at the Royal Danish Naval Museum, the Royal Danish Arsenal Museum and the National Museum of Denmark. His research spans both naval history in the Age of Sail and more recent military and naval history with a Russian perspective.

Lily Style is founder and chair of the Emma Hamilton Society. She has a passion for history and genealogy, and writes regularly for The 1805 Club's *Kedge Anchor*. This is her third *Trafalgar Chronicle* article. She is a direct descendant of Lord Nelson and Emma Hamilton. She appeared in the 2020 French documentary: *Splendeur et Déchéance de Lady Hamilton.*

Andrew Venn is a naval historian from Portsmouth, England. He holds a postgraduate degree in naval history from the University of Portsmouth and has experience working as a visitor guide onboard several museum ships, including HMS *Victory.* He is also the co-author of the *Trafalgar Times*, a quarterly newsletter presenting little-known facts and under-researched topics to new audiences and enthusiasts alike. He often travels to visit museum ships and naval museums around the world and regularly enjoys researching and presenting the history of the Georgian navy, using his youthful perspective to deliver fresh perceptions of the past.

John Wills, Captain RN (Ret) served in seven RN surface ships, including the Royal Yacht *Britannia*, interspersed with shore appointments in leadership training, ship maintenance and defence management consultancy. He served as the UK defence and naval attaché to Athens during the 2004 Olympic Games and concluded his RN service as director of marine services, where he led its privatisation. A most happy and satisfying shore appointment was as second in command of the Portsmouth Naval Barracks, HMS *Nelson*. The role included presidency of the wardroom mess, where in 1990 he hosted a dinner for a stimulating and most interesting gathering of members of The 1805 Club. He joined the club that evening!

Notes

Sir Samuel Bentham – Civil Architect and the First Engineer of the Royal Navy

1   J H Burns (ed), *The Collected Works of Jeremy Bentham*, 'Correspondence 1756–1756', vol 1 (London: Bentham Project, University College London). Burns was editor 1961–79. Kindle edition.

2   F B Sullivan, 'The Royal Academy at Portsmouth 1729–1806', *Mariner's Mirror*, vol 63, no 4 (November, 1977), p315.

3   Mary Sophia Bentham, *The Life of Brigadier-General Sir Samuel Bentham* (Miami, Florida: HardPress, 2017, reprint), pp85–9. Original document published in 1862.

4   Professor Ian R Christie to Jeremy Bentham, *The Correspondence of Jeremy Bentham*, vol 3, January 1781 to October 1788.

5   George Wilson and James Trail to Jeremy Bentham, *The Correspondence of Jeremy Bentham*, vol 3, January 1781 to October 1788.

6   Matthew S Anderson, 'Samuel Bentham in Russia', *The American Slavic and East European Review*, vol 15, no 2, April 1956, pp157–72 (quote on p172).

7   M S Bentham, *The Life of Brigadier-General*, p106.

8   Samuel Bentham, 'Preserving Fresh Water Sweet during Long Voyages, 1800 [on board his Majesty's sloops *Arrow* and *Dart*]', Society for The Encouragement of Arts, Manufactures, and Commerce, Inventory No: 350140.

9   Bentham, 'Preserving Fresh Water'.

10 Bentham, 'Preserving Fresh Water'.

11 Bentham, 'Preserving Fresh Water'; M S Bentham, *The Life of Brigadier-General*, p106; R A Morris, 'Samuel Bentham and The Management of The Royal Dockyards, 1796–1807', *Bulletin of The Institute of Historical Research*, 1981, p7.

12 M S Bentham, *The Life of Brigadier-General*, p6.

13 M S Bentham, *The Life of Brigadier-General*, p7.

14 M S Bentham, *The Life of Brigadier-General*, p127.

15 Wikipedia, 'Samuel Bentham' (accessed 27 January 2022). Original source: Joseph Wickham, *English and American Tool Builders* (New Haven, Connecticut: Yale University Press, 1916), p25.

16 M S Bentham, *The Life of Brigadier-General*, pp114–15.

17 'Simon Goodrich', Wikipedia (accessed 31 January 2022). Due to Bentham's absence in Russia, Goodrich brought the block mills into full production.

18   Catherine Pease-Watkin, *Journal of Bentham Studies*, vol 5 (2002). Part 1 – 'Jeremy and Samuel Bentham – The Private and the Public' (London: UCL Bentham Project, University College London).

19   Felicity Susan Wilkin, 'The application of emerging new technologies by Portsmouth Dockyard 1790–1815', PhD thesis (Open University, 1999).

20   Samuel Bentham, 'Suggestions for the Better Management of Civil Concerns of the Navy', in M S Bentham, *Papers of Sir S Bentham* (Newark, New Jersey: reprinted by Palala Press, 2015).

21   Pease-Watkin.

22   George Bentham and M Filipiuk (eds), *Autobiography 1800–1834* (Toronto: University of Toronto Press, 1997), p262.

23   Wilkin.

The Blomefield Cannon

1   Brian Lavery, *The Ship of the Line* (Annapolis, Maryland: Naval Institute Press, 1983), p179; William James, *The Naval History of Great Britain: During the French Revolutionary and Napoleonic Wars*, vol 1, 1793–1796 (Mechanicsburg, Pennsylvania: Stackpole Books, 2002), p71; E W Allen, *The New Monthly Magazine and Literary Journal*, vol 15, pt 3 (London: Henry Colburn, 1825), pp378–9.

2   The 'firing train' is the building path from spark to explosion. Think of building a campfire. The firing train would be: the spark – dried grass – leaves – small sticks – medium sticks – logs.

3   Donald E Carlucci and Sidney S Jacobson, *Ballistics: Theory and Design of Guns and Ammunition*, 3rd edn (Boca Raton, Florida: CRC Press, 2018), p77.

4   Bernard Ireland, *The Fall of Toulon: The Last Opportunity to Defeat the French Revolution* (London: Weidenfeld & Nicolson, 2005), p248; James, *Naval History*, col 1, p71.

5   Adrian Caruana, 'British Artillery Design', in *British Naval Armaments,* ed Robert D Smith (Dorset: The Dorset Press, 1989), pp12–13.

6   Adrian Caruana, *History of English Sea Ordnance 1523–1875*, vol 2, *1715–1815: The Age of the System* (East Sussex, UK: Jean Boudriot Publications, 1997), p15.

7   Jonathan Spain, 'Blomefield, Sir Thomas, first baronet (1744–1822), army officer', *Oxford Dictionary of National Biography* (28 September 2006) (accessed November 2021), https://doi.org/10.1093/ref:odnb/2666.

8   Friederike Charlotte Luise von Riedesel, *Baroness von Riedesel and the American Revolution: Journal and Correspondence of a Tour of Duty, 1776–1783*, ed and trans Marvin L Brown (Chapel Hill, North Carolina: University of North Carolina Press, 1965), p61.

9   Garith Cole, *Arming the Royal Navy, 1793–1815: The Office of Ordnance and the State, Warfare, Society and Culture*, vol 4 (London: Pickering & Chatto, 2012), pp9, 88.

10   Caruana, *Sea Ordnance*, pp17–18, 22. An 'establishment' is essentially a checklist of what each ship was allotted in men and equipment to make it battle ready.

11   A 'charge' is the bag of coarse-grain gun powder behind the shot.

12   Caruana, *Sea Ordnance*, p11.

13   Double-shotting is firing two cannonballs at a time from the same cannon charge; sixty cannonballs.

14   Edward William Lloyd and Albert George Hadcock, *Artillery: Its Progress and Present Position; In Two Parts, with Appendix* (Portsmouth, UK: J Griffin and Co, 1893), p24.

15   Caruana, *Sea Ordnance*, p23. A foundry would be making multiple guns at once, and several could be produced by a single foundry in seven to eight months.

16   Lloyd, p24; Caruana, *Sea Ordnance*, p16.

17   Robert G Albion, *Forests and Sea Power: The Timber Problem of the Royal Navy 1652–1862* (Cambridge, Massachusetts: Harvard University Press, 1926), pp116–18.

18   Henry Cleere and David Crossley, *The Iron Industry in the Weald* (Chesterfield, UK: Merton Priory Press, 1995), pp209–10.

19   Carlucci, p16.

20   *Handbook of Ballistics*, vol 3, no 29, *Artillery Training, Field Artillery* (UK Ministry of Defence, 2012), pp2–8.

21   Caruana, *Sea Ordnance*, pp9, 12.

22   H A Baker, *Crisis in Naval Ordnance* (London: Wandle Press, 1983), pp1–2.

23   Caruana, *Sea Ordnance*, p22. The five ports were Chatham, Sheerness, Deptford, Portsmouth and Plymouth. Deptford did not have its own gun wharf since it was supplied directly from Woolwich.

24   Caruana, *Sea Ordnance*, p11.

25   N A M Roger, *The Insatiable Earl: A Life of John Montagu, fourth Earl of Sandwich 1718–1792* (London: Harper Collins, 1993), p326.

26   Caruana, *Sea Ordnance*, pp35, 66. Windage is the pressure that leaks around the projectile to exit the muzzle first.

27   Caruana, *Sea Ordnance*, pp16, 257.

28   Guns are measured in calibres and calibre lengths. The calibre is the diameter of the cannonball. Calibre length is that number divided by its total length.

29   Caruana, *Sea Ordnance*, p126.

30   Brian Lavery, 'Carronades and Blomefield Guns: Developments in Naval Ordnance, 1778–1805', in Robert D Smith (ed), *British Naval Armaments* (Dorset, UK: The Dorset Press, 1989), pp15–27.

31   Caruana, *Sea Ordnance*, p126; Lavery, pp24–5.

32   Caruana, *Sea Ordnance*, p257; Lavery, p25; PRO WO 47/108, 29/12/86.

33 Lavery, p24.

34 Peter Padfield, *Guns at Sea* (New York: St Martin's Press, 1974), p102.

35 Peter Goodwin, *HMS Victory Pocket Manual 1805: Admiral Nelson's Flagship at Trafalgar* (Oxford: Osprey Publishing, 2017), p106; Caruana, p16.

36 Goodwin, pp106–7.

37 Lavery, p24; PRO Supply 5/49, 24/8/86, 11/10/86.

38 Baker, p30.

39 Baker, pp38–9.

40 Goodwin, p103; Adam Nicolson, *Seize the Fire: Heroism, Duty, and the Battle of Trafalgar* (New York: Harper Collins, 2005), pp218–19.

41 Nicolson, p225.

42 Goodwin, p98.

Benjamin Robins and the Science of Naval Gunnery

1 Niall Ferguson, *Civilization: The West and the Rest* (London: Allen Lane, 2011), p84.

2 Alessandro V Papacino D'antoni, *A Treatise on Gun-Powder; a Treatise on Fire-Arms; and a Treatise on the Service of Artillery in Time of War.* Translated by Captain Thomson of the Royal Regiment of Artillery (London: T and J Egerton, 1789), xvii–xviii.

3 W Johnson, 'Benjamin Robins, FRS: New Details of His Life', *Notes and Records of the Royal Society of London*, 46 (1992), p235. See also Brett D Steele, 'Benjamin Robins (1707–1751), mathematician and military engineer', *Oxford Dictionary of National Biography*. Retrieved from www.oxforddnb.com/view/10.1093/ref:odnb/9780198614128.001.0001/odnb-9780198614128-e-23823.

4 *Observations on the Present Convention with Spain* (London: George Faulkner, 1739); *A Narrative of What Passed in the Common-Hall of the Citizens of London Assembled for the Election of a Lord-Mayor* (London: T Cooper, 1739); *An Address to the Electors, and Other Free Subjects of Great Britain, occasion'd by the late secession. In which is contain'd a particular account of all our negociations with Spain, and their treatment of us, for above ten years past* (London: H Goreham, 1739).

5 W Johnson, 'Benjamin Robins during 1739–1742: "Called to a Publick Employment … A Very Honorable Post"', *Notes and Records of the Royal Society of London*, 48 (1994), pp31-42.

6 *Report of the Proceedings and Opinion of the Board of General Officers, on their Examination into the Conduct, Behaviour, and Proceedings of Lieutenant-General Sir John Cope …* (Dublin: George Faulkner, 1749).

7 Benjamin Robins, *New Principles of Gunnery: Containing, the Determination of the Force of Gun-Powder, and An Investigation of the Difference in the Resisting Power of the Air to Swift and Slow Motions* (London: J Nourse, 1742).

8   Frederick L Robertson, *The Evolution of Naval Armament* (London: Constable, 1921), p114.

9   *Mathematical Tracts of the Late Benjamin Robins, Esq*, published by James Wilson (London: J Nourse, 1761), vol I, pxxxii.

10 Brett D Steele, 'Muskets and Pendulums: Benjamin Robins, Leonhard Euler, and the Ballistics Revolution', *Technology and Culture*, 35 (1994), p349.

11 N A M Rodger, 'George, Lord Anson, 1697–1762', in Peter Le Fevre and Richard Harding (eds), *Precursors of Nelson. British Admirals of the Eighteenth Century* (London: Chatham Publishing, 2000), pp177–99.

12 George Anson, *A Voyage Round the World, In the Years MDCCXL, I, II, III, IV, by George Anson, Esq; Commander in Chief of a Squadron of His Majesty's Ships, sent upon an Expedition to the South-Seas. Compiled from Papers and other Materials of the Right Honourable George Lord Anson, and published under his Direction, by Richard Walter, M Chaplain of his Majesty's Ship the Centurion, in that Expedition* (London: John and Paul Knapton, 1748).

13 Lord Anson to Benjamin Robins, 22 October 1749, in *Mathematical Tracts of the Late Benjamin Robins*, vol I, xli.

14 Robertson, *The Evolution of Naval Armament*, p121.

15 Peter Padfield, *Guns at Sea* (New York: St Martin's Press, 1974), p102.

16 *A Comparison of the Experimental Ranges of Cannon and Mortars*, in *Mathematical Tracts of the Late Benjamin Robins*, vol I, pp231–2.

17 Howard Douglas, *A Treatise on Naval Gunnery*, 4th edn (London: John Murray, 1855), pp49–51.

18 *An Account of the Experiments, Related to the Resistance of the Air … 1746*, in *Mathematical Tracts of the Late Benjamin Robins*, vol I, pp200–217.

19 Benjamin Robins, *Of the Force of Fired Gunpowder, Together with the Computation of the Velocities thereby Communicated to Military Projectiles,* in *Mathematical Tracts of the Late Benjamin Robins*, vol I, pp218–29.

20 Benjamin Robins, *A Proposal for Increasing the Strength of the British Navy, by Changing all the Guns, from the Eighteen-Pounders Downwards, into Others of Equal Weight but of a Greater Bore* (London: J Nourse, 1747).

21 Robins, *A Proposal*, p5.

22 Quoted in Frederick L Robertson, *The Evolution of Naval Armament*, p121.

23 Robins, *A Proposal*, pp6–7.

24 Robins, *A Proposal*, p13.

25 Robins, *A Proposal*, p16. An embrasure is an opening with sides flaring outward in a parapet to allow the firing of cannon.

26 Robins, *A Proposal*, p19.

27 Benjamin Robins, *A Letter to Lord Anson. Read the 26th of October 1749*, in *Mathematical Tracts of the Late Benjamin Robins*, vol I, p306.

28 Robins, *A Letter to Lord Anson*, p311.

29 Robins, *A Letter to Lord Anson*, p307.

30 Rory T Cornish, 'Robert Melville (1723–1809), army officer and colonial governor', *Oxford Dictionary of National Biography*. Retrieved from www.oxforddnb.com/view/10.1093/ref:odnb/9780198614128.001.0001/odnb-9780198614128-e-18551.

31 Anthony Bruce, 'The Carronade: A Revolution in Naval Warfare', the *Trafalgar Chronicle*, New Series 4 (Barnsley: Seaforth, 2019), pp184–94.

32 Spencer C Tucker, 'The Carronade', *Nautical Research Journal*, 42 (1997), p15.

33 Benjamin Robins, 'Of the Nature and Advantages of Rifled Barrel Pieces', in *Mathematical Tracts of the Late Benjamin Robins*, vol I, p341.

34 Benjamin Robins, 'Observations on the height to which rockets ascend, Read before the Royal Society, May 4, 1749', in *Mathematical Tracts of the Late Benjamin Robins*, vol I, p320.

35 Quoted in W Johnson, 'Benjamin Robins, FRS: New Details of His Life', p243.

36 Charles Hutton, *A Mathematical and Philosophical Dictionary* (London: J Johnson, 1795), vol I, p570.

37 Steele, p368.

38 For example, Francis Holliday, *An easy introduction to practical gunnery, or, the art of engineering* (London: W Innys and J Richardson, 1756).

39 N A M Rodger, *The Command of the Ocean, A Naval History of Britain 1649–1815* (London: Allen Lane, 2004), p420.

40 John U Nef, *War and Human Progress. An essay on the rise of industrial civilization* (Cambridge, Massachusetts: Harvard University Press, 1950), p324.

Robert Fulton's Infernal Machines

1 Alice Crary Sutcliffe, *Robert Fulton* (New York: MacMillan Company, 1915), p55.

2 Bureau of the Port to Robert Fulton, 28 February 1801, in Alice Crary Sutcliffe, *Robert Fulton and the Clermont* (New York: The Century Co, 1909), pp80–3.

3 Robert Fulton to the Committee, 7 November 1801, in Sutcliffe, *Robert Fulton*, p78.

4 *1793–1805 Projets et Tentatives de Débarquement aux Iles Britanniques*, vol 3 (Paris: Librairie Militaire R Chapelot et Co, 1902), p312.

5 William Barclay Parsons (ed), *Robert Fulton and the Submarine* (New York: Columbia University Press, 1922), p72.

6 Letter from Right Honourable Lord Keith, *The Times*, 8 October 1804.

7 Robert Fulton, *Torpedo War and Submarine Explosions* (New York: printed by William Elliott, 1810), pp7–8.

8 Articles of Agreement with Robert Fulton, 20 July 1804, in Parsons, pp83–5.

9 Samuel Bernstein, 'Robert Fulton's Unpublished Memoir to Pitt: Science in the Service of Liberty,' *Science & Society*, 8 (Winter, 1944), pp58–9.

10   Sutcliffe, *Robert Fulton*, pp126–7.

11   'Archimedes', 'For the Balance, Torpedo', *Balance and Columbian Repository*, 11 August 1807.

12   *The Universal Gazette*, 30 July 1807. The demonstration was conducted on 21 July.

13   'Use of the Torpedo in the Defense of Ports and Harbors', 26 February 1810, *American State Papers, Naval Affairs*, vol 1 of 4 (Washington, DC: Gales & Seaton, 1858), p211.

14   Robert Fulton to Secretary of the Navy Jones, 27 April 1813, *The Naval War of 1812: A Documentary History*, vol II, ed by William S Dudley (Washington, DC: Naval Historical Center, 1985), p111.

15   Journal of Commodore Rodgers, 1 November 1810, *American State Papers*, vol I, p238.

16   Journal of Commodore Rodgers, I, p243.

17   Lords Commissioner of the Admiralty to Admiral Sir John Borlase Warren, 26 December 1812, *Naval War*, vol I, pp633–4.

18   Captain Charles Stewart to Secretary of the Navy Jones, 4 April 1813, *Naval War*, vol II, p346.

19   Chapter XLVII, 'An act to encourage the destruction of the armed vessels of war of the enemy', *Statutes at Large*, 12th Congress, 2nd Session, 1813, Library of Congress. https://www.loc.gov/law/help/statutes-at-large/12th-congress.php (accessed 21 December 2021).

20   Fulton, *Torpedo War and Submarine Explosions*, p14.

21   Captain Thomas Hardy to Admiral John Borlase Warren, 26 June 1813, *Naval War*, vol II, p162.

22   Enclosure – List of Killed and Wounded, 25 June 1813, *Naval War*, vol II, p163.

23   John Scudder to the Editor of 'The War', *Weekly Register*, 24 July 1813.

24   *American and Commercial Advertiser*, 4 September 1813.

25   Secretary of the Navy Jones to Captain Charles Gordon, 7 May 1813, *Naval War*, vol II, p355.

26   'Elijah Mix to James Madison, 8 April 1813', US National Archives, *Founders Online*, https://founders.archives.gov/documents/Madison/03-06-02-0175 (accessed 9 January 2022).

27   *Norfolk Herald*, 27 July 1813.

28   *Norfolk Herald*, 27 July 1813.

29   *Bombay Times*, 6 October 1813.

30   Admiral George Cockburn to Admiral John Borlase Warren, 16 June 1813, *Naval War*, vol II, pp355–6. Editors' note: the author surmises that Cockburn was expressing sarcasm in his use of 'humane'.

31   *Weekly Aurora*, 27 July 1813.

32   *The Columbian*, 28 July 1813.

33 Major Benjamin Case to Captain Thomas Hardy, August 23, 1813, *Naval War*, vol II, pp245–6.

34 *Federal Republican*, 2 September 1813.

35 'Original Poetry for the Port Folio', *Port Folio*, 31 October 1807.

36 *Naval Chronicle for 1814*, vol 31 (London: Joyce Gold, 1814), p123.

37 A Crawford, Captain, RN, *Reminiscences of a Naval Officer During the Late War*, vol I (London: Henry Colburn, 1851), p128.

38 Cockburn to Warren, June 16, 1813, *Naval War*, vol II, pp355–6.

39 'A Submarine Boat', *Naval Chronicle*, vol 31 (1814), p287.

40 Crawford, *Reminiscences*, p129.

Charts 'sent by the ever to be lamented Lord Nelson': Some Reflections on Navigational Practice in the Georgian Royal Navy

1   MEDEA CHART Database accessible at https://medea.fc.ul.pt/browse/charts.

2   The National Archives of the United Kingdom, Kew, Surrey, England, Admiralty Papers (hereafter TNA ADM) 1/3522, 10 Oct 1807.

3   National Maritime Museum (hereafter NMM) CRK/13/87.

4   Michael Barritt, 'Agincourt Sound Revisited', *Mariner's Mirror*, 101:2 (May 2015), pp184–99.

5   United Kingdom Hydrographic Office (hereafter UKHO), m13 on Ry.

6   British Library (hereafter BL), Add MS 34966.

7   Copy in Naval Historical Branch, Portsmouth (hereafter NHB/AL), reference Vk5.

8   TNA ADM 1/3522, fos. pp21–6.

9   William Henry Smith, Captain, RN, *Memoir of Sicily* (London: John Murray, 1824), Appendix II; *The Mediterranean* (London: J W Parker, 1854), pp431–59.

10 Editors' note: small-scale charts depict the lowest level of detail whilst covering the largest geographic area. Large-scale charts depict the highest level of detail, covering a much smaller geographic area.

11 NHB/AL Vu3.

12 NMM PBD8166.

13 TNA ADM 52/3711, no 10, 5 February 1805.

14 Pembroke MS22.

15 Colin White, *Nelson: The New Letters* (London: National Maritime Museum, 2005), letter to Lord Hobart dated 21 May 1803.

16 Atkinson's record differs from Nelson's journal at TNA ADM 50/38 where it is stated that when asked to confirm that observed longitude was by timekeeper, the answer from *Leviathan* was in the negative. The longitude reported by timekeeper in *Spencer*, however, confirmed that from *Leviathan* and thus the error in reckoning in *Victory*.

17 Pembroke MS22, entry for 15 April 1805.

18 Tony Campbell and Captain Michael Barritt RN, 'The Representation of Navigational

Hazards: the Development of Toponymy and Symbology on Portolan Charts from the 13th Century onwards', *Journal of the Hakluyt Society* (December 2020), accessible at https://www.hakluyt.com/journal-of-the-hakluyt-society/.

19   TNA ADM 1/5376.

20   John Marshall, *Royal Naval Biography*, vol IV, Part II (London: Longman, 1835), p71.

21   UKHO n31a on Ry is a copy of the chart issued by Arrowsmith. It carries annotations by William Henry Smyth.

22   TNA ADM 1/3522, fos. pp218–19.

23   TNA ADM 52/3711 no 7.

24   TNA ADM 52/3711 no 7.

25   TNA ADM 52/3711, no 10, 22 Feb 1805.

26   See, for example, the portolan made in 1467 by Gracioso Benincasa, Bibliothèque Nationale de France reference DD6269 accessible at https://gallica.bnf.fr/ark:/12148/btv1b55000050r/f5.item.

27   TNA ADM 1/3523, letter dated 5 Mar 1808.

28   Copy at BL 08805.i.6.(7.).

Peter Heywood: Scientific Sailor

1   Madge Darby, 'Lieutenants' Passing Certificates', *Mariner's Mirror*, 87 (2001), p227.

2   See Caroline Alexander, *The Bounty* (New York: Penguin, 2004), pp105–41 for details of these events.

3   Alexander, pp180–302.

4   Edinburgh, National Library of Scotland, Malcolm of Burnfoot Papers 6684/5, Pulteney Malcolm to Mina Malcolm, 8 May 1792; note that this letter must be misdated, since Heywood did not return to Britain until June 1792.

5   Anon, 'Sketch of the Career of the late Capt Peter Heywood, RN', *United Service Journal* (1831, Part 1), p481.

6   Alexander, p293.

7   'Peter Heywood', *Oxford Dictionary of National Biography*, online at https://doi.org /10.1093/ref:odnb/13187.

8   The United Kingdom Hydrographic Office holds several surveys done between 1798 and 1801 by Heywood and Weir, both individually and together.

9   For details of this voyage, see Andrew David, 'Peter Heywood and Northwest Australia', *Great Circle*, vol 1 (1979), pp4–13.

10   Andrew David, 'From Mutineer to Hydrographer', *International Hydrographic Review*, 3 (2002), p9. Heywood also sent these observations to Nevil Maskelyne, the Astronomer Royal; see London, Royal Greenwich Observatory Archives, List of Latitudes and Longitudes of places in the East Indies, RGO4/109.

11   Edward Tagart, *A Memoir of the Late Captain Peter Heywood RN* (London: 1832), p177.

12   Peter Heywood, *Nautical Remarks & Memoranda of Occurrences on board His Majesty's Ships Polyphemus, Donegal and Nereus*, Peter Heywood Manuscript Collection, Rare Books and Special Collections, McGill University Library, Montreal, Heywood, MS 60/3.

13   For details of the early use of chronometers on Royal Navy ships, see W E May, 'How the Chronometer Went to Sea', reprinted from *Antiquarian Horology*, March 1976.

14   Heywood, MS 60/3, pp1–3.

15   Heywood, MS 60/3, pp34–5.

16   Heywood, MS 60/3, p75.

17   Heywood, MS 60/3, pp83–4.

18   Heywood, MS 60/3, pp104, 107.

19   Heywood, MS 60/3, p116.

20   Heywood, MS 60/3, p133.

21   Heywood, MS 60/3, p135.

22   Heywood, MS 60/3, August 17–18, 1810.

23   Tagart, pp196–202.

24   David, 'From Mutineer…', p9.

25   John Marshall, *Royal Naval Biography,* vol II part II (London, 1825), p796.

26   See her letter to *The Daily News*, 26 January 1858.

27   Adrian Webb, 'The Expansion of British Naval Hydrographic Administration, 1808–1829' (unpublished doctoral thesis, University of Exeter, 2010), p265.

28   Webb, p367.

29   'Scrutator', *The Impracticability of a North-West Passage for Ships, Impartially Considered* (London: 1824).

30   The identification of Heywood as the author is provided by Glascock, a naval officer and writer, in: 'An Officer of Rank' [W H Glascock], *Naval Sketchbook; or the Service Afloat and Ashore,* vol I (London: 1826), pp36–7, where after a very positive review of the book, Glascock describes Heywood as 'a highly scientific and experienced officer'.

31   Peter Heywood, *Memoranda on Nautical and Other Subjects*, Rare Books and Special Collections, McGill University Library, Montreal, Heywood, M144 IV, pp23, 45.

32   'Peter Heywood', *Oxford Dictionary of National Biography*, https://doi.org /10.1093/ref:odnb/13187.

Fighting Instructions, Signal Books and the Line of Battle: The Evolution of Sailing Tactics in the Royal Navy, 1740–1815

1   Michael A Palmer, *Command at Sea: Naval Command and Control since the Sixteenth Century* (Cambridge, Massachusetts: Harvard University Press, 2005), p97.

2   Palmer, *Command at Sea*, p98.

3   Edward Vernon, 'An Additional Instruction to be Added to the Fighting Instructions, *c*1740', in *Fighting Instructions 1530-1816*, ed Julian S Corbett (London: Navy Records Society, 1905), pp214–16.

4   Vernon, p214.

5   Michael A Palmer, '"The Soul's Right Hand": Command and Control in the Age of Fighting Sail, 1652–1827', *Journal of Military History*, 61, no 4 (Oct 1997), pp 679–705 (p685).

6   Vernon, p215.

7   George Anson, 'Lord Anson's Additional Fighting Instruction, to be inserted after Article the 4th in the Additional Instructions by Day, *c*1747', in *Fighting Instructions 1530–1816*, ed Julian S Corbett (London: Navy Records Society, 1905), pp216–17.

8   Anson, p216.

9   Palmer, 'The Soul's Right Hand', p688.

10   N A M Rodger, *The Command of the Ocean: A Naval History of Britain, 1649–1815* (London: Penguin Books, 2004), p255.

11   Edward Hawke, 'Memorandum, 1756', in *Fighting Instructions 1530–1816*, ed Julian S Corbett (London: Navy Records Society, 1905), pp217–18.

12   Hawke, pp217–18.

13   Palmer, 'The Soul's Right Hand', pp680–1.

14   Michael Duffy, 'Types of Naval Leadership in the Eighteenth Century', in *Naval Leadership in the Atlantic World: The Age of Reform and Revolution, 1700–1850*, eds Richard Harding and Agustín Guimerá (London: University of Westminster Press, 2017), pp49–57 (p54).

15   Richard Howe, 'Instructions Respecting the Order of Battle and Conduct of the Fleet Preparative to, and in Action with, the Enemy, circa 1778', in *Signals and Instructions 1776–1794*, ed Julian S Corbett (London: Navy Records Society, 1908), pp93–107.

16   Richard Howe, 'Instructions Respecting the Order of Battle and Conduct of the Fleet, Preparative to and in Action with the Enemy, 1782,' in *Fighting Instructions 1530–1816*, ed Julian S Corbett (London: Navy Records Society, 1905), pp239–51.

17   Howe, 1782, p239.

18   Howe, 1782, p239.

19   Howe, 1782, pp246–7.

20   Howe, 1782, p247.

21   Palmer, *Command at Sea*, p126.

22   Palmer, *Command at Sea*, p128.

23   Charles Hardy, 'Orders, Etc Given by Sir Charles Hardy to the Grand Fleet, 1779', in *Signals and Instructions 1774–1794*, ed Julian S Corbett (London: Navy Records Society, 1908), pp124–34.

24   Hardy, pp129–32.

25   Hardy, p134.

26 Richard Kempenfelt and Richard Howe, 'Instructions Respecting the Order of Battle and Conduct of the Fleet Preparative to, and in Action with, the Enemy, 1782', in *Signals and Instructions 1776–1794*, ed Julian S Corbett (London: Navy Records Society, 1908), pp151–67.

27 Julian S Corbett (ed), *Signals and Instructions 1776–1794* (London: Navy Records Society, 1908), pp135–9.

28 Kempenfelt and Howe, p159.

29 Rodger, p345.

30 Rodger, p345.

31 George Rodney, 'Sir George Rodney, 1782', in *Fighting Instructions 1530–1816*, ed Julian S Corbett (London: Navy Records Society 1905), pp225–8.

32 Rodney, p227.

33 Corbett, Fighting Instructions, p253.

34 Palmer, *Command at Sea*, p187; Richard Howe, 'Instructions for the Conduct of the Fleet Preparatory to Their Engaging, and When Engaged, With an Enemy, 1799', in *Fighting Instructions 1530–1816*, ed Julian S Corbett (London: Navy Records Society, 1905), pp268–79.

35 Corbett, *Fighting Instructions*, pp255–9.

36 Howe, 1799, p272.

37 Howe, 1799, pp273–4.

38 Sam Willis, *Fighting at Sea in the Eighteenth Century: The Art of Sailing Warfare* (Woodbridge: The Boydell Press, 2008), p72.

39 Palmer, *Command at Sea*, p192.

40 Palmer, *Command at Sea*, p161.

41 Palmer, 'The Soul's Right Hand', p698.

42 Sam Willis, *The Struggle for Sea Power: The Royal Navy vs The World, 1775–1782* (London: Atlantic Books, 2015), p220.

43 Palmer, *Command at Sea*, p177.

44 Joel Hayward, 'Horatio Lord Nelson's Warfighting Style and the Maneuver Warfare Paradigm', *Defence Studies*, vol 1, no 2 (2001), pp15–37 (p23).

45 Colin White, 'The Nelson Touch: The Evolution of Nelson's Tactics at Trafalgar', *Journal for Maritime Research*, vol 7, no 1 (2005), pp123–39 (pp129–35).

46 David Davies, *A Brief History of Fighting Ships: Ships of the Line and Napoleonic Sea Battles 1793–1815* (London: Constable and Co, 1996. Reprint, London: Constable & Robinson, 2002), p106.

47 White, p131.

48 Horatio Nelson, 'Plan of Attack, 1803', in *Fighting Instructions 1530–1816*, ed Julian S Corbett (London: Navy Records Society, 1905), pp313–16; Horatio Nelson, 'Memorandum, Victory, off Cadiz, 9th October 1805', in *Fighting Instructions 1530–1816*, ed Julian S Corbett (London: Navy Records Society, 1905), pp316–20.

49 Corbett, *Fighting Instructions*, p289.

50 Nelson, 1803, pp313–16.

51 Nelson, 1805, p316.

52 Nelson, 1805, pp316–17.

53 Nelson, 1805, pp317–18.

54 Marianne Czisnik, 'Admiral Nelson's Tactics at the Battle of Trafalgar', *History*, vol 89, no 296 (20 Oct 2004), pp549–59 (p553).

55 Palmer, 'The Soul's Right Hand', p701.

56 David Syrett, 'The Role of the Royal Navy in the Napoleonic Wars After Trafalgar, 1805–1814', *Naval War College Review*, 32, no 5 (Sep–Oct 1979), pp71–84 (p75).

57 Palmer, 'The Soul's Right Hand', p703.

58 Palmer, 'The Soul's Right Hand', p703.

59 Palmer, *Command at Sea*, p209.

60 Corbett, *Fighting Instructions*, p326.

61 Corbett, *Fighting Instructions*, p321.

62 Corbett, *Fighting Instructions*, p336.

63 James J Tritten, 'Doctrine and Fleet Tactics in the Royal Navy', *Naval Doctrine Command Report* (Naval Doctrine Command: Norfolk, Virginia, 1994), pp15–16.

64 Corbett, *Fighting Instructions*, pp336–7.

65 Palmer, 'The Soul's Right Hand', p680.

66 Duffy, p55.

67 Willis, 'Fleet Performance and Capability', p390.

68 Duffy, p54.

Advances in Shipboard Care in Nelson's Navy

1 Richard Gordon, *Great Medical Disasters* (New York: Dorset Press, 1983), front matter.

2 Wayne Biddle, *A Field Guide to Germs* (New York: Doubleday, 1995), p131.

3 Grenfell A Price (ed), *The Explorations of Captain James Cook in the Pacific: As Told by Selections of His Own Journals 1768–1779* (New York: Dover Publications, 1971), p250.

4 Iain, Milne, 'Who was James Lind, and what exactly did he achieve?', *Journal of the Royal Society of Medicine* (December 2012), vol 105 (12), pp503–8. https://www.jameslindlibrary.org/articles/who-was-james-lind-and-what-exactly-did-he-achieve/ (accessed online 4 July, 2021). Raymond E Phillips, 'Bite of the Devil – Scourge of the Long-Distance Sea Voyager', *Sea History*, 172 (Autumn 2020), pp30–3. Dr Phillips also gave a concise explanation of what we now know about the role of vitamin C, essential in the formation of collagen.

5 Milne, pp503–8.

6   Christopher Lloyd and Jack L S Coulter, *Medicine and the Navy 1200–1900*, vol III 1714–1815 (Edinburgh and London: E & S Livingstone Ltd, 1961), p299.

7   Lloyd and Coulter, p303.

8   Lloyd and Coulter, pp320–6.

9   Peter Willoughby, 'Sea Surgeons and the Barbers' Company of London', *Trafalgar Chronicle*, New Series 3 (Barnsley, UK: Seaforth Publishing, 2018), pp213–28. Dr Willoughby gives a detailed account of the process of becoming a sea surgeon in the eighteenth century.

10 Andre Sivla Ranhel and Evandro Tinoco Mesquita, 'The Middle Ages to Cardiovascular Medicine', *Brazil Journal of Cardiovascular Surgery*, vol 31, no 2 (2016), pp163–70.

11 Lloyd and Coulter, p360.

12 Lloyd and Coulter, p62–3.

13 Michael Crumplin, *Men of Steel: Surgery in the Napoleonic Wars* (Uckfield, E Sussex: Naval and Military Press), pp81–3.

14 Lloyd and Coulter, pp215, 229.

15 Lloyd and Coulter, p36.

16 Lloyd and Coulter, p9.

The Navy's Naturalist and Polymath: Sir Joseph Banks 1743–1820

1   The Chelsea Physic Garden still exists today and is an oasis of botanical calm in Chelsea, close to the river. It is well worth a visit and has good facilities with a restaurant and shop. There is a strong relationship with botanical artistry and it houses the Florilegium Society, which has an international reach in botanical painting: https://www.chelseaphysicgarden.co.uk/.

2   Patrick O'Brien, *Joseph Banks, A Life* (London: Harvill Press, 1997). On p161 the author quotes the closing paragraph of Lord Sandwich's letter: 'Upon the whole I hope that for the advantage of the curious part of Mankind, your zeal for distant voyages will not cease, I heartily wish you success in all your undertakings, but I would advise you in order to insure success to fit out a ship yourself; that and only that can give you absolute command of the whole Expedition; and as I have a sincere regard for your welfare and consequently for your preservation, I earnestly entreat that that ship may not be an old man of war or an old Indiaman but a New Collier.'

3   This was the expedition for which the fifteen-year-old Nelson volunteered. Readers will recall the celebrated meeting between young Nelson and a polar bear, amongst other aspects of the voyage.

4   Nepean later became Secretary to the Board of Admiralty, 1795–1804, in which post he is familiar to naval historians.

5   Letter from Captain Arthur Phillip to Joseph Banks, HMS *Sirius* at Sta Cruz, 5 June 1787; State Library of New South Wales (hereafter NSW), Folio 37.01.

6   Tom Fremantle, 'Captain Philip Gidley King', *Trafalgar Chronicle*, New Series 6, vol 2 (2017), pp143–55.

7   King's letters to Banks have been collected into a single folio by the Library of NSW (The Mitchell Library). They are available online on the library's website in Folio 39.

8   State Library of NSW, King Family Papers, vol 8, 1775–1806, ML1980-2 Microfilm CY 906, Paper 52.

9   King to Banks, 9 May 1803, State Library of NSW, Folio 39.78.

10 The innovative Captain John Schank (later Admiral) who had participated in the battle of Lake Champlain during the American War for Independence designed the sliding keel; the *Lady Nelson* was probably the largest vessel to be constructed with this device. Hence the naming of a Cape Schank and a Mount Schank in Australia.

11 Collins was sadly not the right man for the job. After failing to establish a settlement on the Murray River, he moved with all his settlers to the Derwent River and assumed command of the settlement established there under Lt Bowen, much to Bowen's fury and King's disappointment.

12 King Family Papers, vol 8 1775–1806, ML A1980-2 CY906, Item 116. The letter continues, 'I would have justice in the case of those under your command who have already forfeited their lives & been once admitted to a commutation of punishment to be certain and inflexible & no one instance on record where more mercy which is a deceiving sentiment should be permitted to move your mind from the inexorable decree of blind justice. Circumstances may often make mercy necessary; I mean those of suspected error in conviction, but mere whimpering soft heartedness never should be heard.'

13 Readers who would like to know more about Flinders might like to read *The Fever of Discovery; the story of Matthew Flinders*, by Marion Body (New European Publications, 2006). Much of the information given here about Flinders has been taken from this small volume. Reports from governors Hunter and King are contained in the History of New South Wales and much original correspondence is available between both Banks and King papers in the State Library of NSW. Also recommended: George Barrington, *History of New South Wales* (Amazon Kindle edition: 2013 reprint of 1802 publication).

14 An example of Banks's efforts is his letter of 22 August 1804 to Jean Delambre of the Institut, describing Flinders's experiences and seeking his release. State Library of NSW (Mitchell) Folio 39, 13.66.05.

15 Banks to Bligh, 16 September 1805, State Library of NSW Folio 40.002.

16 Banks to Bligh, 5 November 1807, State Library of NSW Folio 40.087.

17 Banks to Bligh, 13 August 1811, State Library of NSW Folio 40.145.

18 This is John Macarthur, former captain in the New South Wales Regiment who almost killed his commanding officer in a duel; who King, as governor, sent home for court martial, which he escaped by resigning his commission; who persuaded the London

Wool Market to acknowledge the quality of New South Wales wool and who convinced the government to grant him 10,000 acres for developing the New South Wales sheep flock for wool production. He was motivated by very powerful self-belief, rather like Bligh.

Family Tradition in the Life of Sir Harry Neale: A Clarification

1 Barry Jolly, 'The Burrard Neale Memorial at Walhampton – Legend and Reality', *Hampshire Studies: Proceedings of the Hampshire Field Club and Archaeological Society*, vol 76 (2021), pp129–46; Barry Jolly, 'Political Admiral and Royal Favourite – The Career of Sir Harry Neale, Baronet GCB', *Trafalgar Chronicle*, New Series 6 (2021), pp70–88; Barry Jolly, 'Let There Be Light: The Story of a Lymington Lamp Standard', *Milford-on-Sea Historical Record Society Occasional Magazine*, NS 7 (2021), pp52–64.

2 Will of Robert Neale, 1776, The National Archives of the United Kingdom, Kew, Surrey, England, PROB 11/1023/201.

3 James Dunn Laird, Dunn Families in North Col Tyrone. https://www.cotyroneireland.com/surnames/dunn.html (accessed 4 January 2022).

4 William R O'Byrne, *A Naval Biographical Dictionary*, vol I (London: John Murray, 1849), pp316–17; *The London Gazette*, Part 1, 1811, p874.

5 Ancestry: England & Wales Marriages, 1538–1988.

6 *A New Guide to Lymington ... By a Resident* (Lymington: various dates).

7 Will of Lady Dunn, wife of Captain Sir David Dunn of Vicars Hill (Boldre), Prerogative Court of Canterbury Wills, 1384–1858, PROB 11: Will Registers 1848–1849 Piece 2094: vol 9, Quire Numbers 401–450 (1849). Dated 8 January 1840 and witnessed by Charles Shrubb, Vicar of Boldre, and William Alex Willis (*qv*) with significant bequest to her brother-in-law Robert Hockings, Captain RN.

8 *Hampshire Advertiser*, 29 February 1840.

9 Edward King, *Old Times Revisited in the Borough and Parish of Lymington* (London: 1879), p233.

10 James Gambier, Baron Gambier, *Trial by Court Martial of the Right Honourable Lord Gambier* (London: Sherwood, Neely, and Jones, 1809), pp vii, 24, 175, 182, 201, 202; Joseph Allen & Charles Haultain, *The New Navy List* (1841).

11 King, p222.

12 *Annual Report of the Committee of Management of the Art-Union of London, with List of Subscribers* (London: The Art-Union, 1850), p84; R C Chater, *The Burning of Moscow: A Poem* (London: Longman, 1838), p8.

13 *Salisbury and Winchester Journal*, 28 October 1833; *Robson's Commercial Directory*, 1839; counterpart lease dated 22 August 1835, St Barbe Museum and Art Gallery, Lymington: accession number LMGLM 2012:117.

14 Census 1841 & 1851; Ancestry: England, Select Marriages, 1538–1973; Chris

Donnithorne, Naval Biographical Database (online), www.navylist.org.

15   Jolly, 'The Burrard Neale Memorial', pp138–9.

16   Milford on Sea Historical Society, Joseph D'Arcy, https://www.milfordhistory.org.uk/content/history/families-and-personalities/joseph-darcy (accessed 4 January 2022).

17   *The Era*, 29 March 1840.

18   Historic England, https://historicengland.org.uk/services-skills/education/educational-images/collingwood-monument-tynemouth-5250.

19   Etching of the design and notes on sale at the time of writing at Grosvenor Prints in London: https://www.grosvenorprints.com/stock.php?keyword=neale&WADbSearch1=go.

20   *Morning Herald* (London), 30 July 1840.

21   George Draper, 'A description of the Burrard Neale Testimonial designed by Geo Draper Esq architect, of Chichester' (RIBA paper 9 January 1843), RIBA Collections MS.SP\3\40.

22   Quoted in Sidney Burrard, *The Annals of Walhampton* (London: 1874), pp153–4.

23   Editors' note: the Nootka Crisis, also known as the Spanish Armament, was an international incident and political dispute between the Nuu-chah-nulth nation, the Spanish empire, the kingdom of Great Britain, and the fledgling United States of America triggered by a series of events in the summer of 1789 at the Spanish outpost Santa Cruz de Nuca, in Nootka Sound, present-day British Columbia, Canada. Outpost commander, Jose Esteban Martínez, seized some British commercial ships engaged in the maritime fur trade at Nootka Sound. Public outcry in England led to the mobilisation of the British and Spanish navies and the possibility of war. Spain called on France, her key ally. France declined to go to war. Without French help, Spain had little hope against the British and Dutch allied forces, resulting in Spain seeking a diplomatic solution and making concessions.

24   David Burrard Smith, *Smith Family History – The Maternal Side* (printed privately: ISBN 0-9682082-2-3: 2001), pp107–9.

25   Vancouver Maritime Museum, Collections: https://vmmcollections.com/Detail/objects/11655 (accessed 4 January 2022).

26   Smith, pp109–11.

27   Sir Nicholas Harris Nicolas (ed), *The Dispatches and Letters of Vice Admiral Lord Viscount Nelson*, 7 vols (London: Henry Colburn, 1844/5).

28   Maurice Rooke Kingsford, *The life, work and influence of William Henry Giles Kingston* (Toronto: Ryerson Press, 1947), p55.

29   Vancouver Maritime Museum, Collections: https://vmmcollections.com/Detail/objects/4388 (accessed 4 January 2022).

30   George Cornwallis-West, *The Life and Letters of Admiral Cornwallis* (London: Robert Holden, 1927), pp266–88, with the offer of the Order of the Bath on p278.

31   Royal Museums Greenwich, Collections:
     https://www.rmg.co.uk/collections/objects/rmgc-object-112895;
     https://images.rmg.co.uk/asset/41561/ (both accessed 4 January 2022).

32   Will of Robert Neale.

George Matcham (1753–1833): A Biography of Lord Nelson's Inventor Brother-in-law

1   M Matcham, *The Nelsons of Burnham Thorpe*, 1st edn (New York: John Lane Co, 1911), pp30–3.

2   J Forbes, *Oriental Memoirs* (1834), Google Books, online at google.co.uk/books (accessed 12 February 2022).

3   Matcham, pp30–1.

4   Robert Markley, "'A PUTRIDNESS IN THE AIR: Monsoons and Mortality in Seventeenth-Century Bombay', *Journal for Early Modern Cultural Studies*, vol 10, no 2 (Indiana University Press, University of Pennsylvania Press, 2010), pp105–25.

5   Charterhouse archivist correspondence with author by email, 2016.

6   George Matcham in 1770, British India Office Births & Baptisms, online at FindMyPast.co.uk (accessed 12 February 2022).

7   Registers of Employees of the East India Company and the India Office, 1746–1939 (online database), Ancestry.com.

8   'Senior Merchant', FIBIwiki, online at Wiki.fibis.org (accessed 12 February 2022).

9   'East India Company', Wikipedia. Online at En.Wikipedia.org (accessed 12 February 2022).

10   'Battle of Plassey', Wikipedia, online at En.wikipedia.org (accessed 12 February 2022).

11   William Dalrymple, 'The East India Company: The original corporate raiders', *The Guardian*, 2022, online at TheGuardian.com (accessed 12 February 2022).

12   P Covey-Crump, 'Glimpses from the life of an 18th century English merchant who made a fortune selling salt in Bengal', *Scroll*, online magazine at Scroll.in/magazine (12 February 2022).

13   'Families in British India', 1765 List of the Hon'ble Company's Marine Officers, Free Merchants & Seafaring Men in private employ in Bombay and Factories Subordinate, online at OurArchives.online (accessed 12 February 2022).

14   *Dictionary of National Biography*, 1885–1900, Matcham, George, online at Wikisource.Org (accessed 12 February 2022).

15   *The Cambridge Economic History of India* (nd), Google Books, Google.co.uk (accessed 12 February 2022).

16   Matcham, p32.

17   Porter Hill, *Bombay Marines* (New York: Random House Value Publishing, 1990).

18   E J Emin, J Emïn, and A Apcar, *Life and Adventures of Joseph Emin, 1726–1809* (Baptist Mission Press, 1792), pp474–5.

19 British India Office Ecclesiastical Returns – Deaths & Burials. Copyright Brightsolid Online Publishing Ltd at FindMyPast.co.uk (accessed 13 February 2022).

20 Matcham, p32.

21 Jstor.org (accessed 12 February 2022).

22 'Eyles Irwin', Wikipedia online (accessed 20 February 2022).

23 Jstor.org.

24 Matcham, pp32–3.

25 Jstor.org (accessed 13 February 2022).

26 Matcham, pp31, 33–4.

27 Matcham, p34.

28 Matcham.

29 Eyles Irwin, *A Series of Adventures in the Course of a Voyage Up the Red-Sea* (J Dodsley, 1787), digitised 2011, Princeton University, p283.

30 Irwin, p290.

31 Irwin, p293.

32 Irwin, p315.

33 'Tigris', 2007 Schools Wikipedia Selection: Geography of Asia, online, at cs.mcgill.ca (accessed 13 February 2022).

34 Irwin, p331.

35 Irwin, p381.

36 *Dictionary of National Biography*.

37 'Maratha Empire', Wikipedia, online at Wikipedia.com.

38 R H Thomas, *Treaties, Agreements, and Engagements, between the Honorable East India Company and the Native Princes, Chiefs, and States, in Western India, the Red Sea, the Persian Gulf, &c: Also between Her Britannic Majesty's Government, and Persia, Portugal, and Turkey* (Government at the Bombay Education Society's Press, 1851), pp707–8.

39 Emin, pp476.

40 *Dictionary of National Biography*.

41 Matcham, pp35–7.

42 Portrait of George Matcham by Gilbert Stuart: Frick Art Reference Library at NYARC.org.

43 Matcham, p36.

44 *Bath Chronicle and Weekly Gazette*, 1 Mar 1787.

45 'Settlements and Entails', Manuscripts and Special Collection, Nottingham.ac.uk (accessed 16 February 2022).

46 'Marriage Settlements (England)', Wikipedia, online.

47 Wiltshire and Swindon Archive photo taken by David Bullock on 4 February 2016.

48 'Barton Broad', Wikipedia, online.

49 Matcham, p59.

50 *Norfolk, England, Church of England Baptism, Marriages, and Burials, 1535–1812* (online database). Ancestry.com.

51 Ancestry.com.

52 John Martin, 'A History of Landford in Wiltshire Part 10 – Newhouse', Landford History online at Wordpress.com (accessed 16 February 2022).

53 Martin.

54 *The St Leonards & St Ives Directory – October 2017*, Dorset Publications online at issuu.com (accessed 16 February 2022).

55 Matcham's folder held by Ringwood Meeting House & History Centre (accessed October 2015).

56 Matcham, p92.

57 Matcham, p135.

58 Matcham, p145.

59 Matcham, p148.

60 Martin.

61 Julie Peakman, *Emma Hamilton* (London: Haus Publishing, 2005), p110.

62 J Sugden, *Nelson: The Sword of Albion, Volume 2* (New York: Random House, 2012), p760.

63 Martin.

64 *Hampshire Chronicle*, 8 December 1800, online at Findmypast.co.uk (accessed 16 February 2022).

65 Martin.

66 Peter Warwick, 'Here Was Paradise – A Description of Merton Place', online at Wandle.org (accessed 16 February 2022).

67 Peakman, p127.

68 'George Matcham Patent', *The Repertory of Patent Inventions*, Google Books, online at google.com.co.uk/books.

69 'George Matcham Patent'.

70 'Plymouth Breakwater', Wikipedia.online at Wikipedia.com

71 Martin.

72 'St James's Park', Wikipedia, online at Wikipedia.org.

73 Ancestry.co.uk (accessed 16 February 2022).

74 Wiltshire and Swindon Archive, record viewed 2 April 2016.

75 *Bath Chronicle and Weekly Gazette,* 31 December 1807, online at Findmypast.co.uk (accessed 16 February 2022).

76 Sylvia K Robinson, *In Defence of Emma* (Croydon, England: CPI Books, 2016), p352.

77 W Gérin, *Horatia Nelson* (Oxford: Oxford University Press, 1970), p100.

78 Robinson, p379.

79 Peakman, p145.

80 Flora Fraser, *Beloved Emma* (London: Weidenfield and Nicholson, 1986), p342.

81 Warwick.
82 Peakman, p147.
83 Robinson, p438.
84 Kate Williams, *England's Mistress* (New York: Random House, 2006), p281.
85 Williams, p329.
86 Peakman, p153.
87 Walter Sichel, *Memoirs of Emma, Lady Hamilton* (University of California: W W Gibbings, 2010). A digital reproduction of the 1882 edition (Gibbings & Co), William H Long (ed), digitised reproduction online at Google books, google.co.uk/books.
88 Sichel, p184.
89 Sichel, p184.
90 Robinson, p438.
91 Robinson, p446.
92 Peakman, p156–7.
93 Robinson, p449.
94 Book shown to author in October 2017.
95 Gérin, p219.
96 Gérin, p218.
97 Gérin, p222.
98 Gérin, p231.
99 Gérin, p224.
100 Gérin, p232.
101 Gérin, p234.
102 Matcham, p293.
103 Matcham, p295.
104 *Dictionary of National Biography*.

Constitution versus *Guerriere*: The Lost Historical Significance of the Single Ship Actions of the War of 1812

1 Wellington to Beresford, 6 February 1813, quoted in Kevin D McCranie, *Utmost Gallantry: The US and Royal Navies at Sea in the War of 1812* (Annapolis, Maryland: Naval Institute Press, 2011), p90. Wellington qualified his view that the American war should end with the proviso that Britain should first take 'one or two of these damned frigates'.

2 Theodore Roosevelt, *The Naval War of 1812 or the History of the United States Navy during the last war with Great Britain* (New York: G P Putnam's Sons, 1882), pp90–2; McCranie, *Utmost Gallantry*, p49; Andrew Lambert, *The Challenge: Britain against America in the Naval War of 1812* (eBook edn, London: Faber and Faber, 2013), ch 2; William James, *A Full and Correct Account of the Chief Naval Occurrences of the late war between Great Britain and the United States of America* (London: Joyce Gold, 1817), pp96–113.

3   See Lambert, *The Challenge*; Andrew Lambert, 'Sideshow? British Grand Strategy and the War of 1812', in Tim Voelcker (ed), *Broke of the Shannon and the War of 1812* (Barnsley: Seaforth Publishing, 2013), pp17–39.

4   N A M Rodger, *The Command of the Ocean: A Naval History of Britain, 1649–1815* (New York: W W Norton, 2005), p516.

5   Nicholas James Kaizer, 'Regret, Determination, and Honour: The Impact of the Single Ship Losses in North American Waters on the British Royal Navy, 1812–1813' (MA thesis, Dalhousie University, 2018), p21.

6   Nicholas James Kaizer, *Revenge in the Name of Honour: The Royal Navy's Quest for Vengeance in the Single Ship Actions of the War of 1812* (Warwick, UK: Helion & Company, 2020), pp72–80.

7   Melville to Warren, 23 Mar 1813, National Maritime Museum, WAR/82/56-64, quoted in McCranie, p121.

8   'First Secretary of the Admiralty John Croker to Station Commanders in Chief, 10 July 1813', in William S Dudley, Christine F Hughes, and Tamara Moser Melia (eds), *The Naval War of 1812: A Documentary History*, vol II: 1813 (Washington, DC: Naval Historical Center, Dept of Navy, 1992), p183.

9   Kaizer, *Revenge*, pp80–4.

10   Kaizer, *Revenge*, p56.

11   Dacres to Sawyer, Boston, 7 September 1812, in William S Dudley, Christine F Hughes, and Tamara Moser Melia (eds), *The Naval War of 1812: A Documentary History*, vol I: 1812 (Washington, DC: Naval Historical Center, Dept of Navy, 1985), p245.

12   Testimony of Dacres, CM *Guerriere*, The National Archives, Surrey, UK (hereafter TNA) ADM 1/5431.

13   'William Henry Tremlett to the Editor, Bath, 21 May 1813', *The Naval Chronicle, for 1812: Containing a General and Biographical History of The Royal Navy of the United Kingdom; with a variety of original papers on Nautical Subjects*, vol 28: July to December (London: Joyce Gold, 1812), p465.

14   'Tremlett to the Editor, 21 May 1813', *Naval Chronicle*, vol 28, p465.

15   Henry Edward Napier, ed Walter Muir Whitehill, *New England Blockaded in 1814: the Journal of Henry Edward Napier, Lieutenant in HMS Nymphe* (Salem: Peabody Museum, 1939), p13.

16   Sir William Henry Dillon, ed Michael A Lewis, *A Narrative of My Professional Adventures*, vol II (London: Navy Records Society, 1953), p278.

17   Library Archive Canada, MG12 ADM 1/1663, Carden to Croker, 28 October 1812.

18   TNA, ADM 1/5436, Carden's Narrative, CM *Macedonian*.

19   TNA, ADM 1/5436, Lt David Hope's Testimony, CM *Macedonian*.

20   TNA, ADM 1/5436, Verdict, CM *Macedonian*.

21   Kaizer, *Revenge in the Name of Honour*, pp103–5.

22 Suffolk Record Office, HA 93/9/124, Philip Broke to Louisa Broke, 26 November 1812.

23 For more on Broke's gunnery training regime, see Martin Bibbings, 'A Gunnery Zealot: Broke's Scientific Contribution to Naval Warfare', in Voelcker (ed), pp103–26.

A Futile Danish Expedition to Morocco – and its Perspectives

1 This article is based on the book: Jakob Seerup, *Flåden*, in the series 100 Danmarkshistorier, published by Aarhus Universitetsforlag, 2021. Further reading on the Moroccan expedition can be found in C F Wandel, *Danmark og Barbareskerne, 1746–1845* (Copenhagen: 1919), and Georg Nørregård, *Fregatten Falster ved Marokko 1753* (Marinehistorisk Selskab, 1956).

2 Jakob Seerup, 'The Danish Naval Academy in the Age of Enlightenment', in *Mariner's Mirror*, no 3, 2007, pp327–34.

3 Jakob Seerup, 'Denmark: The Challenges of Peace', in Evan Wilson, Anna Sara Hammar, and Jakob Seerup (eds), *Eighteenth-Century Naval Officers: A Transnational Perspective* (London: Palgrave Macmillan, 2019), pp161–84.

The 1805 Club

President: Admiral Sir Jonathon Band GCB DL
Chairman: Captain John A Rodgaard USN Ret

The 1805 Club is a registered charity no. 1071871

The 1805 Club was established in 1990, and as of 2022 celebrates its thirty-second year of dedication toward commemorating and conserving the history and heritage of the Georgian Era sailing navies, with emphasis toward the Royal Navy of the period.

No other organisation is so dedicated in its programmes of commemorative and conservation initiatives, education, publications and support to scholastic research of the Georgian era, as exhibited in such a publication as the *Trafalgar Chronicle*.

For thirty-two years, the members of The Club have demonstrated their enthusiasm for all aspects of the sailing world of the Georgian era, and through the partnership of Seaforth Publishing, the *Trafalgar Chronicle* represents such a singular endeavour.

To join The 1805 Club go to www.1805club.org
and download the membership application form.